BREAKING SEAS, BROKEN SHIPS

Front cover: The rudder of the SS *Hoche*, a steamship wrecked at Blegberry, north Devon, 1882.

Back cover top: The battleship HMS *Sans Pareil*, sister ship of the doomed HMS *Victoria*, photographed c 1896, showing the monster guns that equipped both ships.

Back cover middle left: Royal Navy reservists leaving for war, c. 1914–17 (see **Pl 27**).

Back cover middle right: Lifeboat drill on a British liner, c. 1930.

Back cover bottom: An early container facility: the former Victoria Deep Water Terminal at Charlton, London, 1980.

BREAKING SEAS, BROKEN SHIPS

PEOPLE, SHIPWRECKS AND BRITAIN
1854–2007

IAN FRIEL

PEN & SWORD HISTORY

AN IMPRINT OF PEN & SWORD BOOKS LTD.
YORKSHIRE - PHILADELPHIA

First published in Great Britain in 2021
and reprinted in this format in 2025 by
PEN AND SWORD HISTORY
An imprint of
Pen & Sword Books Ltd
Yorkshire – Philadelphia

Copyright © Ian Friel, 2021, 2025

ISBN 978-1-39900-378-0

The right of Ian Friel to be identified as Author of
this work has been asserted by him in accordance with the Copyright,
Designs and Patents Act 1988.

A CIP catalogue record for this book is available from the British Library.

All rights reserved. No part of this book may be reproduced or transmitted in any
form or by any means, electronic or mechanical including photocopying,
recording or by any information storage and retrieval system, without permission
from the Publisher in writing.

Typeset in Times New Roman 11.5/14 by
SJmagic DESIGN SERVICES, India.
Printed and bound in the UK by CPI UK

The Publisher's authorised representative in the EU for product
safety is Authorised Rep Compliance Ltd., Ground Floor,
71 Lower Baggot Street, Dublin D02 P593, Ireland.
www.arccompliance.com

For a complete list of Pen & Sword titles please contact
PEN & SWORD BOOKS LIMITED
47 Church Street, Barnsley, South Yorkshire, S70 2AS, England
E-mail: enquiries@pen-and-sword.co.uk
Website: www.pen-and-sword.co.uk

Or
PEN AND SWORD BOOKS
1950 Lawrence Rd, Havertown, PA 19083, USA
E-mail: Uspen-and-sword@casematepublishers.com
Website: www.penandswordbooks.com

Contents

Author's Notes		vi
Image and quotation credits		vii
A note on tonnage measurement		viii
Introduction		ix
Chapter 1	'Steam has conquered storms and tides': The Passenger Liner *City of Glasgow* (1854)	1
Chapter 2	Message in a Bottle: The Collier Brig *Russell* of Littlehampton (1872)	21
Chapter 3	The Mastermind and the Insubordinate Stoker: The Battleship HMS *Victoria* (1893)	38
Chapter 4	'Last signal giving position…': The Merchant Ship SS *Terence* of Liverpool (1917)	58
Chapter 5	End of Empire: The Heavy Cruisers HMS *Dorsetshire* and HMS *Cornwall* (1942)	78
Chapter 6	The Spill: The Oil Tanker SS *Torrey Canyon* (1967)	98
Chapter 7	Oceans of Stuff: The Container Ship *MSC Napoli* (2007)	118
Endpiece		139
Abbreviations		142
Bibliography		143
Notes		154
Index		168

Author's Notes

I would like to thank the following people and institutions for their help: the staff of The National Archives, Kew; the staff of West Sussex Record Office; the staff of West Sussex Libraries and their excellent reserve book collection; the staff of Merseyside Maritime Museum Archive and Library; the staff of the Library of the Institute of Historical Research, London; Alice Walsh, formerly of the National Museum of the Royal Navy, Portsmouth; Anne Cowne, Lloyd's Register Foundation; the Senior Archivist, and William Bill, Emma Yan and their colleagues, Archives Services, University of Glasgow; Martin Bellamy, Glasgow Museums Resource Centre; Stephanie Markins, Associate Conservator, Collection Care Department, The National Archives for making the original court-martial papers for HMS *Victoria* accessible; Bryan Williamson, Mark Reid, Ross Wilson and the late Jim Murray of the www.britishmedals.us site; Sian Phillips and Rob Lloyd of Bridgeman Art Library Ltd for their help with images.

As will be clear from the text, I have been able to benefit from the work of a large number of other scholars, past and present, and I give my thanks to them. Any errors or misunderstandings are my own.

Special thanks are due to: my agent, Donald Winchester of Watson Little, Ltd, for his support and for his faith in this book and its predecessor; my editor at Pen & Sword, Claire Hopkins, who also saw the potential of the work, and that what started out as one book could become two.

As with my previous two books, my daughter, Helen Friel, turned my scribbled draft images into the beautiful maps and diagrams. With this book and its predecessor, my son David Friel provided key IT advice, and helped me through various laptop crises. My wife Lynne Friel proof-read the text, and prevented me from perpetrating purple passages (and too much alliteration). I want to thank Lynne, and Helen and David, for their love, support and forbearance while I have been writing *Britain and the Ocean Road*, the first book, and this, its sequel, *Breaking Seas, Broken Ships*.

Image and quotation credits

I would like to thank Jack Sullivan/Alamy, the Archives Services, University of Glasgow, the Imperial War Museum and Bridgeman Art Library Ltd for their kind permission to reproduce some of the images in the text. More detailed information on copyright is given in the individual image captions.

In the case of some of the older photographs, it has not been possible to locate copyright holders, if any still exist, despite my extensive efforts. If a copyrighted image has been inadvertently used without permission, I ask the copyright holder's pardon and will make due acknowledgment in any future editions of this book.

Unless otherwise specified, all other images, including maps and line drawings, are the author's copyright.

Quotations from material in The National Archives (TNA) are Crown Copyright, and gratefully acknowledged here. TNA is a resource of international importance, as the sources used in this book show. Much of the newspaper material quoted in this work has come via the indispensable British Newspaper Archive (www.britishnewspaperarchive.co.uk), a hugely useful source for historical research.

A note on tonnage measurement

Tonnage measurement is an issue that can drive you round the bend when discussing ships, past and present. Historically, at least seven or eight different types of ship capacity or size measures have existed in the English-speaking world since the Middle Ages. Each measure could be applied to the same hull, produce a mathematically accurate figure, but each result would be different.[1] In order to reduce confusion to manageable levels, I have tried to explain the meanings of the different tonnage calculation methods as they arise in the text.

Introduction

This book is a successor to my *Britain and the Ocean Road* (Pen & Sword 2020). The first book tracked the story of Britain and the ocean from the Middle Ages to the 1820s, as it grew into the greatest seafaring power the world had ever seen. *Breaking Seas, Broken Ships* covers the period from Britain's imperial zenith to the very different world of the early twenty-first century. As with *Britain and the Ocean Road*, it uses the accounts of a small number of shipwrecks as waypoints on the journey. However, it is not merely an account of 'sea power', or 'sea trade': the more I worked on the book, the more it became clear that it needed to address environmental issues alongside the more conventional concerns of maritime history. This is why the last two chapters have environmental themes at their heart.

This book was completed in the opening weeks of the coronavirus epidemic in Europe. One of the many grim manifestations of the disease across the world was the way it started to spread rapidly through the passengers and crews of various cruise liners, confined as they were aboard ship. Weeks of miserable quarantine followed for many of them, and some people died. It is a reminder that even when the sea is used as playground, as was the case for passengers on the British liner *Lancastria* in the 1930s (**Pl 1 and Pl 2**), subsequent events can turn it into a much darker place. We are none of us insulated from history.

Chapter 1

'Steam has conquered storms and tides'
The Passenger Liner *City of Glasgow* (1854)

William Collis became a regular visitor to the general delivery window at the Philadelphia post office, and the staff there got to recognize him. They thought that this 'intelligent, happy-looking' man was English, aged about forty-five. Collis had moved to the USA with his teenage son, and was looking forward to the arrival of his wife and their five other children. She had planned to travel from Liverpool in the steamer *City of Manchester*, but this did not work out. Mrs Collis had sent her husband a letter, to say that instead they would be sailing in the liner *City of Glasgow*.

The mail steamers were generally faster than the passenger vessels, so Collis knew that if she posted a letter just before embarkation, it could get to America ahead of her. Alongside many other hopeful relatives and friends, he started going to the city's Queen Street Wharf 'to look for the incoming steamer'.

The *City of Glasgow* set sail from Liverpool on 1 March 1854, with 430 crew and travellers on board. The steamer itself was only four years old, an iron-hulled, propeller-driven marvel of Victorian engineering. It was purpose-built to carry cabin-class passengers and large numbers of poorer people in 'steerage', an innovation that was set to make a lot of money for the Liverpool and Philadelphia Steam Ship Company.[1]

The ship and those on board were never seen again, though it took weeks for the truth to dawn. William Collis was shockingly changed when he came back to the post office in the futile hope of new letters. His face was haggard, his eyes bloodshot and glaring. In the end, his despair drove him into the local madhouse for a short while.[2]

The technological advances in nineteenth-century shipbuilding made sea travel safer and more reliable, and gave birth to the first true ocean liners. The mass transportation rendered possible by large ships like the *City of Glasgow* played a key role in the peopling of the Americas and other continents with Europeans. In 1845, a correspondent in *The Spectator* magazine reflected the confidence of the age when he remarked that 'steam has conquered storms and tides'. This blind faith in new technology was misplaced, however: in some ways, the *City of Glasgow* tragedy prefigured that of the *Titanic* fifty-eight years later.[3]

English is now a world language. The origins of this phenomenon lie in Britain's former global reach and the fact that its English-speaking ex-colony, the United States, went on to become a superpower. However, emigration was also crucial to the process – 22.6 million people left the British Isles alone between 1815 and 1914. War, conquest, trade, colonization and emigration spread English speakers and their cultures far and wide across the world between the seventeenth and twentieth centuries, but there were marked changes over time in the nature of emigration from the British Isles itself. In the seventeenth century, between 377,000 and 397,000 British and Irish people sailed for the Americas, nearly ninety per cent of them from England and Wales. The majority of these were indentured servants, bound to work on farms or plantations in North America and the Caribbean for time-limited periods.

The rate of Irish and Scots emigration to North America overtook that of England and Wales between 1700 and 1815. There were attempts to settle loyal ex-servicemen in some places, but the colonies also proved to be a handy dumping-ground for convicts. America was used for this purpose until the War of Independence (49,000 felons went there in the years 1718–75), and then British-settled Australia took over the role, receiving over 29,000 convicted men, women and children between 1787 and 1820.

In the seventeenth and eighteenth centuries, 'educated' opinion tended to see emigration as a good way to get rid of excess population – in other words, the poverty-stricken and other 'undesirables'. Indentured service was a means of survival – not a career move – for many in the seventeenth century. Artisans and other people with skills seem to have made up a larger portion of emigrants in the eighteenth century, and in both periods, there were always minorities of religious separatists, professional people and others who went in search of a better life.[4]

'Steam has conquered storms and tides'

By the 1830s, new attitudes to emigration were emerging in Britain. It began to be seen as a means of peopling the empire with white, English-speaking populations, rather than merely 'shovelling out the paupers', as one proponent put it. In 1840 the British government set up the Colonial Land and Emigration Commission with a remit to oversee emigration issues, encourage colonial settlement and keep a close eye on legal developments in the colonies. The Commission appointed emigration officers to serve in various ports, and began chartering ships for emigrants to Australia and South Africa. Official opinion did not favour emigration to Britain's ex-colony, the USA, because it drained the home countries and empire of people, but this trend was unstoppable.

The Commission also took on responsibility for the administration of the Passenger Acts, which were intended to promote the welfare of steerage migrants, people who travelled in the poorest accommodation in a ship, on the same level as steering gear. Sixteen Passenger Acts were passed between 1803 and 1855. They set maximum passenger numbers for given sizes of ship, stipulated dietary standards and mandated the provision of surgeons and lifeboats (though nowhere was it stated that there had to be enough boats to take *everyone* on board). These laws did not apply to the richer cabin and saloon passengers: by the nineteenth century, 'steerage' merely denoted accommodation for poorer travellers. Penalties for infringements included fines or the forfeiture of a ship, and an emigration officer could stop a ship from sailing if he thought it did not meet legal requirements. However, as the historian Terry Coleman pointed out, the system was undermined by a lack of staff and administrative machinery, and prosecutions were few. In 1855 the emigration officer in Liverpool had six assistants, too few to cope adequately with the passenger traffic in the country's busiest emigrant port. Emigration agents, shipowners and crews were able to get away with abuses, and too often that led to overcrowding, hunger, disease and shipwreck.[5]

In 1853, for instance, the master of the *California Packet* abandoned both his ship and his emigrant passengers in the Atlantic when it began to leak. Two years earlier, in 1851, an American captain had been horrified by the condition of the 174 Irish emigrants he saved from a dismasted British emigrant ship, the *Unicorn*. He wrote that they were dressed in 'miserable rags', and that the British crew treated their charges 'more like brutes than human beings'.

Irish people crossed to America in huge numbers after the Potato Famine began in 1845. They made up around forty-four per cent of the 2.7 million people who left Britain and Ireland for America between 1844 and 1854, and a large number of them travelled via Liverpool. Many suffered terribly in the Atlantic crossing, or succumbed to disease on arrival. Some were treated like garbage. The *Unicorn* emigrants were effectively 'transported' by their landlord, who had paid for their passage – but nothing else – merely as a way of getting them off his land.[6]

Sailing ships were the only vehicles available for mass-migration before the mid-nineteenth century, and their ubiquity meant that emigrants could find ocean passages in many ports. Even places like the small north Devon port of Bideford had an active emigration trade (**Pl 3**). In the 1830s, there were a number of emigrant voyages from Bideford to the USA and Canada, using a range of vessels, including cramped, two-masted brigs. The problem with sail, of course, was that it was dependent on the wind. If the wind dropped, or blew in the wrong direction, a ship could be delayed for weeks. Emigration under sail could be an unpleasant experience.[7]

The growing use of steamships after the early 1850s led to the emigrant business becoming concentrated in a few major ports, where the big shipping lines were to be found. The business was supported by networks of emigration agents across the country and abroad that organized passages for groups and individuals. Some charities also got involved, of which the Salvation Army later came to be one of the most prominent. With more and more effective government regulation, seaborne migration went on to become safer in the second half of the nineteenth century, and less riddled with abuses. One of the other things that helped to make it safer was steam power.[8]

Steam vessels were first developed in the late eighteenth century, but it took decades before they had a real impact on sea transport. Early steam engines could be unreliable, the side-mounted paddles they drove were vulnerable to storm damage, and steam vessels consumed enormous and expensive amounts of coal. The invention of the screw propeller in the 1830s was a step-change in marine engineering. The submerged, stern-mounted screw proved to be a much more efficient way of turning power into propulsion and had none of the vulnerabilities of paddles. For all that, ocean-going steamers of all kinds retained full sets of sail well into the nineteenth century. They were needed in cases where a ship ran out of coal, where the engine broke down, or when there was a chance of getting an extra push if the winds were right.

The first steamer to cross the Atlantic was the American vessel *Nautilus*, in 1819, albeit with a lot of help from its sails. Less than twenty years later, though, ships like Isambard Kingdom Brunel's powerful *Great Western* (1837) showed that it was possible to build more dependable and profitable transatlantic paddle steamers. The drawback of the *Great Western*, however, was that it was built of wood, and wooden hulls did not stand up very well to the intense vibrations caused by steam engines. The solution to the problem was to build ships in metal. Iron hulls were not only stronger than wooden ones, they could be made much larger and their interiors did not require the vast clutter of extra frames, knees and other structural elements needed to keep a wooden ship together. Iron plates and bars suitable for boat- and shipbuilding became available in sufficient quality and quantity in the 1780s, but it was not until 1832 that that an ocean voyage was made by an iron ship.

The first vessel to bring together the iron hull and the screw propeller was Brunel's giant and revolutionary *Great Britain* of 1843 (3,270 gross registered tons – grt were based on the permanently enclosed volume of a ship). Built only seven years later, the *City of Glasgow* belonged to the same technological generation as the *Great Britain*.[9]

Screw steamers did not immediately render the sailing ship obsolete, though. Shipowners were a hard-headed lot, and would only invest in new technology if they could see a profit in it. As late as 1864, ninety per cent of the vessels registered in Liverpool, for example, were sailing ships. Ton for ton, wooden ships were cheaper to build, buy and run than iron ones. It was only the introduction of more efficient and economical high-pressure expansion engines and boilers from the 1860s onwards that really drove the merchant 'steam revolution', and sailing ships did not cease to be competitive in the bulk cargo trades until the 1880s. Steamers were adopted more rapidly in the passenger trade because speed and reliability meant more voyages, which in turn meant more passengers and more profits.[10]

Passenger lines existed before the rise of the steamship, and advertised regular sailings. The famous Black Ball Line began its transatlantic service in 1818, for instance, and the term 'liner' was in use by the 1830s, but sail-driven services were hampered by their reliance on the wind. The first regular steamship services across the Atlantic began in 1838, with the *Sirius* and *Great Western*. The advantages of steam over sail became very clear: by the mid-nineteenth century the average steamer was able to make six return Atlantic voyages in a year, whereas sailing ships could only manage three. Government policy also helped the rise of passenger steamers, through subsidies paid for mail services. Subsidies assisted the growth of steam lines like Cunard, and in the 1840s and 1850s the Royal Mail Steam Packet Company derived almost forty per cent of its income from the mail contract.[11]

The *City of Glasgow* belonged to the unsubsidized sector. It was built on the river Clyde by the firm of David Tod and John McGregor. Scotland lacked a good supply of shipbuilding timber, and back in the 1830s, when Tod and McGregor were starting out, the Clyde was not the great shipbuilding river that it would become. The phenomenal development of the Clyde yards in the mid-nineteenth century relied on the growth of the Scottish iron and later steel production – by 1870, some seventy per cent of all British iron shipping tonnage was being built on Glasgow's river.

Tod and McGregor were the pioneers of the new industry. After working for the innovative Scottish engineer David Napier, they set up as independent engine builders in 1833, and soon after built the first iron ship on the Clyde. Subsequent success led them to move to a bigger site downriver in 1847, where work on the *City of Glasgow* began two years later.[12]

The firm took real risks in building the *City of Glasgow*. Its iron hull, steam engine and screw propeller represented a still-radical combination,

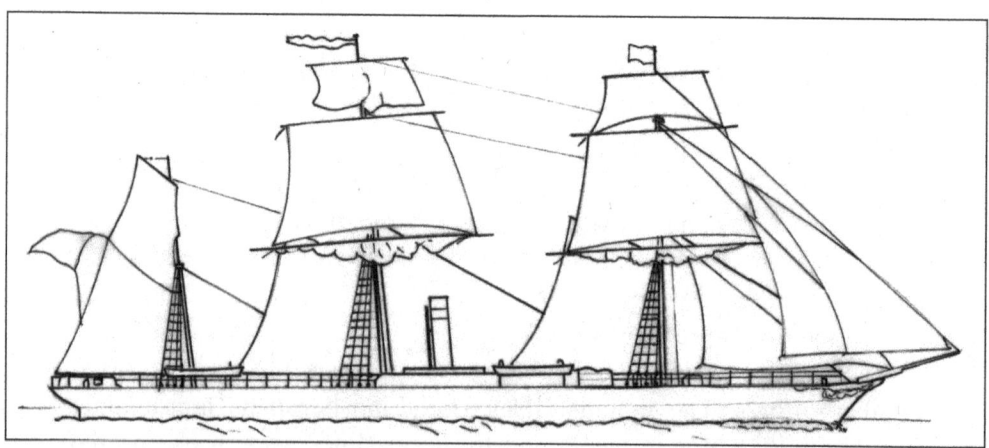

Fig 1 Outline drawing of the *City of Glasgow*, based on a contemporary engraving.

but more than that, the partners designed it to carry steerage emigrants as well as cabin passengers. Tod and MacGregor were the first to see the potential of the mass-emigration market, but their risk was increased because the steamer was built 'on spec', with no prospective purchaser on the horizon. For this reason, they decided to create their own one-vessel shipping line, running between Glasgow and New York. The ship was equipped with machinery made in the company's own workshops and launched on 28 February 1850. After a successful shakedown cruise, the liner returned to Glasgow for final fitting-out, where it became a tourist attraction.

The ship's first captain was Bernard Matthews, a steam veteran who had crossed the Atlantic ninety times as an officer, and had commanded the *Great Western*. The *City of Glasgow*'s crew consisted of forty-one officers and men, along with a dozen stewards, two stewardesses, a baker, a cook, a band of musicians and a ship's doctor.[13]

Unfortunately, the surviving records of the Tod and McGregor yard have little to say about the *City of Glasgow*, but we know that it was a vessel of 1,609 gross registered tons (1,087 tons burden) and had three decks. It measured 237ft (72.2m) from stem to stern, and was 34ft wide (10.4m). Though it had three fully rigged masts, the mechanical heart of the ship was a two-cylinder beam engine, developing 350 horsepower, which turned a single 13-foot diameter (3.97m) propeller. As its service record was to prove, the ship could make a steady 10 knots under steam, and the engine burned coal economically.

A contemporary newspaper description and a surviving cabin-class deck plan of the *City of Glasgow* make it possible to reconstruct something of the interior of the ship. The 'First Cabin' area was behind the funnel. The cabins there generally had more space than those in second class, and were decked out 'with beautiful Tournay curtains, with fringe and silk hangings'. Most first-class cabins had fixed sofas. In fact, the fit-out of the ship betrayed something of an obsession with sofas. Counting a huge curving sofa in the stern (over 20 feet wide), there were over thirty sofas on this deck. Those in the first-class saloon were covered in 'crimson and Utrecht velvet plush', while the second-class sofas were made of mahogany, covered in 'haircloth', and would convert into beds.

Passengers could stroll on the open spar deck of the 'noble steamship', or in bad weather they could relax in the safety of the airy and well-lit main

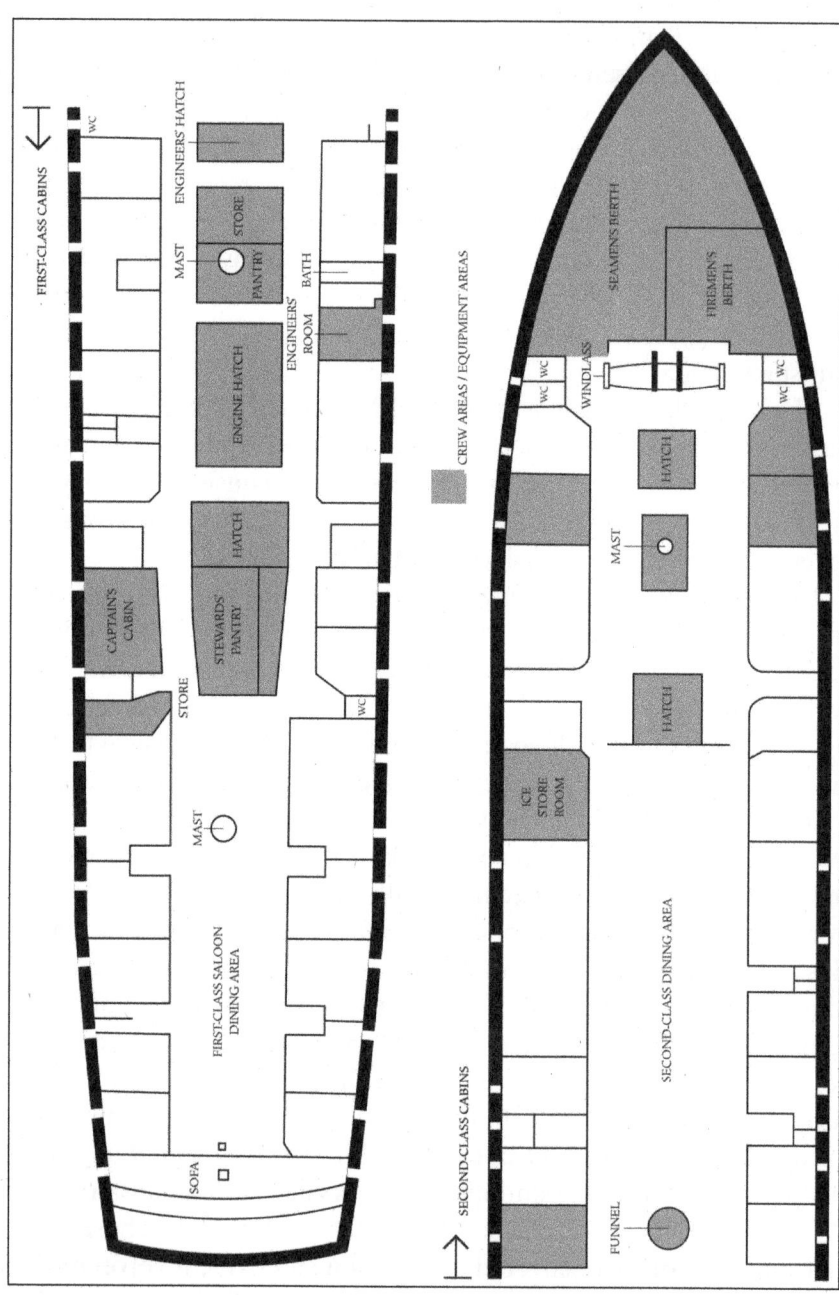

Fig 2 The layout of the main deck of the *City of Glasgow*, based on a contemporary plan in TNA CO 384/89, redrawn and reinterpreted. The original plan had to be split in two in order to fit the company's printed flyer. Shaded areas denote crew accommodation and service areas.

deck, where there was headroom of 7 feet (2.1m). The 'grand saloon' here was the place where the first-class passengers mingled and ate. It was 54 feet (16.5m) in length, with tables that could seat sixty people (second-class passengers had their own dining space). The forward end of the saloon was dominated by a large sideboard topped by a gilt mirror in a carved frame, while at the other end was a gilt clock bearing the arms of the city of Glasgow. The wainscot panelling that lined the saloon carried a dozen large, framed pictures of views from Scotland, Ireland, America and other places. Though described as 'tasteful and genteel' the interior decoration of the *City of Glasgow* was clearly Victorian 'bling' with a vengeance.

Each cabin had its own washbasin and there were nine flushing toilets on the main deck, a considerable advance on the 'heads' found in many contemporary sailing ships (usually no more than a wooden plank with a hole in it, sited in a draughty structure at the bow). Hot and cold showers were available, as well as a salt-water bath, pumped from the sea. The first- and second-class accommodation of the *City of Glasgow* combined luxury and contemporary design in a way that still underlies the fit-out of modern cruise ships.

The steamer was designed to carry fifty-two first-class passengers, eighty-five in second class and '400 steerage emigrants', as well as up to 1,200 tons of cargo. The newspaper account does not mention the layout of steerage and the deck plan offers no clues. It was certainly darker there, as it could only be lit with oil lamps. The main deck above had over fifty portholes, plus skylights, but there were none for the steerage passengers, as their deck was too low in the ship. The Passenger Acts specified that steerage bunkbeds should be no more than two tiers in height, to prevent overcrowding. The ship's final owners, the Liverpool and Philadelphia line, seem to have been scrupulous about following regulations, and it's likely that they kept to the letter of the law.

The 1850 description said that the ship was fitted with 'powerful pumps' to fight fires (always a danger on steamships, even iron ones) and that the hull was divided into compartments by five watertight bulkheads 'so that she would float although several of these divisions were filled'. The ship's 'capacious' lifeboats also got a mention, but the writer did not remark on the disparity between a vessel designed to carry over 500 people that only had lifeboat space for two hundred.[14]

Though they had designed the ship as a vehicle for the mass-migration trade, Tod and McGregor appear to have lost their nerve, probably fearing that the presence of steerage passengers would deter the richer travellers. The advertisement for the first sailing, on 16 April 1850, made a point of saying 'No Steerage Passengers taken'. The ship's departure was a massive public event, with an estimated 100,000 people lining the banks of the Clyde. Amid music, cheers and gun salutes, the *City of Glasgow* smoothly cut its way towards the Atlantic.

The steamer completed four Atlantic round-trips in 1850. The first voyage, with 110 passengers, took 16¾ days, despite 'tremendous gales'. The return trip was even faster, at fifteen days. It's not known what Tod and MacGregor's long-term plans were for the ship, but its potential caught the eye of Liverpool entrepreneurs. They bought major shares in the *City of Glasgow*, and became its new owners. In the autumn of 1850, they relocated the ship to Liverpool.[15]

Once Britain's greatest slaving port, by 1850 Liverpool was a thriving centre for the migrant and general goods trades, and Britain's key Atlantic port. In the mid-nineteenth century over 3.6 million tons of shipping was registered at Liverpool, nearly ten per cent more than in the port of London. However, until the American Civil War of 1861–65, Liverpool still made a lot of money from the product of a slave economy – cotton from the American South, often shipped via New York, Liverpool's counterpart in the USA.

Liverpool had the facilities to support high-volume international trade. By 1836 the walled docklands area of the port occupied nearly 2½ miles (4km) of waterfront, and the huge Royal Albert Dock and its warehouses were added to this in 1846 (**Pl 4**). As well as being a trading hub, Liverpool became Britain's premier emigration port in the nineteenth century. Between 1860 and 1914, nearly nine out of every ten emigrants from the British Isles passed through the port.[16]

Liverpool is famous for its Irish links, and it was the Richardson family from Northern Ireland who helped to inaugurate the mass-migration steamship trade in the city. The Richardsons were Quakers, known for their charitable work, but also canny businessmen, involved in the linen industry. They diversified their business and set up as shipbrokers in Liverpool in the 1830s, importing foodstuffs and other goods. One member of the family, Thomas Richardson, also established an allied firm in the USA, in Philadelphia, Richardson Watson & Co.

'Steam has conquered storms and tides'

The family expanded their activities. They first went into business as emigration agents, and in 1847 set up their own shipping line, with four large sailing ships, equipped to take passengers. The vessels ran between Liverpool and Philadelphia, with monthly scheduled sailings.

In the 1840s a new clerk joined the Liverpool branch of the company, a young man named William Inman. Astute and educated, he quickly rose to be manager of the shipping line, and became a partner of Richardson Brothers in 1849. It is said that he spotted the potential of the *City of Glasgow* as a mass-emigration ship, and persuaded the Richardsons to buy it. The initiative may actually have come from Thomas Richardson in Philadelphia, but of course Tod and MacGregor should be credited with having the idea first, even if they did not follow it up on their own account. They retained an interest in the ship, though Richardson Brothers had the largest group of shares. There were also some other smaller business and individual shareholders in Scotland, Lancashire and Northern Ireland.

Despite the other investors, it was Inman and the Richardsons who ran things, and they announced the formation of the Liverpool and Philadelphia Steam Ship Company in October 1850. Its 'powerful new Screw Steam-Ship CITY OF GLASGOW' would run on the Liverpool–Philadelphia route from December that year, to be joined in 1851 by a larger and more powerful sister ship (this was the 2,125-ton *City of Manchester*, also built by Tod and McGregor). Inman served as the company's 'Passenger Broker', and was directly involved in its operations.[17]

The passengers for the December 1850 sailing of the *City of Glasgow* were all in first and second class, paying ticket prices that ranged from thirteen to twenty guineas (the top price would equate to at least £2,400 today). The company did not embark its first steerage passengers until May 1852, but in the ten months that followed, its two ships took 2,146 of them safely to America. Though company adverts did not use the dread words 'steerage passengers', they offered a coy hint of their existence by stating that 'a limited number' of passengers could be carried for six guineas each. However distasteful it might have been for some cabin and salon travellers, the Liverpool and Philadelphia Steam Ship Company had now entered the mass-migration business. That business would become its lifeblood.[18]

Inman badgered the Colonial Land and Emigration Commission in the early 1850s to exempt his steamers from the Passengers Acts. The subsidized mail steamers were not covered by the Acts, and he saw this as unfair competition. Also, an emigration officer could refuse to clear one of Inman's ships and delay sailing if he felt it infringed the Acts in some way. Inman's position was that his company's ships were fast enough and too well run to need such supervision. Officials had some sympathy with his view, but pointed out that the legislation was there to protect emigrants in ships run by less scrupulous lines.[19]

Modern airlines aspire to provide a service that makes travel as quick and easy for passengers as possible: remarkably, Inman's vision for the steamer company was much the same. In February 1852, he wrote (original punctuation and capitalization): 'Our passengers expect to be able to come to town & walk on board like they would at a Railway Station with a railway train.' If the clearance procedure delayed a ship 'you will be stopping the very element of steam which calls for speed and not for vexatious delay'. As an example, he described how German steerage emigrants travelled to join one of his ships. They took a steamer from Hamburg on a Saturday, arrived in Hull on Monday, cleared their baggage through customs there on Tuesday morning, caught a train for Liverpool, arrived there Tuesday night, and boarded the transatlantic steamer the following day (this also explains, incidentally, why the Welsh emigrants who travelled on the *City of Glasgow*'s last voyage only left home the day before). Sailing vessels could undercut steamers with tickets that could be a third or half the price of those in his steamers, he admitted, and their cargo rates were lower, too. Steam could only succeed if it was punctual, fast and hassle-free.[20]

Life aboard the *City of Glasgow* for the cabin and saloon passengers was luxurious by contemporary standards. No menus seem to survive, but the food on offer was probably pretty lavish. There was an ice store on the main deck that was used to keep meat, milk and other foodstuffs fresh, as well as supplying ice for water. Tea and coffee were served morning and evening to first- and second-class passengers, and they were supplied with all of their crockery, glassware, bedding and soap.

The conditions for steerage passengers in the Richardson steamers were good by the standards of Victorian emigrant vessels, at least as far as food and drink went. They had to supply their own bedding, cutlery, tin plates, mugs and so on, but received standard rations of victuals that exceeded the Passenger Act requirements, served in set menus though the week. Each person was allowed six pints (3.4l) of water per day, and there were three mealtimes, breakfast at 8.00 am, dinner at 1.00 pm and supper at 6.00 pm. Menus varied through the week, but a typical Wednesday menu consisted of porridge for breakfast, pea soup, beef and rice for dinner and tea, sugar and ship's biscuit at supper. It was not an exciting diet, but it was sustaining, and Sundays were enlivened by a 'flour pudding' that contained raisins and molasses.

As the law dictated, the Liverpool and Philadelphia line ships each carried a surgeon and a stock of medicines, but the company also aimed to keep its passengers healthy by refusing to carry sick people. Widows and the disabled were likewise banned unless they had security for bonds to be paid to the US government. The Americans did not want potentially indigent people to become a charge on the state.[21]

The *City of Glasgow* ran successfully on the Philadelphia route for over three years, surviving bad weather and other hazards. The ship's last complete voyage to Philadelphia, in January 1854, was 'a very long and stormy passage of twenty-five days' in which most of the sails were either lost or ripped. Despite this ordeal, the engines kept running throughout, and all of the passengers were landed safely. The return voyage was somewhat faster, and the ship was back in Liverpool by 21 February.[22]

The cost of a Liverpool and Philadelphia line steerage ticket rose to £8/8s (or eight guineas) in 1854, because of growing overheads, but it helped to pay for better conditions aboard ship.[23] There were real profits to be made, from both the cabin and steerage passengers. Allowing for children, the total ticket income for the last voyage must have been in excess of £3,000 (at least a quarter of a million pounds in modern money).[24]

There were 430 people aboard the *City of Glasgow* when it sailed for the last time in March 1854. For some reason, all of the contemporaneous newspaper accounts say that the figure was 480, but analysis of the published passenger and crew lists shows that the true figure was fifty lower. The ship carried seventy-three crew, sixty-four cabin and saloon passengers and 293 in steerage.[25] At least one-third of the passengers were female – though the genders of children and infants are not given. Only fourteen children and infants were recorded – the Collis family made up five of these – but this probably seriously undercounted the total of those aboard, as no children of steerage passengers were identified separately.

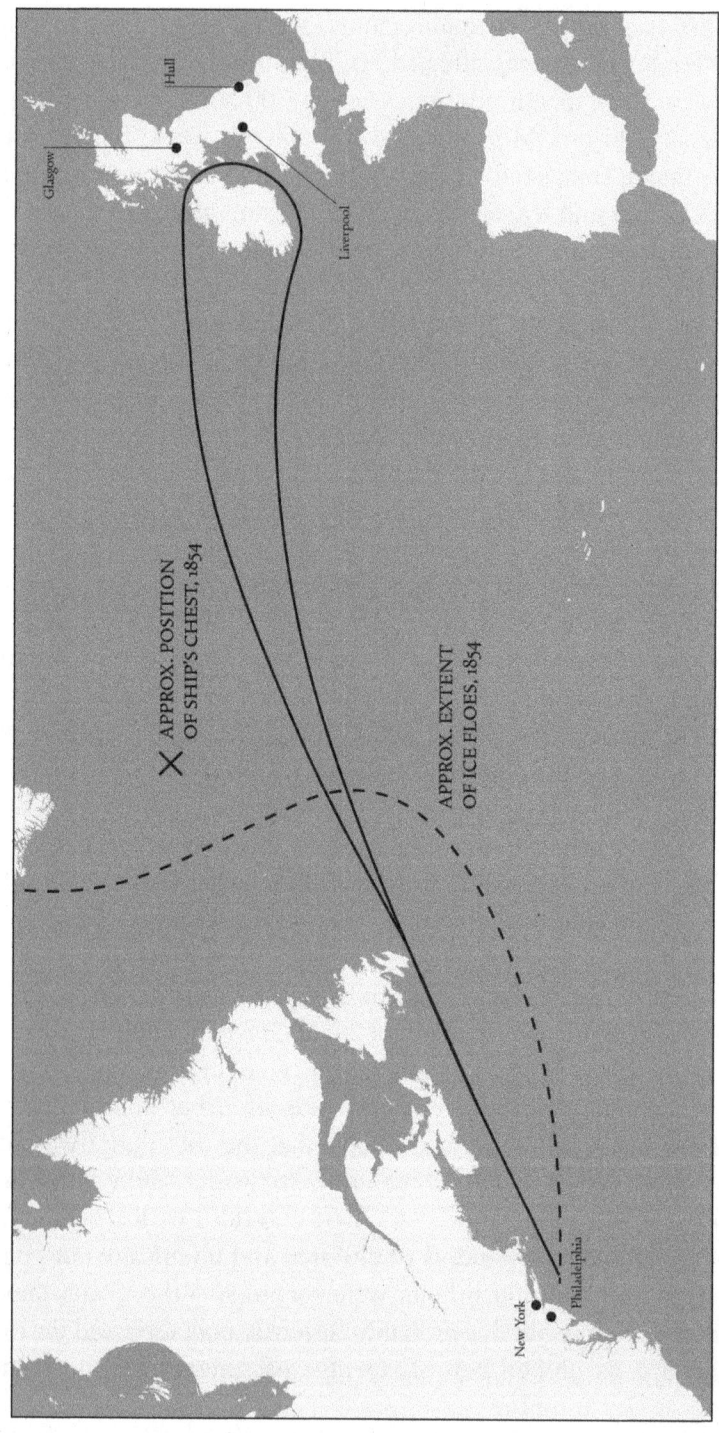

Fig 3 The Liverpool and Philadelphia line's Atlantic passages, showing alternative routes around Ireland, and the approximate positions of the ice and wreckage in 1854. (Redrawn and reinterpreted from an 1855 map in TNA FO 925/4578)

'Steam has conquered storms and tides'

Passenger surnames point to the origins of some of those travelling – sixty-eight had Welsh names, forty-three seem to have been Irish or Scottish and forty-three more came from outside the British Isles. The foreign names sound mostly German or east European, from Monsieur and Mademoiselle Eckstein in the cabin class to William Bechter and the four members of the Weter family in steerage. They were probably German emigrants who had come via Hull.

The large number of Welsh surnames – such as Jones, Roberts, Owens and Williams – was no accident. The steerage passengers included a group of about a hundred people from Bethesda in north Wales, who left their homes for Liverpool on 28 February, the day before the *City of Glasgow* set sail.[26]

The idea of emigration as a way to improve your life chances was definitely in the air in the Britain of the early 1850s. In June 1853 one (not untypical) edition of the *North Wales Chronicle* had five advertisements for emigrant lines on its front page – four sailing to Australia (this was the age of Australian gold rush) and one to America. The same issue ran a very positive piece about emigration, emphasizing the chances of 'immediate employment' and the opportunity to see friends and relatives in the States. Significantly, it also said that the 'facility of crossing the Atlantic at a very low rate of passage, as now offered by the great Screw boats from Liverpool to Philadelphia, has created a strong desire of emigration in the inhabitants of this neighbourhood'.

The paper also singled out a Bethesda man, Mr E. Jones, who had become an emigration agent in Liverpool: 'Mr Jones stands high in Liverpool, and his countrymen in Wales have great confidence in him ...' It was probably Jones who arranged what proved to be a fatal passage for the Bethesda emigrants on the *City of Glasgow*.[27]

By 1854 the ship was commanded by Captain Kenneth Morrison, who led a crew of seventy-one men and one woman, a stewardess. Seamen and engine-room staff moved around a lot, and only about one in five of the crewmen listed for the *City of Glasgow* in March 1853 were still aboard for its last voyage, a year later. Even most of the officers changed, though the first officer, Patrick Tod, remained.

The captain earned £500 per year (at least £46,000 in modern terms) plus perks, such as a pint of wine per day. His pay was more than three times greater than that of the first officer, and over ten times more than that of an able seaman. Interestingly, the chief engineer, John Andrew, earned more than the first officer, a seaman (£14 and £12 per month, respectively), a sign of the growing significance of steam at sea. The importance of the cabin passenger side of the business was reflected in the wage of Chief Steward Archibald Gilfillan, who earned £10 per month, more than the ship's surgeon, Henry Jones, who was a qualified doctor.[28]

The structure of the crew also revealed the impact of steam on seafaring. Some of the job titles and functions had been around since the Middle Ages – seaman, carpenter, boatswain, purser, quartermaster and sailmaker – though the master's mates acquired less salty-sounding titles: first, second and third officer.[29] The ship had eighteen able or ordinary seamen to handle the sails and other traditional gear, but the engine-room complement was almost as large: four engineers, six firemen (stokers) and five coal-trimmers.

The development of ocean liners also transformed the nature of crews. Ships' stewards had worked aboard ship in small numbers for hundreds of years, to serve food and perform other duties, but in liners they became much more important. The *City of Glasgow* had sixteen stewards and one stewardess to attend to the passengers – particularly those in the cabin and saloon class. The stewardess, Mrs Stewart, was one of a small number of women workers who went to sea in the nineteenth-century liner business. The crew also included two cooks, a butcher, a baker and a storekeeper. It was as if a hotel and part of a high street had gone to sea.

There is little doubt that the *City of Glasgow* was a well-run ship, and its hull, boilers and machinery were declared to be in a 'highly efficient state' by a Board of Trade inspection conducted not long before departure. Loaded with passengers and cargo, but without any fanfare for this now-routine voyage, the steamer left Liverpool at noon on 1 March 1854.[30]

There were no verified sightings of the ship once it had sailed. After a month without any news, Inman and his colleagues must have been getting worried, and by mid-April the press was reporting 'great fears' for the safety of the steamer. Information from returning ships said that the ice on the route had been 'greater than had been witnessed for many years, with a compact mass over 300 miles long', and 'numerous bergs 200 and 300 feet high'. The ice was coming down to 40° North, a latitude that runs just south of Philadelphia, and it extended between 100 and 300 miles off the American coast.

'Steam has conquered storms and tides'

The word 'lost' began to appear in stories about the *City of Glasgow* by 19 April, and relatives of those aboard were becoming very uneasy. The shipping line was still trying to reassure the public in late April, but this was whistling in the dark. By early May, parts of the press were saying outright that people believed that the ship had collided with an iceberg. Some clung to hope, but many despaired. The *North Wales Chronicle* of 6 May 1854 reported that 'great distress' prevailed in Bethesda because of the many local people now presumed dead.

There were reported sightings of the steamer, but these were soon discounted. Much more ominous were reports of wreckage. On 30 March, a ship had spotted broken masts and doors in the sea a few hundred miles off Newfoundland. Just over three weeks later, the crew of a vessel which had itself suffered iceberg damage, saw 'a great quantity of wreck' debris, including chests and boxes, floating in the same general area as the ice, around 500 miles off Newfoundland. A couple of sailing cutters went out from Philadelphia to look for the *City of Glasgow*, but governments on both sides of the Atlantic rejected calls for an official search-and-rescue effort. The Liverpool and Philadelphia line seems to have given the ship up as lost by 13 May. By early June, all hope had been abandoned.[31]

The most likely explanation for the loss of the ship is the one that occurred to contemporaries – that it was destroyed in the unusually widespread ice fields, either crushed or fatally holed by a collision with an iceberg. We can get some idea of why it might have foundered from what happened to the *City of Glasgow*'s second sister-ship, the *City of Philadelphia*, in early September 1854. It ran aground on the Newfoundland coast, and became a total loss, though fortunately everyone aboard was saved. Like the *City of Glasgow*, it was fitted with watertight bulkheads, but when it grounded, 'the concussion was so violent, that the bulk-heads were immediately started [i.e. began leaking] and rendered useless'.[32]

Compartmentalizing a hull was a great idea, first introduced in iron vessels in 1834. However, if the bulkheads were too weak, they would give way under water or impact pressure, as in the *City of Philadelphia*. Alternatively, if the bulkheads did not go all the way up to the underside of the open deck, inrushing seawater would simply rise up and go over them. Government regulations of the time did not specify that bulkheads had to reach up to a watertight deck – Brunel's *Great Britain* was built according to such rules (or lack of them). The same applied to the regulations current in 1911, when the mighty RMS *Titanic* was launched. Even though the *Titanic*'s bulkheads exceeded Board of Trade requirements, they were still not high enough, and this vulnerability sank the ship in 1912. The *City of Glasgow* may well have suffered a similar fate to the *Titanic*, for much the same reasons, in the same part of the Atlantic.[33]

On 12 August 1854, a British ship en route for America spotted a green-painted, gilded chest floating in the sea, along with a 12-foot ship's 'headboard' or nameboard. The chest bore the initials 'G B' and the name 'City of Glasgow', though the nameboard could not be read. References to the exact position of the debris are rather garbled, but the majority of them place it several hundred miles from Newfoundland, in the same general area as the other sightings of wreckage. Newspapers suggested that it was the sea chest of George Baker, one of the seamen in the crew. This sombre discovery was taken as final confirmation of the sinking.[34]

Just under three months later, in early November, a ship's nameboard was found lying on the shore near Campbeltown on the Kintyre Peninsula in western Scotland. It bore the gilded words 'City of Glasgow', with 'Let Glasgow Flourish' in one corner. The board was sent to Tod and MacGregor in Glasgow for identification, but nothing more seems to be known about it.[35]

The people in the *City of Glasgow* suffered a terrible death in the freezing waters of the Atlantic, but the horror and misery did not stop there. In Philadelphia, William Collis faced madness; in the English Midlands, a Mrs Fields lost her husband and two children in the wreck, leaving her and her five other children destitute; in the north of England, the Barwise family lost a father and adult son, and a Sheffield factory-owning family, the Moulsons, also lost a son; two Irish families, the Reas and the Wickhams, each suffered the loss of a young man; the Lawlor family of Dundalk in Ireland lost their son, Patrick, who was one of the seamen in the *City of Glasgow*. His brother Thomas not only took over the care of his dead brother's family, he took over Patrick's job on a ferry, but was himself killed in an accident on the vessel at the end of May 1854.[36]

'Steam has conquered storms and tides'

Such tragedies can bring out the best in people, and a public fund was set up for Mrs Field and her children. In Philadelphia, a subscription was got up to relieve families impoverished by the sinking. Unfortunately, the wreck also brought out the worst in at least one person, who sent a fake letter that purported to be from a survivor of the *City of Glasgow*. It said that everyone on board had been rescued. The story was checked out and soon found to be a 'witless and cruel hoax'. Trolls are nothing new.[37]

Despite the loss of life involved, the sinking of the *City of Glasgow* did not linger in the public mind in the same way that the *Titanic* later did. There was no government enquiry into the *City of Glasgow*, no public pinning of blame, no afterlife for the ship as a symbol of courage or vanity or folly, and no movies to explore its human drama. The dreadful truth was that a loss like that of the *City of Glasgow* was not that unusual for the mid-nineteenth century Atlantic.

The company lost the *City of Glasgow* and the *City of Philadelphia* in the same year, but it was not this that destroyed the partnership between the Richardsons and Inman: the Crimean War did that. Inman wanted to hire out the remaining vessel, the *City of Manchester*, to the French government as a war transport. As Quakers, John and Joseph Richardson were pacifists, and could not agree, so Inman bought them out. He took the French contract, acquired another ship and ordered two more from Tod and McGregor. He remained in the emigrant trade and developed what later became the Inman Line into one of the strongest and best-known British shipping lines. However, the company was already in trouble by the time of his death in 1881, and was eventually bought up by an American firm in 1886.[38]

Tragic though they were, the loss of the *City of Glasgow* and other emigrant ships did not stop or even slow the rise of transatlantic migration. Emigration was driven by a mixture of poverty, fear, aspiration and hope, forces too strong to be hampered by the danger of wreck. The technology of larger, faster and more reliable ships facilitated mass-migration. Between 1783 and 1840 the USA received about one million immigrants: the figure rose in the age of steam to fifteen million over the next half-century, with another fourteen million in the years up to 1914. The *City of Glasgow* was just one, small part of a gathering wave.[39]

What became of William Collis and Charles, his surviving son? Collis emerged from the asylum after a short stay. The papers said that he was broke, as the family fortune, worth a reported $20,000, had gone down with the ship.[40]

In fact, William Collis was not English, as the post office staff had thought, but an Irish Protestant from Cork. Neither he nor his son Charles (1838–1902) fell into poverty, and Charles went on to become a successful Philadelphia lawyer. However, before that he achieved fame as a soldier in the American Civil War. He rose to be colonel of the 114th Pennsylvania Regiment, 'Collis's Zouaves', and won the Congressional Medal of Honor for courage in battle. The quartermaster of the 114th was William Collis.[41]

Chapter 2

Message in a Bottle
The Collier Brig *Russell* of Littlehampton (1872)

If marvels of technology like the *City of Glasgow* could be crushed by the sea, what hope could there be for little wooden brigs like the *Russell* of Littlehampton in savage weather?

On 17 December 1872 a great storm drove smashed timbers and wrecked gear ashore on the Northumbrian coast. It's likely that broken bodies also made up part of the monstrous litter left by that winter gale. Bizarrely, an intact soda bottle lay amid the debris, something so small and fragile that you would never have expected it to survive such huge waves. There were two messages sealed inside, written in pencil on the same piece of paper. One was a bald statement of time, position and condition: 'The brig *Russell*, off Huntcliff Foot, on the seventeenth, at five o'clock a.m., making a good deal of water'. The time and position were wrong, or at least out of date, for Huntcliffe Foot was miles away. The second message was personal, addressed to a woman called Ann, her name outlined in dots. Its contents never became public, but 'Ann' was almost certainly either Ann Burtenshaw or Ann Short, wives of two of the crew of the *Russell*. By the time the bottle washed up on that Northumberland beach, both women were widows.

The *Russell* was a collier brig, one of at least five sailing ships lost off the small port of Amble that day. Local people were no strangers to shipwrecks, and first became aware of the impending disasters at about 2.00 pm, when a trio of brigs was sighted two or three miles to the south. Heavy rain was falling, and this probably hid the land from the crews until it was too late for them to tack out to sea and escape. The wind was driving them straight for the shoreline, a situation potentially deadly for sailing vessels, and known as a 'lee shore'.

Groups of rescuers gathered on the coast. William Arkless, a senior customs officer from Warkworth, took charge of operations. Amble had its own twenty-man volunteer lifesaving company, operating rocket and mortar stations on either side of the port. These were peaceful weapons designed to fire lifelines to ships caught close in. The crew of the RNLI lifeboat at nearby Hauxley Haven was also called out in the terrible December weather – Arkless later described it as the stormiest sea he had seen in thirty years.

The first vessel to succumb was the *Father Matthews* of Seaham. At about 4.00 pm its master attempted to run his ship on to the beach, but it was overwhelmed by the sea and vanished. Some thirty minutes later, another brig was seen, just south of Hauxley. This was the *Russell*. It tried to clear the rocks, but struck Bondicar Point. A giant wave, half the height of the mainmast, washed over the ship. None of the six crew was seen afterwards. The hulk careered on towards Hauxley Haven, where the local lifeboatmen endeavoured to launch their boat, but the waves drove the craft back 'like a piece of straw'. The lifesaving brigade fired three rocket lines, but they fell 'a long way short', and rescue efforts were finally abandoned when it became clear that no one was left alive in the vessel. In less than an hour, the *Russell* was gutted by the sea and split apart.

At the same time, the brig *Ocean* of Sunderland drifted behind the north pier at Amble. After repeated efforts, a rocket line was got aboard, but at this moment the ship began to break up and sink, close enough to shore for the shocked onlookers to see and hear the drowning sailors. The *Matchless* and the schooner *Beccles*, both of Seaham, also went down in that storm. In the space of four hours, around thirty-five men died along a five-mile stretch of coast. Just to add to the horror, a boat from a German ship drifted to land, hinting at another tragedy.[1]

But this ill wind did somebody some good. Quite unselfconsciously, on 21 December the *Alnwick Mercury* ran an advertisement for an auction of the 'hull and stores' of the *Russell* that had been washed ashore. It was on the same page as a report of what it called 'this appalling series of disasters'. The same auctioneer also sold off the remains of the *Beccles* and the *Ocean*.[2]

News of the wrecks spread quickly across the country, thanks to the telegraph network and the plethora of Victorian local and national newspapers. People in the *Russell*'s home port of Littlehampton probably knew of the loss within a day or so, and on 19 December the story appeared in the county newspaper, the *West Sussex Gazette*.

The men who died in the brig were the captain, William Belchamber (35), the mate, Thomas Burtenshaw (31) and four seamen, Thomas Short (26), Charles Newell, William Marsh and Thomas Ede. Apart from Marsh, a Kentish man, all of the crewmen were Sussex-born. Three of them cannot be identified in contemporary censuses, but Belchamber, Burtenshaw and Short all had homes in Littlehampton.

William Belchamber and his family lived in St Martin's Lane, on the north side of the High Street. His wife Charlotte was about the same age, and the couple had married in 1862. By 1871 they had five children, aged between 6 months and 7 years. St Martin's Lane itself was mostly a working-class road, home to labourers, craftsmen, transport workers and other seafarers. The Belchambers lived in a rented two-up, two-down cottage on the southern end of a row of six identical dwellings, built in about 1848. As in millions of other homes of the period, at the back of the cottage there was a small garden, coalhouse, privy and a connecting alleyway. It was not a palace, but nor was it a slum (**Pl 5**).

Thomas Burtenshaw's house was in nearby Duke Street, which ran parallel to St Martin's Lane and had a similar kind of community. He was married to Ann (28 in 1871), and they had a daughter of 3 and a 2-year-old son. Ann may well have been pregnant at the time of the 1871 Census, because by 1881 she had a 10-year-old son called Frederick. The 1871 household also included an elderly, unrelated lodger, a sign that the Burtenshaws were in need of some extra cash. The family was part of a small local clan, for the Census lists a total of twenty-two Burtenshaws living in Littlehampton at the time.

Thomas Short lived in Surrey Street in 1871, along with Ann, his 26-year-old wife. They had a 1-year-old daughter in 1871, though apparently another child had arrived by 1872. Surrey Street had a greater social mix than St Martin's Lane or Duke Street, because the road was also home to the owner of the *Russell*, the wealthy Thomas Isemonger (1806–82). Isemonger was well into his sixties and married to 68-year-old Charlotte. They had no children of their own, although Charlotte had some from a previous marriage. Their upmarket household included Charlotte's unmarried daughter and two live-in servants, a cook and a housemaid.[3]

Thomas Isemonger was a member of a long-established family of Littlehampton merchants, shipbuilders and seafarers. Their shipyard had turned out wooden merchant ships, and his father, Thomas Tupper Isemonger, had built a warship for the Royal Navy during the Napoleonic War. The Isemongers also had a long involvement with the coastal coal trade.

Local trade directories give some clues as to how Thomas Isemonger wished to present himself to the world (**Pl 6**). He was described as a shipbuilder in the 1830s and 1840s, though from the 1850s onwards he emerged in new guises. In 1852, he was a 'custom house agent, coal merchant and shipowner'. By 1855, he felt sufficiently qualified to join the column of Littlehampton 'gentry'. At this time, he was also an agent for the London Maritime Association, a marine insurance company, and he retained a connection with the insurance business into the 1870s. An important local man, Isemonger was also on the Works Committee of the Littlehampton Harbour Board.[4] As a 'gentleman', Isemonger was separated from the sailors he employed by a wide social gulf, one measurable in crude economic terms. The total rateable value of his house and other Littlehampton properties was sixteen times greater than that of Captain Belchamber's rented cottage.[5]

Littlehampton stands on the West Sussex coastal plain at the mouth of the River Arun, one of two historic seaports on the river – the other is Arundel, a few miles to the north, at the edge of the South Downs. Arundel is an ancient town and was originally the main local port, whereas Littlehampton was not much more than a village until the eighteenth century. Littlehampton's fortunes improved markedly from the late 1700s onwards, and by the 1820s, four-fifths of the cargo entering the river was unloaded there. Amongst other things, it was easier for shippers to discharge goods at Littlehampton than to make the tricky journey up the winding Arun to Arundel.

The two places were rivals. When Littlehampton's first modern local government body was set up in 1853, it adopted 'Progress' as its motto, perhaps in a self-conscious attempt to differentiate the town from its venerable northern neighbour. 'Progress' could be a bit slow in coming, though. The original Sussex coastal track of the London, Brighton & South Coast Railway (LB & SCR) merely grazed the northern edge of Littlehampton when it opened in 1846, with little effect on the town. However, in 1863 the LB & SCR built a station in the town centre, adjacent to the river, with tracks running on to a nearby wharf. The wharf became the base for a cross-Channel steam ferry service that opened in November 1863 and operated until 1882. The ferries took passengers and cargo to and from the Channel Islands and St Malo in Brittany. Later on, the ferry route was extended to Honfleur in Normandy.

The railway made Littlehampton part of an up-to-date transport economy. Rich holidaymakers had been making their way there since the 1700s, and now the railway brought not just the ferry passengers, but trainloads of middle- and working-class holidaymakers and day trippers, as well. Lazy journalists may have characterized it as just a sleepy seaside resort – 'Emphatically the Sea on the QT' as *Punch* put it – but the people of mid-Victorian Littlehampton had some reason to feel that their town was at the forefront of modern life.[6]

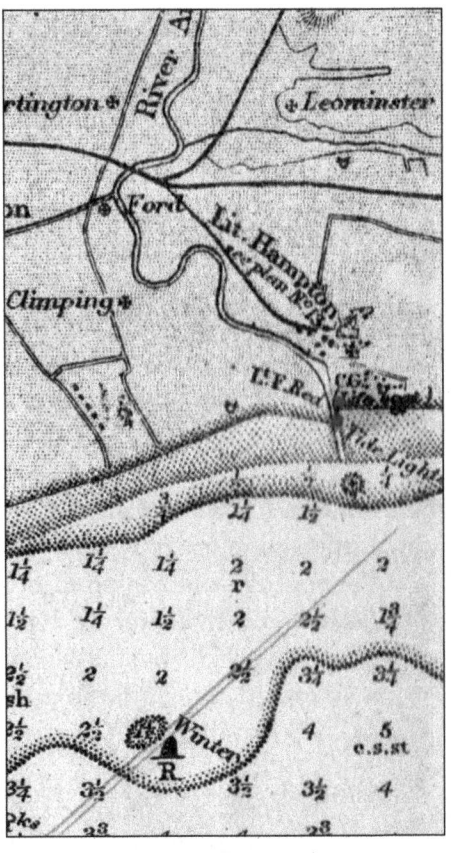

Fig 4 An 1898 chart showing Littlehampton and the Arun. (Hull 1898, pl 10)

Nevertheless, it was still a small place, with only 3,272 inhabitants in 1871. Littlehampton consisted of the old village centre, clustered around the High Street, and a separate area nearer to the shore called 'Beach Town', largely devoted to holiday accommodation. The port itself lay along the banks of the river, giving Captain William Belchamber and Thomas Burtenshaw a very short walk to work. To reach the waterfront from the High Street, they had to take a left into Surrey Street. This road led to the Arun, with houses, pubs, wharves, warehouses and small docks extending in both directions along Pier Road and River Road.

Despite the signs of modernity in Littlehampton, the brig *Russell* was part of an older world. It was a wooden sailing ship in an age when metal hulls and steam were beginning to dominate the oceans. A brig had two masts, with four-sided 'square sails' (hung from yards at right-angles to the keel) and fore-aft sails (rigged in line with the keel). This combination made the vessel manoeuvrable, and was more cost-effective than the conventional three-masted rig, because it required fewer men to manage it. That said, tending the sails of a brig still required a huge amount of work from sailors (**Pl 7**).

The type had been ubiquitous in British sea trade since the eighteenth century, superseding three-masted ships as coal-carriers. A collier brig was basically a mobile container for coal, and in pictures they often look quite boxlike. The hull was deep and generally straight-sided, with a flat bottom that enabled it to sit securely at low tide on a beach or harbour bottom.[7]

The *Russell* was 81 years old by the time it sank in 1872. It was built on the River Tyne in 1791, and was working on the Newcastle–Littlehampton run by 1824. The vessel was bought by Captain George Lawson of Littlehampton in 1827 and re-registered in the port. The *Russell* remained in the Lawson family until 1862, when Thomas Isemonger and a businessman named George Hull purchased it. Each man owned half of the ship – or in the somewhat arcane terminology of ship owning, 32/64ths – until Isemonger bought Hull out in April 1872.

The vessel was reckoned to be able to carry about 200 tons of coal, although the peculiarities of different tonnage *estimation* methods make it sound a lot smaller (118 tons in 1872, officially). The hull measured 74 feet (22.6m) from stem to stern, and 20.7 feet (6.3m) at its widest point. There would have been accommodation at the stern for the master and probably the mate, and a living space for the sailors in the forecastle, or foc'sle, in the bow.[8]

The *Russell* was not the only old ship run by Thomas Isemonger. Between 1855 and 1872 he owned five Littlehampton-registered vessels, either as sole owner or in partnerships. Two of these, including the *Russell*, were lost. The average age of each of the five ships at the time of purchase was thirty-four years. By contrast, the twenty sailing vessels owned by the port's two biggest ship-owning families, the Harveys and the Robinsons, were much newer. On average, Harvey ships were six years old at the time of purchase, and those of the Robinsons were two years old. Newness was not an automatic guarantee of safety – eleven of these twenty ships were lost in wrecks – but the chances for a contemporary vessel were much better than for one built just two years after the French Revolution.⁹

The *Russell* was part of an ancient tradition of shipping – the wooden vessel driven by sail. That tradition was about to die – but not quite yet. The records for ships entering UK ports in 1876 show that the numbers of sailing ship arrivals were still nearly double those for steamships. However, the great maritime technological revolutions of the nineteenth century produced vessels that were faster, more reliable and safer than sailing ships. A metal-hulled vessel could also be built much larger than a wooden one. The greater capacity, speed and reliability of metal steamers meant that by the mid-1870s almost 60 per cent of the cargoes arriving in Britain were carried by them. Sailing ships went into sharp decline from the 1870s and 1880s and by 1913, only around 7 per cent of the British-registered merchant fleet relied on sail.¹⁰

The *Russell* was built to serve the coastal trade in coal from north-east England, a trade that dated back to the Middle Ages. At first, it was based on sea-coal, gathered from the shoreline. London had a 'Sea-Coal Lane' by the 1220s, and in the fourteenth century, north-eastern coal was regularly shipped to other English ports, as well as to the Low Countries and Baltic. By the early decades of the seventeenth century, the Tyne alone was exporting nearly a quarter of a million tons of coal per year.¹¹ The coastwise coal trade was eventually overtaken by competition from rail and later, motor transport. Until that happened, coastal shipping was the only practical and cheap way of moving large amounts of the mineral to places outside the effective reach of the main canal network.

Sussex was further by sea from the English and Welsh coalfields than any other English county. Well-supplied with timber, the county only became a major consumer of coal in the second half of the eighteenth century. By the early 1840s, even a small place like Littlehampton was receiving about 30,000 tons of coal annually. These imports were distributed by horse and cart, and by barge up the Wey & Arun Canal to towns in Surrey like Guildford and Godalming. As in the rest of the country, coal had become an essential fuel for the home, commerce and industry.¹² This was underlined in the winter of 1873, when a strong north wind prevented colliers from getting into the Arun. The *West Sussex Gazette* complained of a 'coal famine' at Arundel and Littlehampton in which 'hardly a ton of coal could be obtained for love or money'.

Eventually, 'a vessel has appeared in the river laden with black diamonds but these are meted out to consumers very sparingly'.[13]

We know so much about the shipping and trade of nineteenth century Britain because the Victorian age was a great era of bureaucracy. Governments made strenuous efforts to measure the social and economic life of the nation, aiming to diagnose problems and improve conditions. Shipping was no exception, though the pace of reform was slow. There were attempts to regulate the safety of the British mercantile fleet from the 1830s, but these met with serious opposition from shipowners.

The general reasons for shipping casualties were well known: they included bad weather, poor construction, bad maintenance, overloading, incompetent masters and owners and inadequate crews. However, detailed data was needed to understand the situation properly, and the Board of Trade was tasked with investigating shipwrecks. By the 1860s the annual Board of Trade *Wreck Abstracts* were fearsomely comprehensive documents. They revealed a desperate situation, but even with all this information, government and its officials could be shockingly complacent about the scale of losses. In a review of shipwreck figures for UK waters in the years 1861 to 1873, the Board of Trade remarked blithely that 'a small proportion only are attended with loss of life'. However, this amounted to totals of 2,038 wrecks with fatalities and *9,384* dead. Between 1853 and 1872 there were nearly 30,000 wrecks and collisions around the British coastline.

The system was also skewed when it came to the interpretation of data. For example, out of 439 ship losses in 1872, bad weather and human error were put down as the two main causes. In other words, either nature or crews were held culpable. It was far less common for the Board of Trade to lay the blame at the door of negligent owners, people who sent out ships that were defective or overloaded. Research carried out by the radical MP Samuel Plimsoll (1824–98), however, suggested that many owners operated vessels that were dangerously overstuffed with cargo. Plimsoll used the Board of Trade data in an ultimately successful campaign to improve the lot of seafarers. In 1876 an official safe load line – later called the 'Plimsoll Line' – was finally made mandatory for British ships. Sadly, this was four years too late for the crew of the *Russell*.

Colliers were a common sight at sea and they routinely made up a third or more of all shipping casualties in UK waters. In 1872 alone, the *Russell*

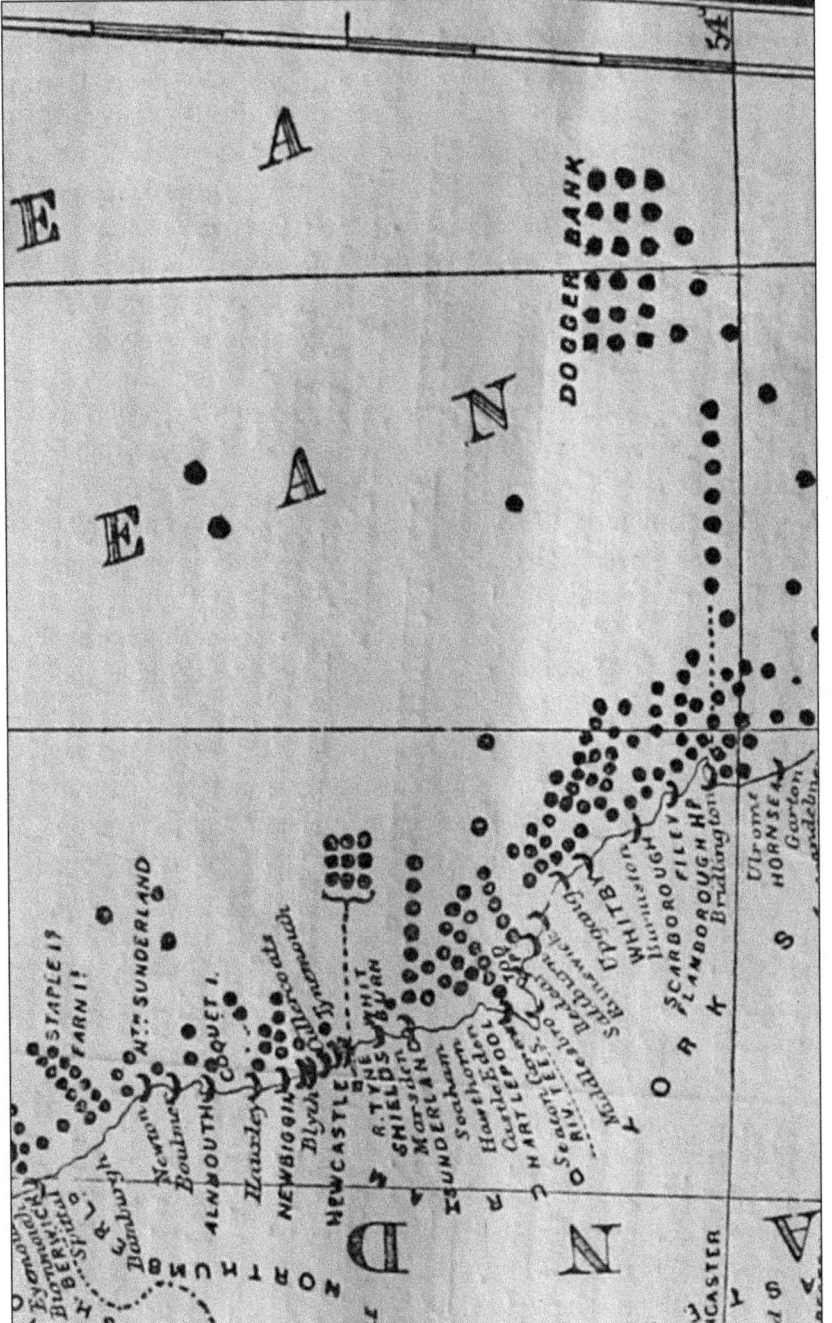

Fig 5 This is an extract from a Board of Trade wreck map for the British Isles, and shows the north-east coast of England. Hauxley, where the RNLI crew tried to launch in an attempt to save the men of the *Russell*, is just south of Alnmouth. Wrecks were appallingly frequent: the map summarizes the shipwrecks and collisions in this area in 1868 alone. The boat shapes on the coast represent lifeboats.

was just one of 421 colliers wrecked or damaged. Even its great age of eighty-one years was not exceptional. Seven older vessels were lost, including two coasters that had racked up more than a century of service apiece. The 1872 *Wreck Abstracts* also highlighted the east coast – the primary coal route – as the most dangerous part of the British seaboard, the scene of 45 per cent of all shipping casualties. The riskiest stretch was the hundred miles between Flamborough Head in Yorkshire and the Farne Islands off Northumberland. The *Russell* was lost in this deadly zone.

On a more optimistic note, the Board of Trade reports showed that between 1855 and 1872, nearly 69,000 lives were saved from wrecks around Britain and Ireland. The majority of these were rescued by the ships' own lifeboats or by other vessels, but about one person in five was saved by lifeboats or shore-based lifesaving societies. The development of a network of lifeboat stations of the Royal National Lifeboat Institution (RNLI) around the British Isles, together with the establishment of many local lifesaving societies, were among the great humanitarian achievements of the nineteenth century. This was made all the more remarkable because lifesaving at sea relied – and still relies, to a very large extent – on the courage and selflessness of volunteers. Everyone who turned out on that terrible December day at Amble and Hauxley was a volunteer.

The government did attempt to increase safety by improving the quality of ships' officers, and from 1850 it was compulsory for all masters and mates in British ships to have certificates of competency based on examination. This did not prevent some owners, like Isemonger, ignoring the law and employing non-certificated officers like Belchamber and Burtenshaw. A mate or a master's 'ticket' was not a magic bullet for safety, but in 1872 the number of wreck incidents where ships' officers had no certificates was just over a third greater than those that involved men with paper qualifications.[14]

The *Russell*'s crew lists survive between 1863 and 1872 (with the exception of those for 1865), and these tell us a lot about its last nine years. Over this time the old brig made at least ninety-two voyages and probably sailed more than 30,000 miles (48,000km), the equivalent of a trip round the world and more.

The cargoes carried by the *Russell* varied little. Typically, it went out either in ballast (with no cargo) or with a load of timber – or tree bark,

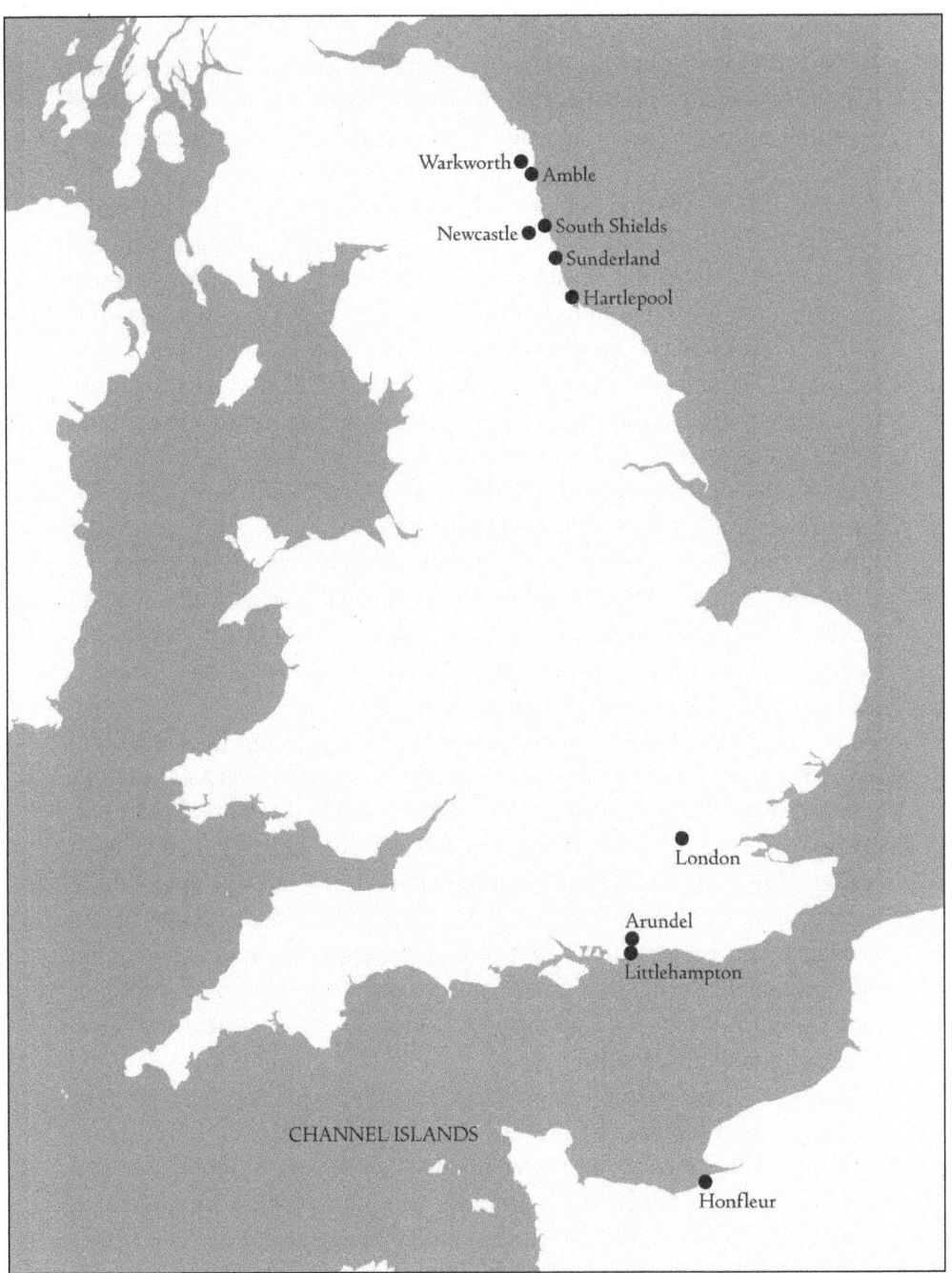

Fig 6 Some of the places connected with Victorian Littlehampton and the *Russell*.

on at least one occasion. Apart from a journey to Llanelli in South Wales in 1866, the north-east was its main destination. Sunderland was the port that the brig visited most frequently, with occasional stops at Hartlepool or South Shields. The return cargoes from the north-east were always coal.[15]

In the 1860s, the normal crew of the *Russell*, counting master, mate, seamen, ship's boy and apprentices, consisted of between seven and ten people. In 1872 the vessel was only crewed by six sailors, and it is possible that under-manning played some part in the eventual disaster.

The vessel was laid up at Littlehampton for two and a half years from January 1870, and only went back to sea in June 1872, after what seems to have been extensive refurbishment.[16] According to testimony at the later wreck enquiry, from William Nutter (a local shipbuilder), Isemonger oversaw the repairs himself and hired seven or eight shipwrights for the work. Nutter said that even though the brig was eighty years old, it was 'a good strong ship' – an opinion general in Littlehampton, he claimed. This was corroborated by three of the shipwrights who worked on the vessel. The one dissenting local voice at the enquiry was Joseph Grafton, the Collector of Customs, who claimed that he had 'heard it said in Littlehampton that the *Russell* was rotten'.

The brig went back to sea on 20 June 1872, arriving in Sunderland five days later. Over the next five months it completed a total of four round trips to the north-east, two to Sunderland and two to Hartlepool; on its last voyage, Sunderland was the port of call (**Pl 8**). On each occasion, the cargo out was timber, and the return load was coal. Of the crew in June 1872, only Belchamber had sailed with the ship before. He had been its mate for much of the period between 1863 and 1867, and in the latter year became its master. Burtenshaw and Short were with him in the ship from June 1872 to the end, Burtenshaw as the mate and Short as an able-bodied seaman.

The other half of the crew changed completely over the course of the brig's final months – Charles Newell, William Marsh and Thomas Ede joined the *Russell* as replacements between late September and late November. This kind of turnover was not unusual for merchant vessels, as sailors were a floating population in more than one sense. It did mean, though, that half of the *Russell*'s crew was fairly new, with little experience of serving together. This might also have affected their performance on the brig's last voyage.[17]

Message in a Bottle

Sussex newspapers treated the news of that last voyage's fatal end in a predictable way. They recounted the events and expressed sympathy for the families, but did not even hint that the brig's owner might bear any responsibility for what happened. Quite the reverse, in fact. In January 1873, six months before the public enquiry, the *West Sussex Gazette* was at pains to exonerate Isemonger:

> It is satisfactory the loss of the Russell has not be [*sic*] attributed to her great age – the ship's register dating from 1791 – she had what in shipping phraseology is called a good constitution – her timbers, which were heart of oak, being found shortly before going to sea remarkably sound.'

Readers were also assured that the other vessels lost on that coast in the storm included 'a fine new ship', which was definitely not true.[18]

The Board of Trade convened the wreck enquiry at Arundel in June 1873. It was chaired by four local magistrates, with two sea captains as nautical assessors to supply technical advice, and lawyers representing both the Board and Isemonger. Most of the witnesses were Sussex men, although three were also summoned from the north-east.[19]

The first of these was John Turpin, master of the tug *Blue Bonnet* of Sunderland. According to his testimony, he had towed the *Russell* to the coal drops (loading chutes) many times. He did so on 13 December, and noticed that the sailors were working at the pumps. After the brig had been loaded, he was concerned to see that there was only 18 to 20 inches (45–50cm) of freeboard, and the men were still pumping. Freeboard is the distance between the water and the open deck level, and this was a perilously narrow margin for a vessel then carrying 184 tons of coal. Turpin was worried, and went aboard at 1.00 am to rouse Belchamber. The captain admitted that the ship was leaking, with about two feet of water in the hold. Despite this, he still decided to set sail later that day, as the wind was favourable.

Isemonger's counsel challenged Turpin and asked 'whether there were not three and a half feet [1.1m] instead of 18 to 20 inches' of freeboard, and the tug master admitted that he could not swear to it. Quite where the lawyer got the 3½ feet figure is not clear – it was probably plucked out of the air in an effort to undermine Turpin's credibility.

The job of guiding the brig out of Sunderland was undertaken by a local pilot, Robert Henry Thompson, who came aboard on 15 December. He testified that the ship was trimmed upright – that is, the cargo had been laid correctly – but

> The men were pumping at one pump only when he went on board on the 15th, and they grumbled at the little decrease in water that was made, and two pumps were then used for about three quarters of an hour. One of the crew said to him that they had had a bad job with her last voyage, but it appeared they were going to have a worse one this time.

Thompson guided the vessel out to sea the following day, by which time the men had ceased pumping. The pilot did not recall the captain making any complaint about the vessel to him. Thompson praised the old brig's sailing qualities, but backed up Turpin's estimate of the freeboard and went on to say that

> She was not sufficiently seaworthy for... [him]... who, knowing how old she was, and that she had made so much water the day before, would not have liked to have gone to sea in her. A ship that would make two feet of water in twenty-four hours [he] should consider to be dangerous.

William Arkless, the Warkworth customs officer, was the third witness from the north-east. He recounted the last minutes of the brig, but was also able to say something about the hull remains that he saw on the beach afterwards: 'The timbers of the ship were inspected, and the bottom found to be good, but she did not seem to be strong, her upper works being very much gone.' He admitted that any ship caught so close to the shore in such a storm could not have saved itself, but also went to say that not one of the ships lost there that day was new: 'If they had been well-found vessels [in good condition]... [he]... did not think they would have been where they were, seeking for a harbour, but would have kept out at sea.'

The evidence from these three men was in marked contrast to most of the Littlehampton testimony. The three northerners saw the ship in its last days, and had no obvious axe to grind about its condition. The

Littlehampton witnesses, by contrast, all knew Isemonger, and some may have hoped for future employment from him. With one exception – the Littlehampton customs officer quoted above – they all said positive things about the *Russell*. The customs officer, it should be remembered, was a state employee and not reliant on Isemonger for work.

Isemonger himself was called as a witness. He said that he had bought the brig, along with a partner, for £327 in 1839. The local registry information shows that he only owned it from 1862: either his memory was at fault, or he was lying, trying to create the impression that he had operated the brig for longer than he did. He claimed that since that time he had spent £1,580/7s/7½d on repairs to the vessel – Mr Isemonger was clearly someone who counted the ha'pennies.

He said that the ship had been 'almost entirely rebuilt', and neither Belchamber nor the crew had ever complained about it being unseaworthy. He tabled a 'lot of letters' written to him by Belchamber during the last voyage, none of which mentioned any problem with the brig's condition. Isemonger also made a point of saying that the *Russell* and its contents were uninsured. Contemporaries were very familiar with the idea that unscrupulous shipowners might send defective vessels to sea in order to collect on insurance, and Isemonger plainly wanted to show that he was not the sort of villain who would do that.

The enquiry lasted five hours. Its verdict was that the wreck was due to the severity of the storm and the vessel's proximity to the coast, making it impossible for the crew to save the brig. It went on to say that: 'The ship was not insured, and there was no evidence to show that the ship was inefficient [sic] in equipment, that she was overloaded, or unseaworthy. The court, therefore, exonerate the owner from in any way contributing to the cause of the disaster.'

In one sense, the judgment was entirely right: a wooden sailing vessel caught in that situation so close to the coast *would* almost certainly be doomed. However, the verdict discounted the evidence of the northerners and of the message in the bottle, all of which made clear that the brig was low in the water and leaking badly. It likewise ignored Arkless's comment about the weakness in the hull, nor did it make any reference to the *Russell*'s extreme age.

All wooden ships will leak somewhat, but the scale of the leaks in the *Russell* suggests that there was a hole in the hull or something was seriously wrong with its caulking, the mixture of rope and tar that was supposed to seal the gaps between planks. Serious leaks were not always immediately fatal to a vessel, because a ship might take in a lot of water and still stay afloat. However, it would acquire the sailing characteristics of a log and become uncontrollable, at the mercy of the waves. As Arkless noted, well-found ships – that is, well-equipped vessels in good condition – would have been able to keep out to sea on the day of the storm.

As master, William Belchamber was accountable for the loss of the *Russell*. He was an experienced seaman, and his lack of complaint about the vessel is strange, though explicable. Professional pride or a dislike of whingeing may have played a part in his disastrous decision to take the leaky old brig to sea. However, I suspect that there was another consideration at work here: shipwreck was a *possibility*, but the dire consequences of not sailing were a near certainty.

Although called 'captain', William Belchamber was far from rich and ranked very low in the Victorian maritime world. His pay rate of £4 a month was only £1 more than that of the able-bodied sailors in his crew. He had no paper qualifications. He had been employed by Isemonger on and off for at least nine years, and must have relied on the man for his future prospects. A decision not to sail would have had immediate consequences: stoppage of the crew's wages, the sack for him, his career blighted or even terminated, and potential destitution for his wife and children.

Despite the 1873 verdict and Belchamber's fatal decision, in my view Thomas Isemonger bore a heavy responsibility for the loss of the *Russell*. The vessel was far too old to be at sea on the east-coast route, whatever reconstruction work had taken place. It had serious leaks, and a hull that looked weak to an independent, experienced observer. It is difficult to believe that Isemonger, a man with a shipbuilding background, could have been ignorant of the vessel's shortcomings. He may simply have accepted them as 'normal', a risk worth taking because, for decades, the brig had always come through. His complacency may well have killed the men of the *Russell*.

We don't know what the grieving families thought about all this. The approach of a Victorian local newspaper was often strictly top-down, even with members of the 'deserving' poor, and no one seems to have sought the opinions of the widows. It was reported that Charlotte Belchamber was heavily pregnant at the time of the sinking, but if this was true, she lost the baby. There is no record of a sixth child.

There is a terrible irony in the fact that Isemonger was the local representative of the Shipwrecked Mariners' Society, which raised money for wreck survivors and the families of lost seamen. By 9 January 1873, the Society had donated the equivalent of several months' wages to the bereaved, and it was said that 'a good local subscription is also being passed'.[20]

No doubt the money tided the families over for a while, but the loss of their main breadwinners must have had dire financial repercussions for them. There were signs of this, ten years on, because it is possible to trace Charlotte Belchamber, Ann Burtenshaw and their children in the 1881 Littlehampton Census returns.

The Burtenshaws had moved to St Martin's Lane by that time, and both women were near neighbours. Neither family had prospered, the women getting by on ill-paid menial work. Ann worked as a laundress, sharing her cottage with two schoolboy sons; Charlotte still had four children living at home, three boys in low-paid jobs and one girl at school. Charlotte herself worked as a charwoman.

In the scale of nineteenth-century shipping casualties, the loss of the *Russell* was not a major one, and around twenty-nine other men also died off Amble in that terrible storm. However, the story of this tragedy is a stark illustration of the precarious lives led by many ordinary sailors and their families, from the Middle Ages to modern times. On the one side was casual employment in a dangerous environment, working in vessels that could be unseaworthy: on the other side lay family disaster, poverty and death. Shipowners like Isemonger, however, could often walk away from a tragedy like this without any public sign of reproach.

Charlotte Belchamber never remarried, and outlived William by just over twenty-three years. She died on 13 February 1896 at the age of 58, and lies in Littlehampton Cemetery, under a headstone that also commemorates her husband:

WILLIAM BELCHAMBER
WHO WAS DROWNED
17th December 1872

Chapter 3

The Mastermind and the Insubordinate Stoker
The Battleship HMS *Victoria* (1893)

If complacency may have helped to sink the *Russell*, then other kinds of folly sank HMS *Victoria*.

The *Victoria* was sunk in a collision with another British warship in the eastern Mediterranean on 23 June 1893. The collision was the fault of Vice-Admiral Sir George Tryon, commander-in-chief of the Mediterranean Fleet, who 'flew his flag' as admiral in the *Victoria*. However, the disaster was aided and abetted by a number of senior officers who failed to question the mistaken order that led to the tragedy. Tryon and 363 of his crew perished, but among the 291 survivors was a man who normally worked in the bowels of the ship and stood at the opposite end of the chain of command from Tryon. He was Stoker (2nd Class) James Curran. It is sometimes said that tragedy repeats itself as farce, but in Curran's case, it was repeated for entertainment and profit, as he took the stage and recounted his tale in a late Victorian multimedia show. The stories of these two men, and of the *Victoria*, have a lot to say about the navy, the nation and naval warfare in the years leading up to the First World War.

Understandably, earlier studies of the sinking of the *Victoria* have focused on the failings of Tryon and other officers, and the confused contemporary ideas about naval warfare that contributed to the tragedy. However, the story has other dimensions, one of them captured by the *Portsmouth Evening News* on Saturday, 24 June. News of survivors was still:

> awaited at the Dockyard gates by a considerable number of the relatives of the crew, who, with tear-stained faces

and eyes swollen by prolonged weeping, had been in attendance at the main entrance of the establishment since the early morning, watching for the appearance of the official communication which would disclose the fate of their loved ones.[1]

George Tryon (1832–93) (**Pl 9**) came from an old-established Northamptonshire gentry family, and joined the navy as an officer cadet at the age of fifteen. He served with distinction in the Crimean War, and in 1861 was one of the officers of HMS *Warrior*, the original British ironclad. Clever and experienced, Tryon had a distinguished career in the navy: he reached the rank of rear-admiral in 1884, and was knighted in 1887. Amongst other things he reorganized the defence of the Royal Navy's Australia Station and in Britain set up a naval intelligence committee that would later evolve into the Naval Intelligence Department. In public, he raised the thorny issue of government insurance of sea trade in wartime – something that became a matter of desperate urgency a little more than twenty years after his death (see Chapter 4).

Tryon believed that the Victorian navy had become over-reliant on a complex system of signalling that stifled the initiative and daring of individual commanders and would serve the fleet badly in wartime. As he pointed out, random shots in battle could take out signal flags or signallers, making it impossible for a fleet commander to transmit orders. His innovative approach was known as 'TA', after a signal code that signified that a captain should observe the movements of the admiral's ship in a squadron, and be prepared to copy them, with or without signals. Tryon went on to train the Mediterranean Fleet in 'TA'. In his classic study of the Royal Navy from the Victorian era to the Great War, *The Rules of the Game*, Andrew Gordon points out the paradox that Tryon's immense knowledge and ability, when coupled with his forceful personality, led his subordinates to see him as infallible. As Captain Bourke, commander of the *Victoria*, put it at the court martial that followed the disaster: 'Sir George Tryon had a master mind. He loved argument, but was a strict disciplinarian. He always used to say that he hated people who agreed with him; but that was different from arguing against a direct order …'

The 'mastermind' ended up leading himself and hundreds of his men to their deaths. The testimony of the survivors of all ranks featured at the subsequent court martial, and some appeared in the press. However, one of the truly unusual features of the loss of the *Victoria* and its aftermath is that a very lowly crew member, Stoker James Curran, got to appear on the public stage and give his side of the story.[2]

The details of James Curran's life are far less well documented than those of Tryon. Curran was born in Dundee in 1873, though unfortunately he is difficult to track in the censuses (**Pl 10**). He briefly served in the army, and then deserted, joining the navy in August 1892 for a twelve-year stint. He came aboard the *Victoria* on 1 April 1893. According to his enlistment form, the young Scotsman was of average height, just over 5½ feet, with dark brown hair, grey eyes and a sallow complexion. Like many other sailors, he had a tattoo – in his case, the figure of a woman drawn on his right upper arm. He gave his trade as 'seaman', avoiding all mention of his previous army service.[3]

The third 'character' in this account was the battleship HMS *Victoria*. It belonged to a two-ship class, with HMS *Sans Pareil* as its sister ship (see back cover). The *Victoria* was built by Armstrong, Mitchell and Co. in their Elswick yard on the River Tyne and launched in April 1887 (the *Sans Pareil* was constructed on the Thames, and launched in the following month). They each had a displacement of

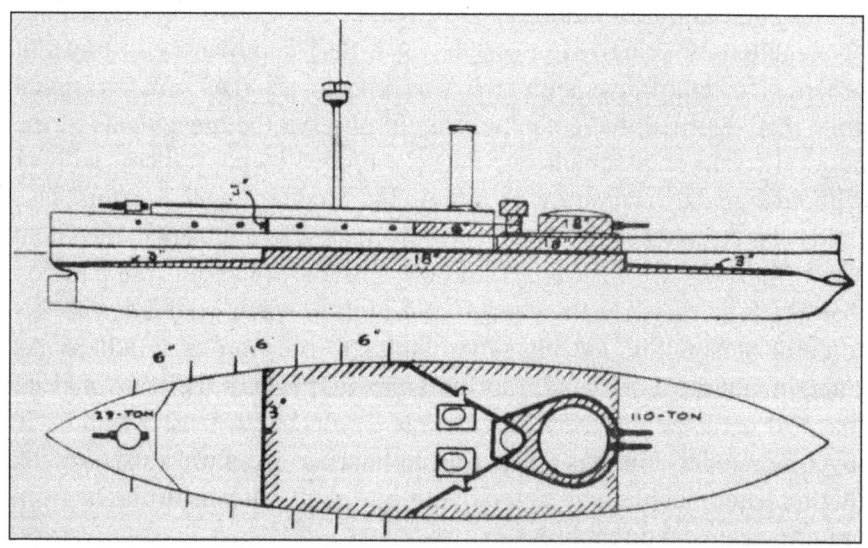

Fig 7 Plan and elevation drawings of HMS *Victoria*. The hatched areas represent armour plating. (Hovgaard 1920, p 15)

10,470 tons, a length of 340 feet and a beam of 70 feet (104 x 21m – displacement tonnage represents the weight of water displaced by a vessel). The ships were built of steel and were the first in the Royal Navy to be powered by triple expansion engines, of which each had two, driving twin propellers (see Chapter 4).

Both were armoured ships, though it was never practical or desirable with any armoured vessel to protect every part of the hull. As with other ships, the armour in these vessels was concentrated to cover vital spots. For example, an 18-inch thick (457mm) belt covered around one-thirds of each side of the hull, just above the boilers, there was a 3-inch armoured deck and 17 inches of armour around the main gun turret.

The ships cost around £777,000 each. As a share of GDP, this would equate to about £1.1 billion today. The vessels bristled with twenty-seven guns apiece, besides six torpedo tubes, but their chief armament comprised a pair of massive, turret-mounted guns, each weighing just under 111 tons and built by an Armstrong subsidiary, the Elswick Ordnance Company. The gun barrels had bores of 16¼ inches (413mm), firing projectiles of 1,800lb weight (818kg).

The ships had a wide field of fire at the bow – the turret could traverse through 300° – but if they had ever gone into combat, the limitations of their big guns would have been quickly exposed. Only a dozen of these monster weapons was ever built: the design was 'tweaked' with each example, and they were reckoned to be able to fire just seventy-five times before they wore out and needed replacing. Though their range exceeded 12,000 yards (3.7km), it's unlikely that they could hit anything with any accuracy beyond a few thousand yards, given the limitations of contemporary gunsights. Besides these huge guns, both the *Victoria* and *Sans Pareil* had ram bows that projected outwards in their underwater parts – every other major warship of the period had this feature.

The design parameters of warships were laid down by the Board of Admiralty, in a period when the Royal Navy was experimenting with a multiplicity of battleship types. There was little data on what designs would or would not work in combat, because there had been very few major fleet actions since the Napoleonic War, nearly three-quarters of a century earlier. Naval strategy and tactics were in flux, which accounted for the wide range of warship designs that appeared, and the questionable value of features such as the ram. It is possible that the powerful bow armament of the *Victoria* and *Sans Pareil* was the result of an Admiralty requirement for ships capable of blasting their way through the Turkish-held Dardanelles to the Black Sea. This is not certain, though both ships did serve in the Mediterranean.

The technology that went into the *Victoria* was the product of a long period of development and expensive trial and error, reaching back to the early decades of the nineteenth century and the introduction of steam power. Like other navies, the Royal Navy was building steam-powered warships by the 1830s, but these were all fairly small vessels, not line-of-battle ships. They were also driven by paddles, which would be vulnerable to damage in battle and took up space in the sides normally used for guns. Paddles were rapidly superseded by screw propellers, which produced more power and were far less vulnerable because they were mounted at the stern, below water (see Chapter 1). New wooden line-of-battle ships were built with propellers, and some existing big vessels were converted to use steam power and screws, though all warships would retain their masts and sails until the 1870s or later (engines were not always reliable, and sail-trained naval officers could also be *very* conservative).

In the 1850s the French began building armoured warships, though their first effort, *La Gloire*, was a wooden warship with applied iron armour. This helped spark an arms race. Arms races of one kind or another have been a feature of human history since a warrior with a flint dagger found himself facing someone waving a metal sword, but nineteenth- and twentieth-century industrialization speeded the process up in unprecedented ways. The Royal Navy feared that the French fleet might have a technological edge in any conflict, a recurrent nightmare through the rest of the nineteenth century (until it was supplanted by the threat from Germany in the early 1900s). Britain went one better than *La Gloire*. In 1861 it commissioned HMS *Warrior*, the world's first iron-hulled ironclad, complete with a steam engine and propeller – though it still had a full set of sails and most of its guns fired out from the sides of the ship, in broadsides (batteries of weapons, firing through gunports in the side of the ship).

A better kind of mild steel became available from the 1870s, one that was stronger and more malleable than iron. Hulls and armour made of steel became practical propositions, and began to replace iron. At the same time that hull construction and propulsion were changing, naval armament was also evolving. Rifled breech-loading guns were developed that proved more accurate than the existing muzzle-loading guns, but early experiments with them, and with explosive shells, were not wholly successful. Muzzle-loading guns, firing solid shot, continued in use into the second half of the nineteenth century, as did the arrangement of guns in broadsides. Eventually, reliable breach-loaders and shells supplanted the older weapons and ammunition, and the biggest guns aboard ship came to be positioned in rotating turrets, which gave the guns a much greater field of fire than was possible with broadsides. Such was the speed of change that HMS *Devastation*, completed just ten years after the *Warrior*, became the first seagoing ironclad to be equipped with turrets, and the first to be without any sails.

Naval officers appreciated that steam power made new tactics possible. The older line-of-battle tactics, developed in the seventeenth century, had been based on sailing ships whose main firepower lay in their broadsides. Steam vessels could move independently of the wind, opening up a potentially greater range of tactical options. One of these options was an ancient method, given a new lease of life: ramming. Experience from the 1861–65 American Civil War and the 1866 Austro-Italian naval battle of Lissa, in which two Italian ironclads were sunk by ramming, suggested that it could be a viable tactic. The appeal of ramming, if one can call it that, lay in the limitations of solid shot. Solid shot was still widely in use, but its impact was often blunted by iron hulls and iron armour. The result was that major warships, until the early decades of the twentieth century, were built with reinforced rams at their bows. The *actual* evidence to support the tactic was very slight, but this near-suicidal vogue appealed to the offensive mindset inculcated in naval officers of all nations. As the sinking of the *Victoria* was to show, ramming did work, but it could also put the ship that did the ramming at serious risk.[4]

The Royal Navy of the late nineteenth century was a very different kind of organization from the one that had won the Napoleonic War at sea. The professionalization of the officer corps had begun in the later seventeenth century, and the navy came to offer a career, albeit mainly for men of middle or upper-class origins. This had not been the case for most common seamen in the days of sail. They were mainly recruited or (often in wartime) pressed into service from the poorer sections of society, the majority serving with little hope of anything better beyond prize money for captured ships or eventual demobilization.

Problems in manning the Victorian navy, and the increasing need to have people able to operate machinery, led to changes in the mid-1800s. The Continuous Service Act of 1853 enabled boys to sign on for ten years' service at the age of 18, and if they served for twenty years, they became eligible for a naval pension. Pay was increased for continuous service men, and the creation of new ranks, below officer level, opened up more chances for promotion, as did a growing number of specialist courses in areas such as gunnery or engine-room work. One very visible sign of change came in 1857, with the introduction of an official naval uniform for seamen – though it came in more than a century after officers had first received government uniforms. Life in the navy was no picnic for anyone, as discipline was tight: to take one instance, the use of flogging as a punishment was not suspended until 1879. However, with all its imperfections, naval service gradually became much more of a career for the men and boys of the 'lower deck' than had been the case in earlier times.

The introduction of steam into the navy in the early decades of the nineteenth century created a need to recruit significant numbers of men who were not sailors. Engineer officers and stokers became essential, the officers to manage the engines and the stokers to keep the boilers supplied with shovelfuls of coal. Though the work of the stoker was vital, and the navy introduced an improved career structure for these men in the 1870s and 1880s, in terms of status stokers existed, both literally and figuratively, at the bottom of the ship.[5]

Whether they were senior officers or stokers, the 655 men and boys aboard the *Victoria* on 22 June 1893 all underwent the same ordeal, and over half of them were drowned.

The *Victoria* was commissioned as the flagship of the British Mediterranean Fleet in 1890, the most powerful single force in the Royal Navy. This fleet defended Britain's interests in the Mediterranean, particularly the vital route through the Suez Canal that gave a shortcut to India and the rest of the British Empire in Asia. Tryon was appointed commander-in-chief of the fleet in 1891, a sign of the trust that the navy had in his abilities.

Exercising a fleet was important both to maintain battle readiness and to 'show the flag', and on 27 May 1893, the fleet sailed from Malta on its summer manoeuvres. It was divided into two divisions, the first led by Vice-Admiral Tryon in the *Victoria*, which was captained by Maurice

Fig 8 The eastern Mediterranean, the Dardanelles and the southern Black Sea, from an early 1920s map, showing the Dardanelles in the north-east, and the Suez Canal to the south-east. The black dot marks the approximate position of the loss of the *Victoria*.

Bourke. The second division was under Rear-Admiral Albert Markham in the *Camperdown*. The ships called in at Nafplio in Greece, and then at Marmaris (Turkey), Acre (then in Syria) and Beirut in the Lebanon. On 22 June, the fleet up-anchored and set sail northwards, for Tripoli.

Midway through that afternoon, the *Victoria* was rammed and sunk by the *Camperdown*, following a manoeuvre ordered by the commander-in-chief. The fleet was sailing in two parallel columns, one led by Tryon, the other by Markham. 'TA' was not in use – in other words no ships' captains were being called upon to use their initiative. Tryon ordered both columns to turn towards each other, preparatory to entering Tripoli Bay and anchoring. The problem was, the columns were only 1,200 yards apart (six 'cables' in nautical measurements – 1,098m), less than the combined turning circles of the two battleships. It made a

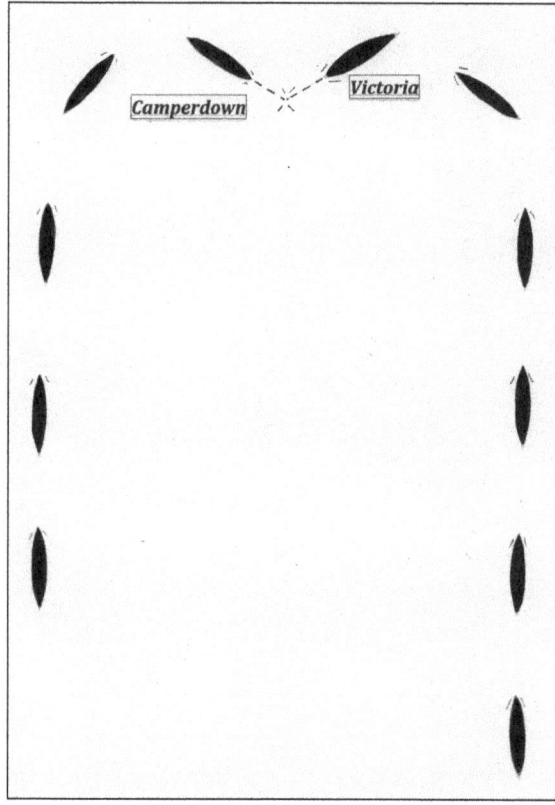

Fig 9 The fatal manoeuvre: the positions of the *Victoria* and *Camperdown* three minutes after Tryon sent his turn order. (Redrawn and reinterpreted after a chart in TNA MFQ 1/235)

collision likely. Officers in the *Victoria* knew this, but did not challenge Tryon directly about the danger. No naval officer of the time – perhaps of any time – would risk his career by telling an admiral that he was dead wrong. Added to that, Captain Bourke of the *Victoria*, like others, trusted the mastermind to perform some brilliant manoeuvre at the last moment. That trust was misplaced.

Rear-Admiral Markham in the *Camperdown* had misgivings about the order, too. He hesitated, but complied after Tryon tetchily signalled 'What are you waiting for?'

The *Camperdown* gashed a large hole in the starboard side of the *Victoria*, with a force reckoned to be equivalent to 17,000 or 18,000 tons concentrated into its steel ram, which penetrated some 9 feet (2.75m) into the *Victoria's* hull. The ships were only locked together for a minute or so, but in that time their sterns swung towards each other, widening the breach like a can opener working at a tin.

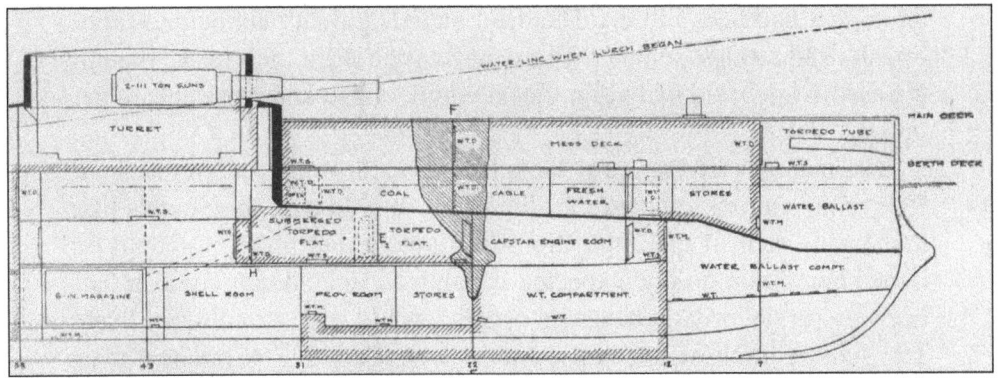

Fig 10 The fatal impact. The hatched area shows the hole made by the *Camperdown*'s bow, and the diagonal line above the deck marks how far the water got before the *Victoria* lurched over and sank. (Hovgaard 1920, facing page 69)

An order had gone out a minute or so before the collision to close watertight doors and hatches in the *Victoria*, but it normally took three minutes to close all of them. Out of around sixty doors, scuttles and hatches in the fore part of the vessel, at least thirteen were still open when the *Camperdown* struck. As Markham's vessel withdrew, hundreds of tons of water flooded into the bow of the *Victoria*, dragging it down: the massive weight of its big guns contributed to the downward pressure.

Within the space of four minutes, nineteen compartments below the weather deck were full of sea water. The bow sank by 10 feet, and the ship began heeling over to starboard by about 20°. An attempt was made to steam towards land, to ground the ship, but this probably just increased the inrush of water. The hydraulic steering gear failed at this point, but even if it had been working, it is doubtful that a functioning helm would have affected what came next.

The water reached the two forward 6-inch gunports on the starboard side. They were open, allowing water into the superstructure. The ship gave a sudden lurch, turned over on its starboard side, and then sank, bow first and upside down. It was around thirteen minutes after the collision. Staff-Commander Hawkins-Smith, who had been standing on top of the chart house with Admiral Tryon, was washed into the sea along with the admiral, who was never seen again. Hawkins-Smith survived and later noted that his watch stopped at 3.44 pm and 50 seconds.[6]

What became of the crew of the *Victoria* in the disaster? Some may well have died in the flooded sections, perhaps trapped behind watertight doors that had been closed. The dead included eighty-six engine-room officers and ratings, some of whom may have died at their posts, though it was also later said that a significant number of stokers were able to get into the water.

The majority of the crew, though, mustered on the quarterdeck, in four rows, waiting to board the ship's lifeboats. In case this sounds like nothing more than the imposition of mindless discipline, it should be remembered that no one expected the ship to sink so quickly. If it had been slower, an orderly boarding process would have saved many lives. The sudden lurch of the ship came as a shock to all. A junior officer shouted 'Jump!' when this happened, the only 'abandon ship' order that was issued: the angle of the vessel meant that the lifeboats were unusable.

The testimony of one of the gunners, Frederick John Masterman Johnson, gives a vivid impression of what happened. Aged about 42, he was an experienced hand, and had been in the navy since 1867. He was near the stern of the ship just before it turned over:

> Directly she gave the heavy lurch to starboard, I managed to succeed in catching hold of the poop rails, and only just. I had got one leg over, I thought of letting go [i.e. releasing] the port lifebuoy, but the ship was heeling over too far and it would not act. I got as low as the lower guard and looked down. By that time the ship had heeled over so that I was practically lying flat on the ship's side.

Johnson was washed off the side of the ship, and sucked down 'a great distance'. Coming up for air, he grabbed a floating timber, and was able to count thirty or forty heads around him. Then he was dragged down for a second time, by what appeared to be an explosion. He banged his head on some wreckage on resurfacing, but fortunately stayed conscious. He looked about, and counted the heads nearby. Only ten were visible. There was a moment for one short breath before he went down again. By the time he bobbed up once more, only three or four men remained in his immediate vicinity.[7]

The 'explosion' mentioned by Johnson also features in Captain Bourke's testimony. The captain ended up in the water along with everyone else. It was a very crowded patch of sea – to begin with. Men were 'very, very thick' in the water, some flung off the ship: 'those who could not swim, or who were hurt in any way, clutching at those who could swim...' The ship disappeared almost immediately, quickly followed by a boiler explosion, caused as Bourke thought by the bow hitting the seabed. Many men were struck by spars and other wreckage carried up by the 'enormous swirl' of water that followed; some suffered broken ribs. The 'swirl' drowned many men, but Bourke attributed the heavy loss of life to the fact that many of the stokers and Royal Marines aboard did not know how to swim. Lieutenant Heath, the ship's executive officer, said much the same thing – he reckoned that most of the swimmers were the 'bluejackets', the sailors.

The 'swirl' was probably a mixture of air and escaping steam. In recent years, research has shown that gas rising up through sea water can reduce its density, causing a deadly reversal of Archimedes' principle: things that would normally float become heavier than the water that they displace. This likely explains why even a good swimmer like Frederick Johnson found himself going down for the second and third times, and why so many of those around him never returned to the surface alive.[8]

Boats from some of the other ships picked up survivors, including Johnson. The *Camperdown* and the rest of the fleet sailed into Tripoli Bay, where it anchored just before sunset. Markham's flagship was badly damaged at the bow, but a desperate repair effort managed to keep it afloat. The British Consul-General at Tripoli, Colonel Trotter, had been travelling with the fleet in HMS *Edinburgh*, and witnessed the disaster. His draft report of 23 June contains what may be the earliest rough plans of the incident. Trotter offered his services to Markham, and went ashore to send off the stricken admiral's first report. The following day, Trotter also arranged the funerals of six dead in the local American Protestant cemetery.

Those six bodies had been picked up by the rescue boats: no others were ever recovered from the wreck, despite a subsequent search by ships from the fleet. Aside from wreckage, all they found was a patch of oil leaking from the sunken vessel. The injured and other survivors were taken to Malta on 25 June. Of the *Victoria*'s crew, 291 survived. Figures for the number of dead vary: 358 is often quoted, but the memorial to the *Victoria*'s crew in Victoria Park in Portsmouth lists 364 names.

Markham's telegram reached the Admiralty early on 23 June 1893. As with the *Russell* in 1872, the telegraph system spread the news rapidly across the country and beyond – the information had reached the USA by that evening. There was widespread shock in Britain, coupled with great sympathy for the crew and their families. A relief fund set up by the Lord Mayor of London raised £72,000 in two months – just over £32 *million* in terms of modern wages. Less seriously, there was a story that 'a well known lady' guest at Tryon's London house had seen his figure walk down the stairs there on the evening of the disaster, before the news had reached Britain. Another lady also claimed to have seen him. The account added a supernatural frisson to the catastrophe, and was avidly recounted by the press.[9]

The navy held a court martial for the loss of the *Victoria* at Malta between 17 and 27 July. Many people gave evidence, both officers and ratings, though Captain Bourke had effectively tried to pervert the course of justice beforehand, telling his officers that they should do all they could to preserve Tryon's reputation. This could not prevent the court from holding Tryon entirely responsible. The admiral might well have agreed with this, had he lived, because witnesses had heard him blame himself in the last minutes of the *Victoria*. Why he made such a terrible mistake can never be established with absolute certainty. He may have simply forgotten that the ships needed more space for the turn, or confused the space needed for a quarter-circle turn with that required for a half-circle turn (as Andrew Gordon and others suggested).

Despite the fact that none of the officers present had directly challenged Tryon's dangerous order, the court martial board did not find them culpable and merely expressed regret that Markham had not queried the command, as he had intended. It could not, however, fault him for obeying the direct order of his commander-in-chief. The whole navy, after all, functioned on the basis that subordinates would carry out the orders of their superiors.[10]

Though the careers and reputations of Markham and some other officers may have suffered as a result of the wreck, the living victims of the tragedy were the families of the men and boys lost.

Most of the dead crewmen probably came from the UK. For example, the personnel records of some of the ship's Royal Marine detachment list the following (ages approximate): Francis Cole (30), came from Peckham in London; Joseph Kent (21) was a former barman and came from Brentwood in Essex; Henry Lodge was an ex-seaman from London; 25-year-old Ferdinand Edward Boileau Hughes had, despite his exotic name, been an Essex labourer; William Hillery (23) had worked as a labourer in Hampshire; Charles Lane (21) was another former labourer, from the inland town of Hereford; William Ellis (30) came from Londonderry in northern Ireland and had been an engineer of some kind. Whatever their backgrounds, these men and many others ended up with the odd-sounding and brutally bureaucratic phrase 'Discharged Dead' scrawled on their service records.[11]

At least thirty men of Maltese or Italian origin served alongside the Britons, of whom seventeen were lost. The ship's band was mainly composed of Italians, led by Chief Bandmaster Giuseppe Olivieri, who survived along with a minority of his musicians.

Beside the London Lord Mayor's relief fund, another was quickly got under way in Portsmouth. Once it was closed, the Lord Mayor's fund was handed over to a body called the Royal Patriotic Fund for distribution. The amount of money raised was a testament to public generosity, and perhaps also to the sentimental regard that many had for the 'British Bluejacket'.

The Patriotic Fund had been established originally to pay pensions to widows and orphans of men killed in the Crimean War, but in the case of the *Victoria* families it proved to be penny-pinching, inflexible and strangled by red tape. The 364 dead of the battleship left around 89 widows and 143 orphan children, along with aged parents – mothers in particular – who had relied on part of their sailor sons' wages being remitted home. Just over five months on from the tragedy it was said that a 'great delay occurred in issuing pensions to the widows and orphans, and as yet very few of the dependent relatives have derived benefit from the *Victoria* Fund', but it was also remarked that 'Splendid work was carried out by Miss Agnes Weston in relieving the temporary needs of the sufferers and £5,000 was raised in Portsmouth alone'.

Agnes Weston (1840–1918), known to generations of sailors as 'Aggie Weston' (though probably not to her face) was a formidable campaigner for social reform and temperance, driven by a strong evangelical Anglican Christian faith. In the 1870s she became involved with missionary work in the Royal Navy, and established Sailors' Rests at Devonport (1876) and Portsmouth (1881) that provided decent, alcohol-free overnight accommodation for ordinary sailors. She also took up the cause of sailors' wives and children, working to improve their lot.

It appears that it was thanks to Agnes Weston that any of the families of the *Victoria* dead received any money in the months immediately after the disaster, money drawn from the fund established in Portsmouth. Various reports indicate that the Royal Patriotic Fund did little or nothing to begin with. This was despite Agnes Weston assiduously gathering information on dependents and forwarding it to the Fund. Official support for the widows and their children of ordinary sailors was largely absent. In 1894, Weston set the matters out starkly:

> There is a shadowy idea that a 'grateful country' always takes care of Jack's wife, whether he dies in battle, by disaster, or wears away by inches in hospital; but the real truth is, that the grateful country does nothing of the kind, and Jack's wife may drift, and often does, to the workhouse when a terrible disaster shakes the country to its centre... The breadwinner cut off, poverty and distress fall like a thunderbolt.

A sailor had to pay for his own uniform, and when he went to sea, his pay changed from weekly harbour pay to monthly pay, with two months' money kept in hand in case the man should desert. Men who were at sea could, and usually did, assign half of their pay to their wives, who had to go to the local royal dockyard to collect it. This could be a difficult journey for women who lived a long way off, or had very young or sick children.

Though the nineteenth century navy did improve the lives of ratings in some ways, the welfare of sailors and their families was not a high priority. Individual officers had responsibilities in this regard, but this was not a substitute for an adequate welfare system that was service-wide, and widows' pensions were not automatically granted.[12]

Stoker Curran was discharged from the navy soon after the disaster. Despite his background as an army deserter, neither the army nor the navy pursued him over this – perhaps it was not felt expedient to prosecute a survivor. The War Office did not take him up as a deserter, and the navy did not reclaim the clothing and bedding allowance of £3/10s that he had received as an advance (pretty much all his kit had gone down with the *Victoria*, of course). This was despite his 'fraudulent entry' into the fleet. As Bryan Williamson has pointed out, however, he was not given any further allowances.[13]

Curran's next move was apparently inspired by a childhood experience. As a boy in Dundee, he had seen a survivor of the battle of Rorke's Drift

(William Jones VC) recounting his experiences as part of a show by Hamilton's Panorama that featured the battle (much later retold in the 1963 film, *Zulu*). Curran must have realized that people might pay good money to listen to his account. In the autumn of 1893 he was engaged to appear in a show run by an impresario called Frank Howe, along with an illusionist act called 'The Montanas'. Howe advertised that a 'Large, Beautiful Coloured Photograph of the Victoria and Curran' would be hung in theatre lobbies, with Curran appearing 'in the Identical Suit of Clothes that he wore when the sad disaster occurred in which the *Victoria* went down'. He was also supposed to be part of the magic act, stepping into a disappearing cabinet to be replaced by 'a Beautiful Young Lady'.

Curran's involvement with Howe did not last very long. By mid-February 1894, the ex-stoker had been recruited by Joseph Poole's Myriorama show. Poole's show had included a piece on the loss of the *Victoria* as early as November 1893, and he probably saw Curran as a 'hot property', able to give authenticity to the whole thing.

The Myriorama was a panorama, a type of entertainment first developed in the Georgian era. At its simplest, it consisted of (literal) moving pictures – large paintings on canvas set on revolving vertical rollers – so that the audience saw a continuously moving spectacle. The Myriorama also involved sound effects, lights, smoke, music, moving models, variety performances and narration, including Curran's account of the shipwreck. The sinking itself was dramatized with two models of the *Camperdown* and the *Victoria*. They were made to collide, the *Victoria* model turning turtle at the end of the sequence. The panorama showed scenes of nature and of foreign places as well, but its big attractions were disasters, battles and shipwrecks – later on, even the *Titanic* received the Myriorama treatment. Shows of this kind were hugely popular – the Poole family had six separate Myriorama shows on tour around the country in the mid-1890s – nowadays it might be called 'infotainment'. Contemporary press reports do not suggest that audiences found the slick repackaging of human suffering at all tasteless.

Between February 1894 and April 1897, Curran appeared in at least thirty-four venues with the Myriorama, ranging from the Channel Islands to north-east England, and from London to south Wales. Notably, the show does not seem to have fetched up in Portsmouth, the *Victoria*'s home port – perhaps it would not have been welcome. The last recorded performance by Curran was at Hull, and interestingly, that Myriorama production involved a cinematograph film (unrelated to the *Victoria*), just a year after moving pictures had first been shown in Britain.

The full content of Curran's script is uncertain, though as he himself admitted (below), the original was written by one of Poole's staff, based on details that he had supplied. His text was auctioned off in 1997 and its current whereabouts are unknown, but a part of it is quoted on the 'British Medals' site in a section authored by Mr Bryan Williamson. According to this extract, Curran was on the 'debris deck' at the time of the collision, the First Dog Watch, perhaps dumping boiler-room clinker, as Williamson suggests. He heard a loud crash and felt the ship shake. A friend stationed at a nearby watertight door alerted him with a shout, and he just managed to get through before the door was closed, trapping 100 men of the watch below. He reached the quarterdeck to find men lined up in fours, facing outwards. No orders were given to lower lifeboats, but the ship started heeling over to starboard, loose guns crashing about inside the hull, and the sailors were ordered to jump. A sudden lurch flung Curran into the sea, fortunately clear of the propellers, which were still turning and cut some men to pieces. The suction from the hull dragged many down; Curran also claimed that others were drowned by panicking Maltese and Italians, who grabbed on to them. Curran himself stayed afloat for forty minutes until he was rescued by a boat from HMS *Dreadnought*. He was unconscious by the time he reached the ship.

In the introduction to the talk, Curran apparently likened the disaster to the Charge of the Light Brigade in 1854, picking up a word from Tennyson's famous poem about the event – 'blunder'. When the show was touring the Channel Islands, a naval officer, signing himself 'Commissioned Officer' wrote to the Guernsey *Star* in August 1895 with a complaint about Curran. He claimed that some in the Myriorama's management had 'blundered, and in very bad taste, too, in allowing James Curran, one of the survivors of the ill-fated *Victoria*, too much license of speech in his account of the disaster'. He decried 'the man's intemperate language and insinuating invective against his late officers… a disgrace to the uniform he no longer has any right to wear.' He admitted that 'the man who is supposed to have been the cause of the terrible disaster paid the penalty of his mistake with his own life, and there the matter ends'. 'Commissioned Officer' also deprecated a comparison with the Charge of the Light Brigade, stating that 'Tommy Atkins' had never got up on stage to criticize his superiors: 'Let Mr Poole see to this point; his excellent performance requires no gilding in the form of claptrap sentiment poured forth, not by a hero, but by an insubordinate marine stoker'.

That was probably the nub of the complaint: the officer objected to a member of the 'lower deck' criticizing the actions of his superiors. Curran wrote to the paper with a reasoned and cogent defence of his performance. The officer had said that the sooner Curran was returned to the navy, the better: Curran's reply was that, as a reservist, he could be recalled at any time:

> but as for my future welfare I am looking after that by staying with Mr. Poole... at present I am earning with Mr. Poole and honestly too, four times the amount I earned in the navy... I don't think I say anything that isn't creditable to a British sailor. Of course I am not an educated man like the gentleman who wrote to you. If I was I don't suppose I should ever have been a stoker. I speak of the disaster on the stage the same as I spoke to the gentleman who came to see me when I came home and who put it all in the paper. I never accused anybody (*as he now does in his letter*) of being the cause of the disaster. My words (or rather the words of Mr. Poole's lecturer when I first came, for I copied them from him) are, whether the disaster occurred through the blundering of man or the failure of machinery, it is difficult to say.

Curran also challenged the charge of intemperate language and insubordination: his conduct was rated as good when he was discharged, and although he admitted that he had been punished before, it was never for insubordination. He was happy to show his papers to anyone who asked.

This brief newspaper spat – the only sign of criticism of Curran's performance to come to light – did not damage the show, which continued for more than a year and a half afterwards. Newspaper reports spoke of it as 'thrilling' or 'realistic', with Curran delivering his piece in a 'manly, sailorlike fashion'. The *Sheffield Independent* wrote that Curran's story 'never fails to touch the hearts of hearers'.

All good things come to an end, and Curran's theatrical career seems to have finished in the spring of 1897. The Myriorama tried to keep up with (reasonably) current events, and by then, the loss of the *Victoria* must have felt like old news.

My efforts to trace James Curran definitively after that date have been unsuccessful: he cannot be conclusively identified in the 1901 or 1911 censuses. However, there are two later service record forms for a naval reservist named James Curran, born at Dundee in 1873, but names of his parents and his physical details do not match those of the 'other James', and there are even discrepancies between the two forms. This man enrolled on 11 December 1902 and remained on the books until 1934, though he was demobbed from active service in 1919, after serving in various ships and shore stations during the First World War as a stoker. His conduct was described as 'good' or 'very good' at points, and the navy's final summation of him was that his service had been 'satisfactory'. Given the disparities in the records, he may have been a completely different man from the James Curran of the *Victoria*. However, it is also possible that the latter simply re-enlisted in search of work and blurred some of the details of his background to avoid being identified as the stage performer.[14]

The navy that 'our' James Curran rejoined – if it was him – was changing fast, along with international politics and technology. The Naval Defence Act of 1889 had introduced a 'two-power standard' into British naval policy – that is, the Royal Navy should be as strong as the next two naval powers combined. Seventy new warships were ordered, including powerful battleships that combined speed, protection and well-distributed armament.

When the *Victoria* was built, the Royal Navy still regarded France as its potential future enemy, but in the 1890s a new opponent emerged. Germany embarked on major naval build-up, as part of an expansionist policy. Britain and some other major powers came to perceive the German Empire as a threat. Alliances shifted. France and Russia, long seen as rivals to Britain, became allies.

Naval technology also changed rapidly between 1893 and 1914. HMS *Dreadnought*, completed in 1906, introduced an eponymous, new kind of warship that made all other battleships obsolete. The ship was heavily armoured, but fast, driven by the new steam turbines, and its main armament consisted of ten 12-inch guns that could be controlled centrally. By 1914, advances in range finding and mechanical computers had pushed accurate gun ranges out to at least 12,000 yards. The introduction of the 'dreadnoughts', as they came to be called, also intensified the naval race between Britain and Germany, as each sought to out-build the other, destabilizing international relations.[15]

In the 1914–18 war that followed, the great test of the British surface fleet came at the battle of Jutland in 1916, when the German High Seas Fleet attempted to break out of the maritime blockade imposed by Britain. The British suffered higher losses in men and ships than the Germans, but at the end of the day it was the High Seas Fleet that retreated, and never attempted to come out again in force. Merely by existing, the strong and technologically advanced British fleet justified its existence because it served as a deterrent, however much naval officers and the public at large might have expected (and wanted) a Trafalgar-like crushing of the enemy.

The commander of the British Grand Fleet at the time of Jutland was a survivor of the *Victoria* disaster – Sir John Jellicoe. Jellicoe had been the ship's executive officer, but at the time of the collision was sick below decks in his cabin, and so not on duty. He escaped from the ship, and the illness meant that he also escaped from any career damage.

The *Victoria* disaster showed aspects of the Royal Navy at its worst – a blind reverence for command authority, hero worship and an ingrained reluctance to question orders, even when they were patently dangerous. The irony is that the 'mastermind' responsible for the catastrophe was a man working to modernize the fleet. James Curran, the 'insubordinate stoker' was nearly killed by Tryon's mistake. More than half of his shipmates were not so lucky, but Curran lived to tell the tale – literally, on a stage and in spotlights.

One might question that he and Poole's Myriorama empire chose to make money out of the calamity, but was it really so different from the ways in which modern media organizations produce 'based on a true story' versions of recent wars, terrorist attacks and other catastrophes? Like the audiences of the 1890s, modern viewers like to be both thrilled and moved by other people's tragedies. Shipwrecks and other disasters were served up as entertainment long before James Curran set foot on a stage, and there is no sign that the public appetite for them has diminished.

The wreck of the *Victoria* was rediscovered in 2004 by divers Christian Francis and Mark Ellyatt. The ship sank bow-first and stands with nearly one-third of its length buried in the seabed, like a grisly cartoon caricature of a shipwreck, a monument to the futility of arms races and the dangers of unquestioning obedience.[16]

Chapter 4

'Last signal giving position...'
The Merchant Ship SS *Terence* of Liverpool (1917)

It looked, thought Captain Frodsom, like a caterpillar. Daydreaming was dangerous in the Atlantic in 1917, and it took only a moment for him to realize that the distant object was in fact a German U-boat. Within hours, his ship, the SS *Terence*, would be sinking, holed by a torpedo – but only after a determined fight for survival.

The primary function of the *Terence* was to transport South American beef, either on the hoof or in tins. Britain relied heavily on sea trade by 1914, especially when it came to food. As the historian François Crouzet remarked, British farms only fed the nation for three days out of every week. The rest came from imports: four-fifths of all cereals, 40 per cent of meat, nearly two-thirds of butter, just over a third of vegetables, close on three-quarters of all fruit and all of the sugar (**Pl 11**). The picture was much the same with raw materials. Cotton, rubber and oil came from abroad, of course, but so did 75 per cent of all wool, about a quarter of iron ore and almost all the manganese used in high-quality steel.

The First World War brought home to the British people just how much their way of life depended on shipping and sea trade. Britain was imperilled by the world's first submarine war, and the *Terence* was just one small part of the massive effort to keep the country afloat.

The *Terence* was a mid-sized oceangoing cargo ship, fairly typical of its time – a time when Britain owned just over one-third of the world's total merchant tonnage. It was built in 1902 for the Liverpool, Brazil and River Plate Steam Navigation Co. Ltd, a subsidiary of a long-established Liverpool shipping line, Lamport and Holt. The ship was used in the Atlantic trade, linking South America and New York with the UK. Its story highlights the nature and extent of Britain's global maritime reach before and during the Great War, and shows how a failed strategy helped to sink the *Terence*, and almost sank the country along with it.

'Last signal giving position...'

In the nineteenth century, government decisions not to protect native farming against imports played a big part in the decline of British agriculture. As a result, cheaper foreign grain and other foodstuffs began to flood in from the 1870s onwards. Food became cheaper, but less and less of it was home-produced.

The First World War turned Britain's reliance on the import trade from a free-marketeer's dream into a national nightmare. By the end of 1916, the crisis was acute. Lost supply ships, poor harvests in North America, increased consumption by armies and industrial workers, and the need to support Britain's French and Italian allies – all of these put the food supply under pressure and the wider economy under great strain. The effect of the U-boat campaigns is shown starkly in the volume of British imports, which in 1917 were only two-thirds of the 1913 level, though the actual value of the imports still far outstripped that of exports.

Government shied away from compulsion in food issues during the early years of the war, and relied on propaganda to try to make people consume less and grow more. Home-grown produce from gardens or allotments helped somewhat, but this softly-softly approach led to higher food prices and discontent, made worse in 1916 by a poor domestic harvest. The situation did not stabilize until the tide turned in the submarine war in 1917, and the government took proper control of consumption, prices, and food production. Even then, rationing was not tried until 1918, when the food crisis was almost over.[1]

Both before and after the Great War, the British mercantile marine was one of the lifelines that kept the country fed, but it did not treat its seafarers well. In 1914, less than three weeks before the outbreak of the Great War, a conference of British Port Sanitary authorities was scathing in its condemnation of British seamen's living conditions, 'the lowest of all countries': 'The mercantile sailor... is housed in a dark, damp, overcrowded, ill-ventilated forecastle, his food is of the worst description, and the cooking is usually beyond description'. The medical officer for the Port of London described shipboard accommodation as worse than that in prison, deterring men of good character from a life at sea.

Regarding shipboard food, a correspondent wrote this to *Lloyd's List* in 1910:

> under ordinary circumstances on a tramp steamer, a lump of meat is thrown into a dirty, half-rusty tin... and I have seen

in ship's forecastle [*sic*] the potatoes almost the same as when they came out of the garden… the coffee quite black, with no taste, sugar like wet sand.

In theory, seafarers' food was not bad – the 1906 Merchant Shipping Act laid down a bill of fare that included more enticing victuals such as soft bread, marmalade, jam, condensed milk and curry powder. The problem was that the government largely left it up to shipping companies and their officers to see that it was provided.

The shipowners' organization, the Shipping Federation, blamed all this squalor on the neglectfulness and obstinacy of the seafarers themselves. There may have been some truth in this, but most shipowners could have improved the conditions if they had been prepared to put money and thought into it. It was not rocket science. Some shipping companies, such as the mail lines, were able to provide decent accommodation and food for their crews.[2]

The Board of Trade was the government department responsible for regulating merchant shipping. It had acquired the responsibility under the Mercantile Marine Act of 1850, and in 1854 the first Merchant Shipping Act brought together all existing relevant laws. Apart from brief periods in the two world wars, the Board retained its responsibility for merchant shipping regulation into the second half of the twentieth century. Broadly speaking, that shipping was of two kinds: liners and tramps. Liners were vessels that ran to a published schedule on set routes, and the term embraced both passenger liners and cargo ships. 'Tramps', on the other hand, traded from port to port, picking up whatever cargoes they could.

The rise of shipping lines was due in part to the steamship, which could run to a timetable much more reliably than a sailing vessel, and to the limited liability laws of the mid-nineteenth century. The new laws made it possible for people to invest in shipping *companies*, rather directly than in individual ships, as part owners. This reduced their financial risks and in turn made much more capital available to the shipping firms, covering both their huge costs and providing investment for expansion.

Lamport and Holt was one of the firms that grew out of these changes. It was founded in Liverpool in 1845, but did not invest in steamships in a big way until the 1860s. It came to specialize in particular trades, as did

'Last signal giving position...'

a lot of contemporary lines – in its case, this included routes to South America and the USA.

Like so many other shipping companies, Lamport and Holt was later swallowed up by a conglomerate. The firm became a public company in 1911, but the Royal Mail group promptly snapped it up. Lamport and Holt foundered along with the Group in the wake of the 1929 Wall Street Crash, only to be reborn in 1934. However, independence did not last long and the company was acquired by the Vestey group ten years later. Lamport and Holt survived into the early container age, but finally ceased to be in 1974 (**Pl 12**).

In its heyday, though, Lamport and Holt was an efficiently run company that kept up with changing technology and renewed its fleet, with ships like the *Terence*. The same could not be said of many tramp companies, which might consist of a single ship run by slipshod managers. They were very numerous, however. In 1914, tramps made up between 33 and 40 per cent of British tonnage.[3]

If living arrangements aboard many British ships were not good in the early 1900s, nor were the conditions of service. The employment of ordinary seafarers was always casual in nature. Pay began and ended with a voyage, and if a ship went down, all pay stopped on that day. Charitable or religious organizations tried to help sailors ashore, with Seamen's Missions or sailors' homes, but life remained hard for many seafarers.

Not all seafarers were sailors, anyway. The introduction of steam in the nineteenth century had created an entirely new kind of maritime workforce (see Chapter 1). Alongside traditional groups like sailors and stewards, there were firemen (stokers), coal trimmers and greasers (trimmers moved the coal around in the coal bunkers to stop it destabilizing the ship as the coal was shovelled into the boilers). These men laboured in the heat and dirt of the claustrophobic bunkers, boiler and engine rooms. Working in these conditions, it is doubtful if many of them were contented, and it is probable that most felt even more disconnected from the ship in which they served than did merchant seamen. They required some skills for their jobs, but they were not those of a sailor, and seamen tended to see them as a race apart. Captain David Bone, a liner master who served through the Great War, described them as 'uninfluenced by the traditions of sea-service'. A euphemism, if ever there was one.

It was difficult for seamen as a group to oppose the combined wills of masters and owners. Given the nature of their work, they were a fragmented body of workers, lacking cohesion and organization. Things began to change in the late nineteenth century, though. Local seamen's unions had existed in earlier days, but in 1887 a merchant seaman from Sunderland, J. Havelock Wilson, formed the first national sailors' union, the National Amalgamated Sailors' and Firemens' Union. The union grew in strength and by 1911 was able to mount the first-ever national seamen's strike, which successfully wrested improvements in pay and conditions from the owners.

The shipmasters employed by those owners did not have an easy time of it, either. The duties of a captain included (and still include) being able to navigate and run a ship safely, to look after cargo, to deal with commercial agents and officials, to manage a crew, to see to their provisioning and pay, and to meet whatever statutory requirements were in force in different countries. Crew management could be especially difficult, as the Merchant Shipping Acts gave shipmasters only a limited degree of disciplinary control, and the companies recognized this. Lamport and Holt's 1914 *General Instructions to Masters*, for instance, warned them against being too indulgent to their crews, but also cautioned them not to be 'overbearing'. All a captain had in the way of lawful sanctions against offenders were fines, the threat of demotion or the possibility of getting them arrested when the ship reached port (if the offence was serious enough). Masters also had to know when to turn a blind eye, or as Captain Bone put it, to tolerate a degree of indiscipline 'for the sake of a quiet commercial life'.

The master of the *Terence* in 1917 was Captain William Frodsom (the name is given in some sources as 'Frodsham', but he spelled it 'Frodsom'). Frodsom was born at Maryport in Cumberland in 1857, the son of a sailor. He went to sea aged 17 in 1874, and by 1885 was qualified as a shipmaster. His early seafaring experience was in sailing ships, but he joined Lamport and Holt in the late 1880s and must have served on steam vessels for most of his career. Frodsom settled in Liverpool with his wife Mary and their children, finally making their home in Milton Road, a couple of miles from the waterfront. He was master of the *Terence* for its last nine years of service.

The official logs of the *Terence*, for six voyages between 1913 and 1916, give us an insight into the life of the ship and how the pressures of

'Last signal giving position...'

war changed things. The logs are principally a disciplinary record. The first three voyages, between November 1913 and November 1914, largely reflected peacetime conditions, even though the last one overlapped with the first three months of the war. In this time, the logs record a total of thirty-four offences, committed by fourteen men. The offences were mostly minor, and included drunkenness, missing a day's work, and so on. Only three men deserted during this year, which suggests that conditions aboard were tolerable. Desertion was in fact fairly common in the British merchant fleet – there were 14,000 deserters in 1899 alone.

The war changed things, or at least, changed the nature of the crews. Many merchant officers and sailors either volunteered for naval or military service after the outbreak of war, or were already naval reservists. Merchant ships, especially big ones, were faced with manning difficulties. Men laid off from the civilian industries filled some of the gaps, but Captain Bone claimed that not more than one in five stayed in seafaring, put off by 'the class of men with whom they had to live and work'. The worst losses were among the stokers. Paradoxically, Bone claimed that the manning problem improved with the advent of unrestricted submarine warfare, as more survivors from sunken ships became available. He also said that U-boat attacks inspired a spirit of patriotism that induced better men to sign up for the merchant fleet.

The three *Terence* logs for the period from May 1915 to October 1916 show a very different situation, as the stresses caused by unrestricted submarine warfare took hold. The total number of recorded disciplinary offences shot up from the earlier thirty-four to 274, and involved seventy-four men, not fourteen. Most were not serious – the taking of unauthorized days off, for example – but drunkenness seems to have played an increasing role in such problems.

More seriously, the number of desertions rose to thirty-five. New York was the port favoured by deserters, probably because many could speak English and they felt it was easy to get berths in American ships, which were then neutral and had better conditions than British ones. Significantly, sixty-five of the eighty-eight men who committed offences on the *Terence* between 1913 and 1916 were firemen, trimmers or greasers, the most notoriously discontented members of merchant crews. Some of them had little respect for officers. Frodsom found himself roused from bed in New York harbour one night in October 1915 by two drunken firemen, who swore at him and demanded to be paid, so that they could leave the ship. He was not a man to put up with this treatment, and he took them to court, where each got five days' jail for using threatening or abusive language.

Even with such problems, the *Terence* was not a dysfunctional ship. There was only one case of serious violence, when a crewman wounded two shipmates with a razor, and he also ended up in a New York jail. Writing in the log, Frodsom consistently rated the abilities and character of most of his men as 'very good' or 'good'.[4]

The normal peacetime complement of the *Terence* was around sixty-two men. There were fifty-one aboard at the time it was sunk in 1917, forty-six British, three Japanese and two 'Russian Finns'. Crews of mixed nationalities were not at all unusual in British ships, and this had been the case for centuries. Inevitably, the proportion of foreign sailors often rose in wartime. In one 1915 voyage, only one-third of the *Terence*'s crew was British: the rest came from sixteen different countries, including Belgium, Russia, Cyprus, Spain, the USA, Brazil and Australasia.[5]

The pay of ordinary seafarers was low, even with a £2 monthly 'War Bonus'. The basic pay of a coal trimmer in 1916 was £6, whereas the first mate of the *Terence* earned £13. Most sailors were poor and those on the *Terence* typically owned no more than 'one bag containing clothes'. Officers, of course, had more possessions. In May 1916, Hugh Howell, the first mate, tragically fell to his death in No. 2 hold. His effects had to be listed, and they comprised a wicker chair and three bags. The contents of the bags included a tweed suit, a uniform coat and vest, eight shirts, four pairs of shoes and boots, three navigational reference books and a watch. This was much more than the average seaman or fireman possessed, though it's clear that Howell was far from rich.[6]

The temporary home and workplace of these men, the *Terence*, was one of four 'T-Class' ships launched for Lamport and Holt in 1902. The vessel had a gross registered tonnage of 4,309 grt, a size that the company clearly found useful. The ship measured just over 390 feet in length, with a beam of 50.2 feet (118.92 x 15.3m), and was driven by three triple expansion engines, that gave it a maximum designed speed of 13 knots (**Pl 13**).

The *Terence* had a number of holds for stowing general cargo, but it could accommodate a small number of passengers and was also designed to transport live cattle. There were two decks in the hull and a 'shelter

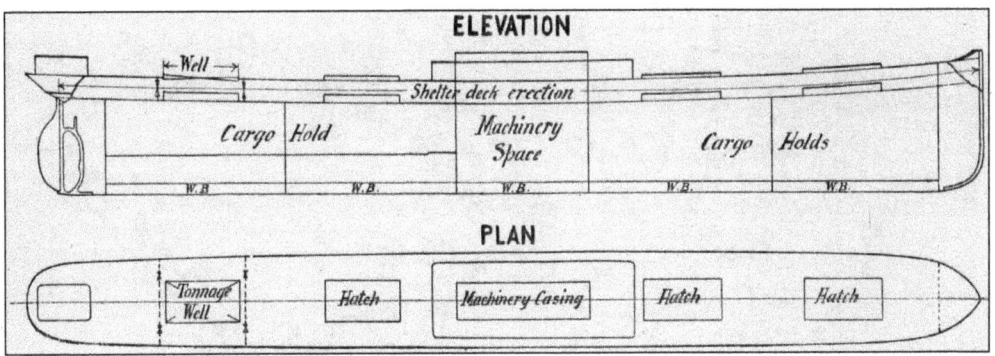

Fig 11 Drawings of a generic shelter-decked cargo ship. (Nicol 1912, p 356)

deck' on top of these that provided additional cargo space, and probably accommodated the cattle. The crew lived in the forecastle, as was usual, and the officers inhabited the 'round houses' in the superstructure amidships. When cattle were embarked, the cattlemen bunked in quarters at the stern.[7]

The *Terence* and its engines were built by David & William Henderson Ltd of Glasgow. This shipbuilding firm had taken over the old Tod and MacGregor yard in 1873 (where *City of Glasgow* was earlier built – see Chapter 1) and renamed it. The company launched around 470 ships of many different kinds over the next sixty years, making it one of the twenty most prolific yards on the Clyde.

The *Terence* was the product of several revolutions in shipbuilding. It was constructed of mild steel, not iron, because steel was stronger, lighter and more durable. Steel had become available in cheaper, mass-produced form in the 1850s, but it took some time for the quality to improve and it was not until the 1880s that the tonnage of steel ships built in British yards began to overtake that of iron vessels. Iron construction declined rapidly thereafter. Britain itself led the world in ship construction: in 1902, for example, 70 per cent of steamships in service across the world were British-built. The strength and falling cost of steel made it much easier to build bigger ships. Lamport and Holt, for instance, acquired its first 3,000-tonner in 1888: a couple of decades later, the company's fleet included ships of 7,000 and 8,000 grt.

The new giant steamers could carry cargoes in much greater quantities than ever before. Across the world, the volume of international trade increased fivefold between 1860 and 1914. The process was helped by

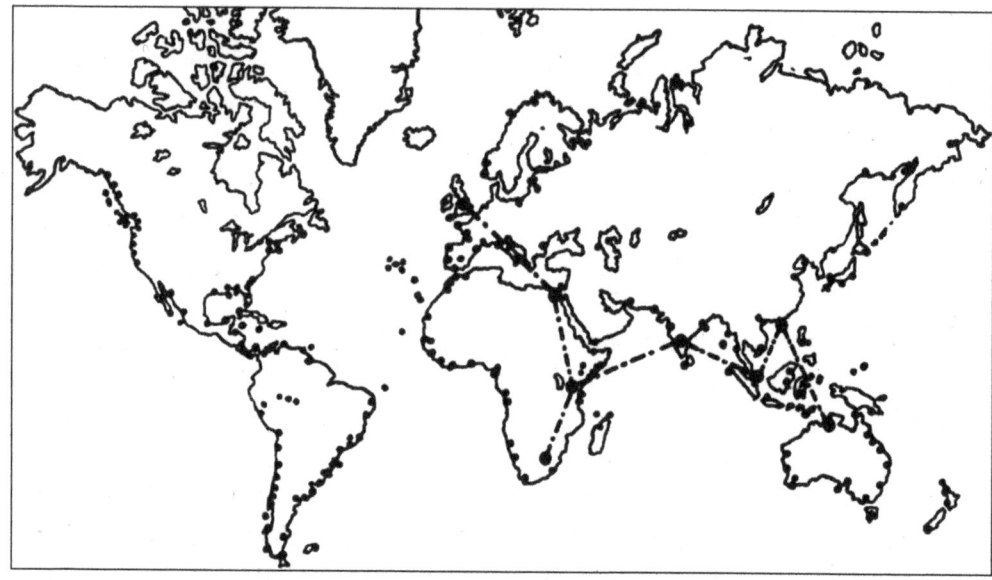

Fig 12 A 1913 map showing the global network of wireless stations that existed even before the Great War: each dot represents a station. (Cressy 1914, p 317)

the construction of new ports and docks, and developments like the Suez Canal (opened 1869) and the Panama Canal (1914), which cut voyage and turnaround times. Like the later container vessel, the steel steamship helped to feed an increase in world trade, and conversely, its development was fed by this growth.

The wheel of commerce was given an additional spin by another new invention – the marine triple expansion engine. This came into use in the 1870s and 1880s, and consumed much less coal than earlier types. The engine was also generally more compact than its predecessors, and required fewer men to tend it. Coupled with the introduction of new boiler types that could take higher pressures, the engine helped to make sea transport cheaper and quicker. Though it was later overtaken by steam turbines (first developed in the 1890s) and diesels, the reliable and economical triple expansion engine continued chugging its way across the oceans through peace and war well into the twentieth century.[8]

The *Terence* combined two relatively new technologies, its construction and its engines, with a third that was very new – wireless. The invention of wireless had a profound effect on sea trade and sea war. The Italian inventor Guglielmo Marconi made his first transmission

'Last signal giving position...'

across water in 1897, a mere 3½ miles from Lavernock Point in South Wales to Flatholm Island in the Bristol Channel. Just four years later, in 1901, he was able to send the first transatlantic wireless signals, between Land's End and Newfoundland. Navies quickly saw the advantage of wireless, which enabled ships to report home regularly, and gave admiralties much closer control of their fleets. The Japanese were the first to use wireless in a naval battle, in 1905, and it was standard equipment for all significant war fleets by 1914. Transmissions were made using Morse code, though both naval ciphers and codes were developed to encrypt the messages sent via the Morse key.

Commercial marine wireless developed rather more slowly. International conventions for its use were established between 1903 and 1912, and a worldwide network of land-based transmitting stations existed by 1914. It was agreed in 1906 that 'SOS' would become the standard international signal for a ship in distress, replacing the earlier 'CQD' (though the latter remained in use for some years; the resemblance of 'SOS' to the phrase 'Save Our Souls' was accidental). Most merchant ships did not carry wireless in 1914, but it was adopted much more widely during the war, when wireless became a lifesaver. It enabled ships to pick up the warning broadcasts sent out by the Admiralty at set times during the day, and made distress calls possible, which could increase the chance of rescue.[9]

If new technologies built and sustained the *Terence*, they were also used to sink it. The ship's nemesis took the form of the German *Unterseeboot U81*, commanded by Kapitänleutnant Raimund Weisbach. Aged 30 in 1917, Weisbach was a veteran submariner. As a junior officer in May 1915, he had pressed the firing button for the torpedo that sank the liner *Lusitania*: in his later career as a U-boat captain he destroyed thirty-six ships (**Pl 14**).

Most major navies did not begin to adopt submarines in regular service until the early 1900s. Neither the British fleet nor the German navy saw the submarine as much more than a coastal defence weapon, and concentrated on trying to out-build each other with dreadnoughts and other surface vessels. Britain's investment in its ships paid off: when war came, most German warships outside Europe were quickly eliminated, and the Royal Navy penned the main High Seas Fleet in the North Sea and the Baltic for the duration of the war. At the same time, the underrated submarine emerged as weapon of mass destruction. The touch of Weisbach's finger led to the deaths of 1,198 men, women and children in the *Lusitania*.

In earlier centuries, maritime trade wars were usually conducted by privateers (ships licensed by states to attack enemy merchant vessels), but privateering had been abolished by international treaty in 1856. Pre-1914 thinking about trade warfare was governed by a convention known as the 'Cruiser Rules'. These dictated that warships could not sink merchantmen on sight. A cargo vessel could be searched for enemy goods or 'contraband', but could only be sunk if contraband was found. Even then, the crew was supposed to be allowed to abandon ship first.

German submarines began the war by observing the Cruiser Rules. However, this negated one of the chief advantages of the submarine, which is stealth. Some German naval officers began to think, correctly, that a submarine war could undermine trade-dependent Britain. The Royal Navy (RN) saw that Germany was also vulnerable in this way, and in November 1914 began a total maritime blockade of German sea trade, though the RN mostly used surface vessels to maintain it. This seems to have persuaded the German high command to let the U-boats off the leash. They brushed aside politicians' worries about the potential effect on neutral opinion, and in February 1915 the German navy instituted its first unrestricted U-boat campaign against merchant shipping.

Neutral countries did protest, particularly the USA – more than one in ten of those lost in the *Lusitania* were Americans. Eventually, at the end of August 1915, these protests led to the suspension of the unrestricted campaign. U-boat attacks resumed between 29 February and 24 April 1916, but were suspended once more in the face of an American ultimatum. Rightly, the Germans feared that America might join the Allies.

Submarine warfare seriously damaged the British war effort. The majority of the 3,098 British cargo ships lost between August 1914 and December 1916 (totalling 2.3 million tons) were sunk by U-boats. Along with these, 1,850 merchantmen from Allied and neutral nations (3.9 million tons) also went to the bottom.

Germany resumed unrestricted submarine warfare in February 1917. British losses in the first six months of that year, before the convoy system really took effect, were close to catastrophic: 2.1 million tons of shipping, almost the same amount as the country had lost in the previous *twenty-eight* months of war. The *Terence* was one of 2,274 British ships sunk in that time. America entered the war against Germany in April 1917, but at first it could offer little help. The First Sea Lord, Admiral Jellicoe, feared that if merchant shipping losses went on at their current rate, it would be impossible for Britain to continue the war.

The U-boat menace was defeated in the end by a passive measure: the use of merchant convoys. However, in the early part of the war, Royal Navy officers pursued an offensive strategy against the submarines, one that included hunting patrols. Their training and instincts led them in this direction, but it was only a partial solution, at best, because anti-submarine technology was in its infancy. Just under half of the 178 U-boats sunk in the Great War are known to have been lost through direct combat with surface ships or other submarines: the others fell prey to mines and other causes.

The British Admiralty had not given much thought to trade protection before 1914. It assumed that danger came only from surface 'commerce raiders', which could be destroyed quite rapidly – as actually happened – and only a few merchant ships were given guns for self-protection before the war. The arming of British merchantmen proceeded slowly even after the conflict began and by April 1916, no more than 1,100 of them had been armed. These vessels were known as 'Defensively Armed Merchant Ships' or DAMS: each had a single weapon, usually an obsolescent naval gun, mounted in a defensive position at the stern, to make clear that the vessel was not an auxiliary warship. The weapons were manned by a couple of naval or Royal Marine gunners, assisted by members of the ship's crew. By 1917, the *Terence* was one of these armed vessels.

The Admiralty issued its first instructions to merchant ships in August 1914. They were based on the assumption that trading vessels would only be attacked by surface craft. In case of attack, the advice was to make a run for it: a 'stern chase is a long chase', said the document, a phrase that sounded almost Nelsonian. As the U-boat threat grew between 1914 and 1917, the navy still continued to counsel that ships should sail independently in a war zone: 'Masters should remember that the object is to scatter vessels as widely as possible'. It was a disastrous strategy. Scattering merchant ships across the ocean merely gave U-boats a multiplicity of targets, especially in relatively busy areas like the south-western approaches to Britain and Ireland.

Later tactical recommendations included zigzagging in danger zones, to throw off a submarine's aim. However, in the event of an attack, a ship was advised to pile on speed, to make a smokescreen and use its gun – if it had one – to deter the U-boat. Statistics from 1916 and early 1917 did indeed show that DAMS had a much better chance of surviving an attack. This was because U-boat commanders at that time still favoured surface attacks, which gave the submarine more tactical options, even though it made them vulnerable to the DAMS guns. Unfortunately, the arming of more merchant ships led the Germans to change tactics, and by spring 1917, 60 per cent of attacks were delivered from below the waves.

In 1917–18, convoys proved to be the solution to the U-boat danger, but back in 1914 they were out of favour with the navy. Convoys were a medieval idea, based on the principle of safety in numbers, and later proved highly effective in the wars between 1793 and 1815 (especially when the navy provided escorts). However, by the start of the Great War, the Royal Navy saw convoying as an out-of-date defensive tactic that was incompatible with its aggressive mindset. It was also believed that the differential speeds and variable crew abilities of liners and tramps would make it impossible to keep a convoy together, and that a convoy would just present the enemy with a bigger target.

This was a fallacy. Convoys were big targets, but they could be as difficult to locate in the vastness of the ocean as a single vessel. If a U-boat did find a convoy, it could attack, but then risked destruction by the escorting warships. These factors help to explain why convoys became so important in 1917–18 and later, between 1939 and 1945.

The Great War placed enormous strains on Britain's shipping capacity. Despite this, both the British government and the Admiralty were slow to take control of merchant shipping and the submarine crisis. For one thing, there was no single body that could collect statistics on shipping losses and act on them. The Admiralty's over-centralized system was poor at processing data and it did not have a separate Anti-Submarine Division until December 1916, the same month in which the first (merchant) shipping controller was appointed at Cabinet level.

Radio direction-finding made it feasible to locate enemy vessels at sea, and to read their messages, if the codes had been broken. The Royal Navy's codebreakers in Room 40 at the Admiralty were able to do this

'Last signal giving position...'

Fig 13 Outline of a U-81 Class U-boat.

for much of the war. On the evening of 25 April 1917, one such 'sigint' intercept placed submarine *U81* off the north-west coast of Ireland. What the intercept did not reveal was that the U-boat was heading for the vulnerable south-western approaches.

U81 was a big vessel, built on one of the great glass-covered slipways at Krupp's Germaniawerft yard at Kiel, and entered service in August 1916. It measured just over 70 metres in length and displaced 946 tons when submerged. Its two MAN diesels gave a surface speed of 16.5 knots, double the submerged speed provided by its electric motors. The vessel had a range of 12,445 miles (20,742km), and could dive to around 50 metres (164ft).

Its primary armament in April 1917 consisted of eleven 50cm-diameter torpedoes. Viable self-propelled torpedoes had been invented in the 1860s, and developed into devastating weapons. *U81*'s torpedoes could travel at least 5.7 miles (9.2km) at a speed of 27 knots, carrying a 160kg (352lb) high-explosive warhead. The submarine was also armed with a powerful 105mm deck gun and a supply of about 240 rounds of ammunition (**Pl 15**).

Weisbach assumed command of *U81* in summer 1916. He and his crew undertook four patrols between October 1916 and May 1917, and sank thirty ships. *U81*'s last cruise began on 18 April 1917, when it left its base at Emden, on the German North Sea coast. The submarine headed north to sail round Scotland and Ireland, with thirty-six men packed into its dank, smelly and claustrophobic interior. There were no suitable targets off Scotland, so the U-boat sailed to the waters west of Ireland, where it went on to attack ten vessels in seven days. One of those ships was the SS *Terence*.[10]

The last hours of the *Terence* were chronicled in brief radio messages. The first distress call from the ship was picked up by a wireless station at Valentia, in the south-west of Ireland, at 2.45 pm on the afternoon of 28 April 1917: 'SOS. SSS sighted s/m 51.28 N 14.19 W Course S. 65°

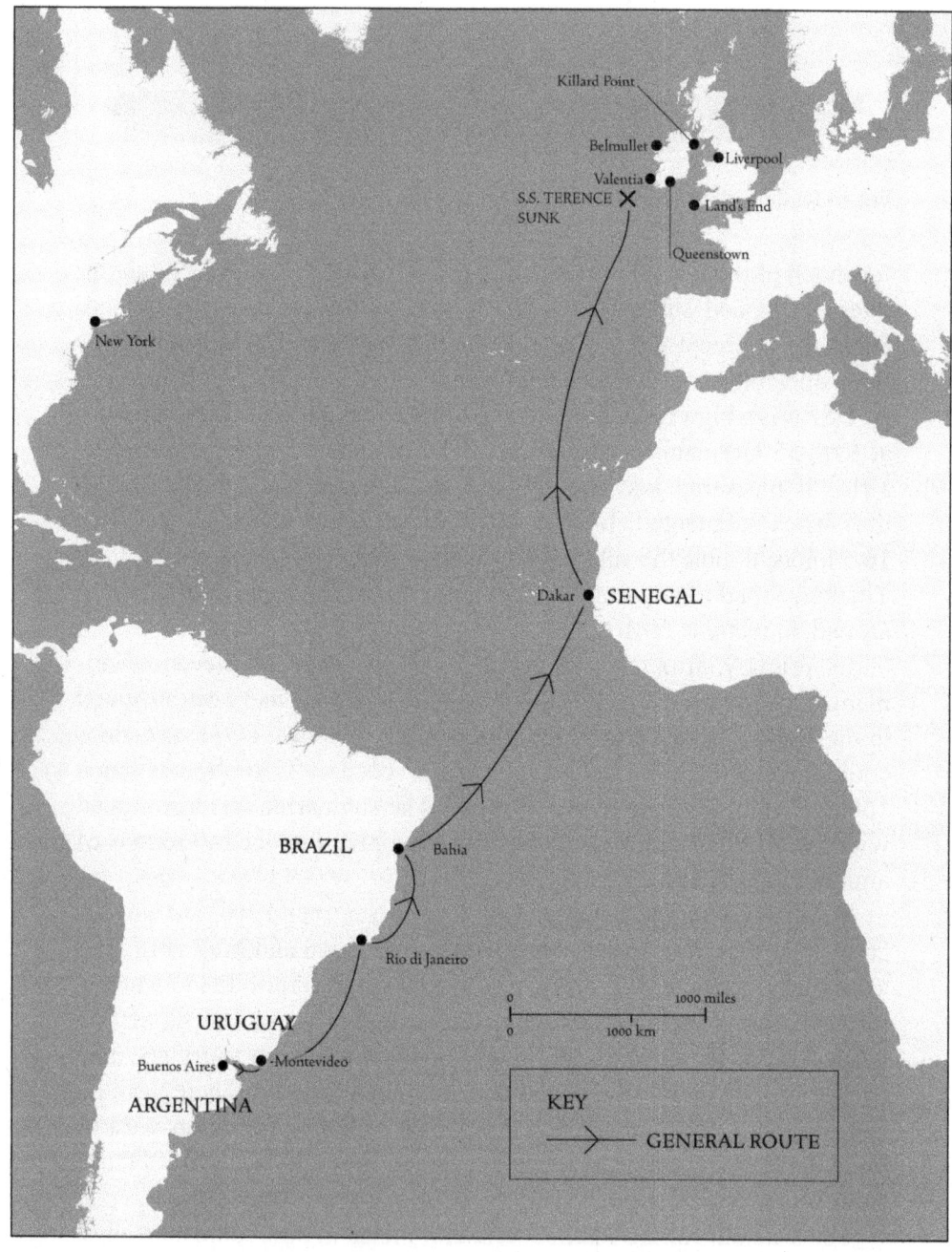

Fig 14 The general route taken by the *Terence* on its last voyage from South America, 1917.

'Last signal giving position...'

E. speed 12 knots'. This was followed by five other signals over the next six hours or so, the last at 9.06 pm. They were received at Valentia, as well as at two other stations, Queenstown in Ireland (now Cobh) and Land's End in Cornwall.

The *Terence* had left Buenos Aires on 26 March, calling at Montevideo in Uruguay and then two Brazilian ports, Rio and Bahia. It then crossed the Atlantic to Dakar in Senegal, to pick up route instructions for the final leg of the voyage home to Liverpool. The ship departed Dakar on 17 April, and nine days later was close enough to the danger zone of the south-western approaches to begin zigzagging.

The *Terence*'s final cargo included beef, wool, hides and piassava (palm fibres used to make brushes and brooms) from both Argentina and Brazil. The insured value of the goods came to £55,968, with the beef making up nearly 60 per cent of the total. In terms of modern economic output, the cargo was worth about £25.9 million – underlining just how damaging the loss of any cargo could be to the Allied war effort.[11]

The *Terence* was sunk on Saturday, 28 April 1917, a day of fine weather and light winds, with a 'summer haze' on the horizon. The haze probably helped to conceal the first submarine, which had got to within two miles of the ship before Captain Frodsom spotted it at 1.20 pm. He turned the ship round immediately, putting the U-boat behind the *Terence*. The ship's siren screamed to alert the gunners and crew, and down below the engine-room telegraph rang for maximum speed. The firemen double-banked the boilers and the ship now ploughed along at 14 knots, faster than its nominal top speed.

The submarine still lay broadside-on to the *Terence* as the merchant ship's stern swung round. The ship opened fire, loosing-off seventeen rounds until the target vanished into the haze just after 3.00 pm, apparently unscathed. The *Terence* returned to its original course and resumed zigzagging. A wireless message came in from a shore station in reply to the ship's first SOS signal, and said that help was on its way. Given the immediate circumstances, this was not much use.

At 4.55 pm, the ruler-straight wake of a torpedo was spotted just 600 yards to starboard, heading for the ship. The *Terence* turned, but the torpedo passed close enough to streak right underneath the counter, the part of the upper hull that projected out at the stern. Soon after, the conning tower of a submarine rose from the water, about 5,000 yards distant. The *Terence*'s siren sounded again, and its gun crew opened fire, their first shots going over the target.

The U-boat's gun returned fire, and Frodsom zigzagged the ship 'to disconcert his aim'. The submarine commander ran his boat at top speed, 'burying himself in foam', in an effort to catch up with the merchant ship. Once the U-boat got within range again, it turned side on and stopped, to give its two gun crews a stable firing platform (the boat was clearly not *U81*, which had only one gun). U-boats had special shells, designed to drive DAMS gunners away from their weapons. They worked. The shells burst right over the *Terence*, and the rattle of the shrapnel fragments hitting the ship must have been terrifying. By this stage the ship only had sixteen shells left, and Frodsom decided that it was better for his gun crew to take shelter.

At nine minutes past seven, another torpedo track appeared off the ship's port bow, heading towards the location of the bridge. This came from another submarine.

The ship's wheel was spun to starboard, but the *Terence* answered sluggishly. By chance, the torpedo was set to run too low in the water and it went harmlessly underneath the ship. Despite this piece of luck, Frodsom was beginning to think that they would not make it, because he ordered all of the ship's confidential papers to be thrown overboard. The *Terence* now turned back to port to avoid the shells from the first submarine. Yet another torpedo passed under the ship's stern, probably from the second U-boat, which was on the surface. This boat also began firing its gun.

The shelling stopped at about 8.15 pm, after the first U-boat had fired an estimated 120 shells – though with no hits, beyond the dangerous showers of shrapnel. Frodsom carried on zigzagging, but knew that the *Terence* was trapped between the two submarines (it's not known if one of these was the U-boat spotted at 1.20, or not: the *Terence* may have encountered three submarines in total). The ship's bulk and the smoke billowing from its funnel meant that the submarines could keep it in sight, even at night. All they had to do was for one to turn east, and the other to the west, so that they could catch the ship as it zigzagged (**Pl 16**).

At five minutes past eleven, a huge bang jarred the *Terence* as a torpedo struck No. 3 hold, about 15 feet below the waterline. The ship started to sink.

'Last signal giving position...'

One report of the sinking says that the *Terence*'s crew acted with 'Perfect behavior & discipline'. Frodsom's account is different. 'It was not necessary to call the men to the [lifeboat] stations, all their nerves were gone after the shelling they had been subjected to'. The engines were stopped and the four lifeboats descended to the water, 'but there was a regular panic at the starboard lifeboat, one man apparently jumped into the sea.' The panic is entirely understandable. These were civilian sailors, not servicemen, and they had just endured a shelling on a scale with those experienced by soldiers in a trench on the Western Front (**Pl 17**).

The boats were all away within three or four minutes, leaving just Frodsom and his chief officer on the ship. The idea of a captain going down with his ship has long seemed no more than a joke, but it looks as if this is what Frodsom intended to do. This was not just stiff-necked nautical pride. He had reason to fear being taken prisoner. In 1916, the Germans had shot Captain Fryatt, a captured British merchant shipmaster, because he had tried to ram the U-boat that attacked his ship. They claimed that he was a *franc-tireur* – a 'terrorist' because of this. Frodsom had just fought a running battle with two, or possibly three, U-boats.

The chief officer, however, talked him out of staying on the ship. Fortunately, the second officer knew that both men were still aboard, and came back to rescue them. Frodsom and the chief went round the *Terence* to make sure that no one was left on the ship, and then boarded the lifeboat. Frodsom again declared that he would not let the Germans take him. It was reported later that the captain was prepared to jump overboard if captured by the submarine – taking a German officer with him, if he could.

By now, the lifeboats had become separated. One of them was stopped by a U-boat, the vessel that had torpedoed the *Terence* – *U81*, as it turned out. An officer asked questions of the British sailors in 'broken English'. Whoever replied, they lied to the Germans, as the U-boat's survivors later reported that they had sunk the 7,000-ton SS *Achilles*. Frodsom's party sighted the conning tower of the submarine while this was going on, but rowed away quietly in the darkness without being spotted.

The *Terence* was last seen by Frodsom at 0040 hours, at which time it was still afloat. The captain reckoned that his boat was far enough away from the U-boat to make it safe to raise its sail. They set course for the coast of Ireland, about 200 miles away, and reached Killard Point on

1 May, after a sixty-one-hour voyage, where they had 'a real hospitable welcome, everyone doing their utmost to help us'. A second group of survivors also endured a long open-boat voyage, and arrived at another Irish port, Belmullet, on the same day. The other seventeen crew were picked up at sea by the steamer *Chirripo* on 29 April.

Only one of the *Terence*'s crew died as a result of the attack. He was John William Lee, a married 40-year-old cook who lived in Seaforth, Lancashire. It's likely that he was the man who dived into the water during the panic at the starboard lifeboat. Lee was one of more than 17,000 seafarers killed while serving in British merchant ships during the Great War.[12]

U81 went on to sink another vessel and damage two more over the next two days, before it was itself sunk. On 1 May, *U81* was busy shelling a British merchant ship, the SS *Dorie*, when it was struck by a torpedo fired from a submerged British submarine, *E54*. It sank very quickly. The majority of the crew was on deck, and should have survived, but most of them probably drowned in the huge gout of oil fuel that welled up from the U-boat's ruptured tanks. Twenty-nine German sailors died, though Weisbach and six other survivors were picked up by *E54* about a quarter of an hour later, and taken prisoner.[13]

There is no question that *U81* sank the *Terence*, though the identities of the other one or two U-boats that attacked it are not known. The fact that so many were in the vicinity at all, underlines the scale of the submarine threat to British sea trade.

The answer to the threat was to introduce regular convoys with naval escorts. The problem was that, aside from its tactical objections to convoys, the navy thought that it simply did not have enough ships to escort convoys properly, because it had overestimated the scale of the challenge. Some 5,000 merchant vessels entered or left the UK each week, but when this figure was properly analysed, it became clear that the actual number of weekly sailings by high-value oceanic merchantmen was only around 280, *eighteen* times fewer. Once this was realized, ocean convoys were implemented rapidly. The first convoy of the new system sailed on 10 May, less than two weeks after the *Terence* was sunk. Lloyd George, the prime minister, later claimed that this was done on his initiative, but the decision was made before his intervention.

The convoy system was not a total panacea – many ships still sailed independently and some were sunk. However, out of 9,250 ships travelling in Atlantic convoys between May 1917 and the end of the war in November 1918, only 104 were lost, a loss rate of just over 1 per cent. In April 1917, alone, 18 per cent of all merchant ships bound for Britain had been sunk.[14]

The German submarine siege of Britain could have decided the war in its favour. It failed largely because of the convoy system and Britain's efforts to control food consumption and agriculture. The British maritime blockade of Germany was more brutally successful. More than three-quarters of a million people died as a direct result of the blockade, and the strategy also undermined the German war economy.[15]

In June 1917 Captain Frodsom was awarded the Distinguished Service Cross for his 'zeal and devotion to duty'. He retired in 1928, after more than forty years' service. William Frodsom died in early 1945 at the age of 87, though his wife Mary had predeceased him.[16] Raimund Weisbach lived until 1970.

By the time the Second World War started in 1939, the Royal Navy had learned from history: convoys were instituted immediately. In spite of this, new technology made U-boats even more dangerous than they had been in the Great War. Between 1939 and 1945, just over two-thirds of all British merchant losses were caused by submarines – 2,775 ships. The total tonnage destroyed by submarines was more than twice that of 1914–18, and the death-toll among British merchant crews was much higher – nearly 32,000. Likewise, the German U-boat arm endured far greater casualties. It lost 5,087 men killed and 178 U-boats sunk in the first war; in the second conflict the numbers came to 33,087 men and 999 boats.[17]

Somewhere, in the depths of the ocean off the south-western approaches to Ireland lie the wrecks of the *Terence* and *U81*, along with many other ships, submarines and aircraft destroyed in both world wars. They offer silent testimony to the new ways in which technology was used to turn the sea into a graveyard.

Chapter 5

End of Empire
The Heavy Cruisers HMS *Dorsetshire* and HMS *Cornwall* (1942)

The telegram from South Africa summarized the fates of two British warships and their crews – and most of what it said was accurate, if misspelled in places:

> DURBAN SAFRICAN SURVIVORS RECENTLY ARRIVED ESTIMATE TEN MINUTES ATTACH* FORTYEIGHT BOMBS HIT BRITISH CRUISERS CORNWALL DORSETSHIRE LOST INDIOCEAN 4/4 BOTH SUNK WITHIN TWENTY MINUTS STOP SUVIVORS VIVID STORIES 40/60 JAPANSE PLANES DIVING THREES EXGREAT HEIGHT SUCH STEEP ANGLE SHIPS GUNS UNGETABLE THEM
> END MGE ++++2200++++28/4/42++++[1]

By 28 April, the destruction of the *Dorsetshire* and *Cornwall* off Ceylon[2] (actually on 5 April) was old news, superseded by other events, such as the daring American strike on Tokyo.[3] Time and the war had moved on.

The two cruisers were lost at a time when the British, Americans and the other Allies were still reeling from the Japanese advance that had begun with the attacks on Pearl Harbor and many other places on 7 December 1941. By early April, the Japanese had conquered Hong Kong, Malaya, Singapore, the Dutch East Indies, much of Burma, the Philippines and many islands in the Pacific. In February 1942, Japanese carrier planes had even raided Darwin in northern Australia.[4] Large

---

* for ATTACK

parts of the British Empire in the East were gone, and the rest was under a very real threat (**Pl 18**).

One of the things that reinforced the British Empire, like many other empires, was a sense of racial superiority. That feeling of ascendancy evaporated between December 1941 and the spring of 1942, as the Japanese, an Asian people, drove the white Europeans and Americans to retreat and near-defeat. A shrewd Australian politician, Sir Bertram Stevens, who also knew India, observed at the time:

> If Japan is defeated, a new order in Asia is inevitable. We must think of Chinese, Indians, Malayans and Javanese as equals. European prestige in the form in which it used to exist has been shattered.[5]

Stevens' comments were widely disseminated. Independence movements had existed in India and other colonies before the Second World War, but the near-collapse of imperial power helped to pave the way for early postwar independence.

Japanese propaganda certainly linked the defeat of the Royal Navy with the decline of the British Empire, and this claim was echoed in much postwar historical writing. There was some truth in this, even though the Navy's performance at the time and in the following years was much better than has often been supposed.[6] The losses of the *Dorsetshire* and *Cornwall* were signs of the way the world was going, both in geopolitics and the nature of war at sea. But that was not the whole story. The events surrounding the sinking of these two cruisers also have something important to say about the men who served in Britain's last imperial navy.

The two cruisers were part of a revolutionary process of innovation that went back over one hundred years. Steam power, iron, steel and other new technology transformed the nature of warships and war at sea in the nineteenth century. The technological changes that produced vessels like the *Victoria* and the *Dreadnought* (see Chapter 3) also had a profound effect on war vessels of all kinds. New types of warship appeared. The battleship was menaced by the development of fast torpedo-boats, and 'torpedo-boat destroyers' (later, just 'destroyers') were built to counter them. There was also the 'cruiser'. In the early 1800s the word had been 'cruizer', denoting a warship sent on detached duty. Steam-powered 'cruisers' started to appear from the 1860s, primarily intended as commerce raiders. Britain, with its long trade routes and maritime empire, built cruisers to protect its sea lanes, to act as fleet scouts and to police the empire. These vessels had lighter guns and armour than battleships, but they were fast.

Changing technology also began to have an impact on world politics. The Royal Navy's decision to change its ships' boiler fuel from coal to oil in 1909 gave a new level of significance to oil and oilfields in regions such as the Persian Gulf (see Chapter 6).[7]

When the Napoleonic War had ended in 1815, the Royal Navy was the premier naval force in the world. Though it faced challenges over the next century, it did not fight another major war until 1914. Its performance during the First World War was patchy, but it did score some important strategic victories. The navy contained the German surface fleet, helped to break the German economy through blockade, and beat the U-boats.

The post-1918 world was not an easy one for the navy, though. The economy was ailing, defence budgets shrank sharply and there was widespread revulsion against wars and weaponry. The strategic picture was different, too. Since the Naval Defence Act of 1889, the development of the Royal Navy had been governed by the principle that it should be stronger than the next two largest naval powers combined. With shrinking economic performance, this was no longer possible. Britain had to acknowledge that it now had to share the top spot as the world's number-one sea power.

The *Cornwall* and the *Dorsetshire* were products of something new in the world –international arms limitations agreements. The Washington Naval Treaty, concluded in 1922, was epoch-making for Britain. For the first time, the country had to accept naval parity with another power – the United States. The USA, Britain, France, Italy and Japan all agreed to limit the sizes and composition of their fleets, though Britain was still allowed to out-gun the next two smaller navies. In reality the treaty was an admission of the limits of British naval and economic power, though it was sold publicly as a peace measure. There were other naval agreements and negotiations into the mid-1930s, but all hopes of disarmament evaporated with the rise of fascism and militarism in Italy and later, Germany and Japan.

The *Cornwall* and the *Dorsetshire* were 'Treaty Cruisers', designed to fit the 10,000-ton limit for the type set by the Washington Treaty, which also restricted them to guns of no more 8-inch (203mm) calibre.

They belonged to different sub-groups of the thirteen-strong 'County Class', launched between 1926 and 1929. The ships measured just over 630 feet (192m) in overall length, and around 68 feet in width (20m). They had a high freeboard (high sides), and were very seaworthy, which made them stable gun platforms. The hulls were made of a new, high-tensile metal known as 'D-steel', but this could not be welded effectively. Traditional riveted construction was used instead, something still favoured by conservative shipbuilders. Because the cruisers needed to be fast, and because displacement was limited by treaty, the armour used in them was restricted to the magazines and engine machinery, though the *Dorsetshire* did have some additional protection. Both ships were built in royal dockyards: the *Cornwall* was completed at Devonport in May 1928, and the *Dorsetshire* at Portsmouth in September 1930.

Redefined as 'heavy cruisers' under the 1930 London Naval Treaty, the County Class ships were expensive. The whole group cost around £33 million – equivalent to about two-thirds of all UK expenditure on armaments in 1932–33. The cruisers were a disappointment to the navy, however, seen as unsuitable for fleet work. They were expensive to run, with less manoeuvrability and a lower rate of fire than smaller cruisers. For these reasons, they tended to be relegated to colonial policing and trade protection. *Cornwall* underwent a major refit in 1936/37, which included the construction of a large box-like hangar to accommodate two amphibian Walrus reconnaissance aircraft. The *Dorsetshire* carried just one aircraft, but both cruisers had upgrades to their anti-aircraft equipment and later, in 1941, the *Dorsetshire* was equipped with a primitive air-warning radar set.

The industry that built the County Class and other British warships was spread across the UK. It included southern English royal dockyards of Devonport, Portsmouth and Chatham, companies like Armstrong-Whitworth on the Tyne, Cammell-Laird at Birkenhead, Vickers-Armstrong at Barrow, John Brown on the Clyde and Harland & Wolff in Belfast. These companies were supported in turn by steel producers, as well as many private and state facilities that designed and made guns and other items of equipment.

Even in 1935, before the major pre-war rearmament programmes began, the industry that underpinned the navy employed over 158,000 people, a figure almost a sixth higher than it had been in 1907. Britain managed to retain a substantial naval shipbuilding and armament industry in the interwar period. These enabled the country to rearm quickly before the war, and made it possible for British yards to build more than 940 combat ships and submarines, and many smaller naval craft, between 1939 and 1945.

The *Dorsetshire* and *Cornwall* spent much of the 1930s 'showing the flag' on the navy's Far-Eastern 'China Station', but like the rest of the navy they were put on a combat footing in 1939. There was no 'phoney war' for the Royal Navy: it was on active duty from 3 September 1939 to the Japanese surrender in August 1945, losing 50,962 men and women killed and just over 1,500 vessels.

The two cruisers were deployed on numerous operations in the Indian Ocean and the Atlantic between 1940 and early 1942. The *Dorsetshire* took part in the hunt for the German battleship *Bismarck* in 1941, and fired the torpedoes that finally sank it; the *Cornwall* sank a German commerce raider. March 1942 found them back in Indian waters.[8]

The men who crewed the *Dorsetshire* and the *Cornwall* in 1942 comprised sailors from the old regular navy and volunteers from empire countries like South Africa. There was also a newer group, 'citizen sailors', that included many officers and men who had been conscripted for wartime service only.[9]

The quality and quantity of training for both officers and men increased markedly between the mid-nineteenth and mid-twentieth centuries. This was demanded by the increasingly technical nature of ships and weapons, and after elementary education became compulsory in the 1870s, the educational standards of naval recruits also began to rise (see Chapter 3).

An officer-cadet scheme was also introduced, offering a broader education than the one that had been available in the old sailing navy. Britannia Royal Naval College, the navy's school for officer cadets, can trace its origins back to 1859. A few years later, in 1873, Greenwich Royal Naval College was opened to provide continuing education for senior ranks.

Changes of this kind did not, and could not, address the social gulf that existed between most officers and their men, as officers came from predominantly middle and upper-middle class backgrounds. They enjoyed much better conditions than most of their crews, and accommodation and food for the 'lower deck' remained unsatisfactory even into the 1930s and 1940s. Discipline was strict, and sometimes applied unthinkingly, and conditions of service could be harsh for seamen. A teenager was able to sign on – or be signed on by parents or guardians – as a boy sailor at 15 and find himself stuck in uniform until he was thirty. The engagement period was for twelve years, but only began at 18 – the three previous years were not counted. This system endured for a long time after the Second World War and discontented sailors had an acronym – 'ROFT', 'Roll on My Fucking Twelve' – to describe their plight.

The worldwide deployments of the navy during the Second World War required a huge increase in personnel. Conscription provided many people for this, as did the Royal Naval Reserve and the Royal Naval Volunteer Reserve (RNR and RNVR – founded 1859 and 1903, respectively). Naval manpower rose more than fourfold between 1939 and 1945, to a peak of over 850,000 men and women (by which time 8 per cent of the 'manpower' consisted of Wrens serving in the Women's Royal Naval Service). Of the 1.1 million people who passed through the navy during the war, over two-thirds were short-term conscripts or volunteers: 'Hostilities Only', as the official phrase had it. For all these vast changes in personnel, the navy's overall performance during the Second World War was better than it had been during the Great War. Amongst other things, the RN played a major part in the defeat of a German U-boat campaign that was, if anything, more dangerous than that seen in the 1914–18 war. It was also largely responsible for containing and then breaking both the German and Italian surface fleets.[10]

The Royal Navy was not as effective when it confronted the Japanese fleet, however, and there is an awful historical irony in the fact that the Imperial Japanese Navy (IJN) owed part of its development to Britain. In the mid-1800s, Japan had emerged on the world stage after centuries of isolation, and in less than fifty years turned itself into a military and industrial power. Though forcibly 'opened up' by Western countries, Japan remained independent and, in many ways, very traditional.

Japan's modernized army and navy were used as instruments of colonial aggression on the Asian mainland in successful wars against China (1894–95) and Russia (1904–05). Britain cultivated Japan as a counterweight to the Russians and French in the Far East, and sold ships and equipment to the country. There was admiration among some in Britain for the naval prowess of another island nation, and the IJN returned the compliment. The museum at its Etajima Naval Academy had what was effectively a shrine to Nelson, complete with a lock of the hero's hair.[11]

Japan and Britain were allies in the First World War, and co-operation continued after 1918. The IJN was keen to develop its own naval aviation, and Britain sent the Sempill Mission there in 1921 to offer assistance and to sell British aircraft, equipment and expertise to the Japanese. The mission made a material contribution to the early development of the Japanese naval air power, but it was eventually withdrawn at the insistence of the United States, which already saw Japan as a serious rival.[12]

By the time of the Second World War there were three ways in which an aircraft might sink a ship: by torpedo, by bombs dropped from level flight and by dive-bombing. Dive-bombing was first developed by the United States in the 1920s, but other nations soon adopted the tactic, including Japan. This method offered a high degree of accuracy if the pilot could keep the target ship in his sights during a dive, and Japanese naval aircrew were highly proficient in this form of attack by 1941.

The First World War had shown just how vulnerable surface ships were to submarines. The Second World War showed how vulnerable they were to aircraft. In the years 1940 and 1941, air attack was the biggest single cause of loss for British warships, sinking more than a quarter of the 601 RN ships destroyed in those years. The Royal Navy itself used aircraft to sink or disable three moored Italian battleships at Taranto in

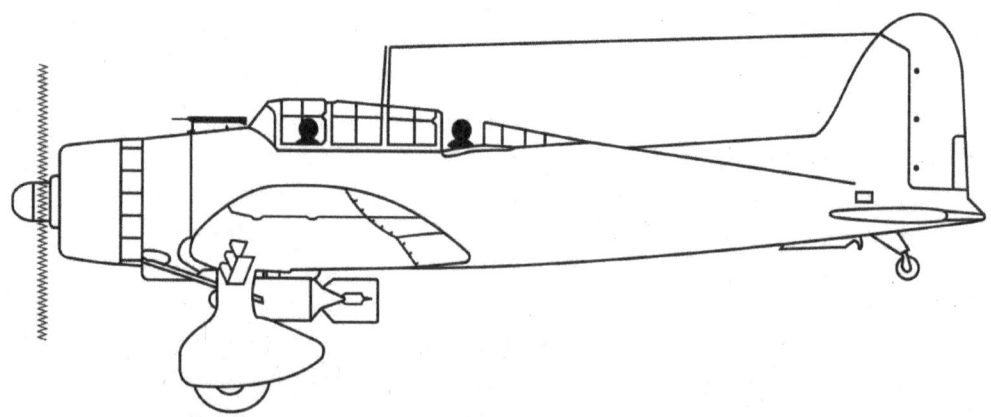

Fig 15 Line drawing of a Japanese Aichi D3A, 'Type 99' dive-bomber.

1940, and the Japanese attack on Pearl Harbor in 1941 did much the same thing, but on a bigger scale.

Dive-bombing imposed huge strains on an airframe, so specialized aircraft were needed to cope with them. In the early 1940s, Japan's principal dive-bomber was the Aichi D3A, commonly known as the 'Type 99', though the Allies later codenamed it 'Val'. It entered service in 1940, and could carry a crew of two, with one 250kg (551lb) bomb under the fuselage, and two 60kg (132lb) weapons under the wings. The aircraft's slow rate of climb and low speed (240 mph maximum) later made it a sitting duck for Allied fighters, but the Type 99 sank more Allied vessels than any other make of aircraft in service with Japan, Germany or Italy. That list of ships included the *Dorsetshire* and *Cornwall*.[13]

Britain came to view Japan as a possible enemy in the 1930s, a threat to its empire and commercial interests in the East. The British adopted a strategy of deterrence against the Japanese, and this included the construction of hugely expensive naval dockyard at Singapore, finally completed in 1938. It was thought that if deterrence failed, naval forces based there might at least buy time for Britain to reinforce its overstretched fleet in the Far East.

In late 1941, with the rising danger of a Japanese war, the Admiralty (not Winston Churchill, as often claimed) decided to send 'Force Z' as a deterrent to the Far East, with the new battleship *Prince of Wales* and the battlecruiser *Repulse*. Sailing without air cover, both were sunk on 10 December 1941 by Japanese planes, with heavy loss of life. This was the first time that capital ships had been sunk at sea by aircraft, and it was a profound shock to both the nation and the navy. The British had possessed reasonably good intelligence about Japanese intentions and capabilities, but failed to appreciate the range and striking power of Japanese naval aviation.

The first months of the war in the Far East went very badly for Britain and its allies. The Royal Navy and the Far Eastern naval forces of its American, Dutch and Australian allies were beaten, losing many men and vessels, and the surviving ships withdrew to wait for what would come next.[14]

The British Eastern Fleet left Singapore, and eventually ended up in Colombo, the principal port of Ceylon (now Sri Lanka). On 24 March 1942, Admiral James Somerville arrived to take command of what, on paper, was a powerful fleet, comprising five battleships, three aircraft carriers, eleven cruisers, fourteen destroyers and seven submarines. The fleet had serious weaknesses, however. Some of the vessels were old and slow, only ninety-four carrier aircraft were available, and the ships had not operated before as a single fleet.

The Japanese navy had wanted to mount a full-scale offensive in the Indian Ocean and capture Ceylon, but the Japanese army said that it did not have enough troops for this. In its place, the IJN developed 'Operation C', a plan for a major naval raid. Its aims were to destroy the British Eastern Fleet, to interdict British sea trade and communications in the Bay of Bengal, and to support Japanese land operations in the region.

The commander of the Indian Ocean force was Admiral Nagumo Chuichi, who had led the Pearl Harbor attack. His fleet was more modern than Somerville's and included five carriers, four battlecruisers, two heavy cruisers, plus other vessels. The carrier air groups had about 275 dive-bombers, torpedo planes and fighters, flown by men with recent combat experience, unlike many of the Fleet Air Arm crews on the British side.

On 26 March 1942, Nagumo's fleet left the Celebes and headed for the Indian Ocean. Separately, the Bay of Bengal raiding force sailed for the Bay of Bengal, commanded by Admiral Ozawa Jisaburo.[15]

Somerville was under orders to protect communications in the Indian Ocean, but also to keep his fleet in being and avoid unnecessary risks. As Andrew Boyd and others have pointed out, losing control of the Indian Ocean could have been disastrous for the British war effort. The routes across the Indian Ocean made it far easier to support British forces in the Middle East and to maintain contact with Australia. Crucially, it also gave access to the oil supplies of the Persian Gulf, vital to both Britain and its new ally, Russia.

Radio intercepts told Somerville that Japanese ships were on the way, but naval intelligence seriously underestimated the scale of the forces involved. Catalina flying boat patrols were sent out in an effort to detect the Japanese, but only a few of them were available. Somerville divided his fleet into two groups, Force A, with the faster and more modern vessels (including *Dorsetshire* and *Cornwall*) and Force B, with the older ships. The admiral took his fleet to sea on 30 March, both to avoid being caught at anchor in Colombo and in an attempt to intercept the Japanese. He put the ships through some rapid work-ups in an effort to turn them into a more cohesive fighting force.

Right: **Pl 1** An unknown photographer's memento of a relaxing day on a British cruise ship in the 1930s…

Below: **Pl 2** … the cruise ship was the RMS *Lancastria*, seen here anchored off Funchal, Madeira, between 1932 and 1939. In June 1940, the *Lancastria* was pressed into war service to evacuate British servicemen and civilians from western France. It was bombed and sunk by German aircraft. The number of dead is believed to have exceeded 3,000, making it the worst shipping disaster in British history.

Pl 3 Pen and ink sketch, by an unknown artist, of brigs at Bideford, north Devon, c. 1830. With the crowd gathered on the quayside and people embarking in the ships, this could be a scene from Bideford's brief period as a port for transatlantic emigration.

Pl 4 Part of the Royal Albert Dock, Liverpool, opened 1846.

Pl 5 Though now much altered, the Belchamber family home in St Martin's Lane, Littlehampton, was the building at the end of this row, nearest the camera.

Pl 6 Thomas Isemonger's 1830 warehouse on the Littlehampton waterfront in River Road, photographed before modern redevelopment.

Pl 7 The entrance to the River Arun at Littlehampton, c. 1900, with the tug *Jumna* towing a brig out to sea. There was no harbour tug there when the *Russell* sailed in 1872, but otherwise the view would not have been much different.

Pl 8 A paddle tug, sailing vessels and a steamer in Sunderland harbour, c. 1900.

Pl 9 The 'mastermind'. Sir George Tryon, photographed in Malta some years before the loss of the *Victoria*.

Pl 10 The 'insubordinate stoker', James Curran, photographed while on tour with Poole's Myriorama, probably in spring 1894.

Pl 11 A steamship being loaded with bags of coffee in the port of Santos, São Paulo, Brazil, around the time of the First World War. In August 1916 the *Terence* loaded over 42,000 bags of coffee at Santos. (According to *Wileman's Brazilian Review*, Vol 4, 1916, pp 575, 577 and 578)

Pl 12 Part of the magnificent Liverpool waterfront, now a UNESCO World Heritage Site. The Albert Dock is in the foreground, with, in order, the Mersey Docks and Harbour Board Building (1907), the Cunard Building (1917) and the Royal Liver Building (1911), collectively known as the 'Three Graces'. Lamport and Holt moved their head office to the Liver Building in 1912.

Pl 13 The SS *Terence* during sea trials in 1902, a photograph taken by its builders, D. & W. Henderson Ltd. of Glasgow. (© University of Glasgow Archives & Special Collections, Adamson & Robertson Collection, GB248 DC 101/607)

Pl 14 A pre-war vision of the future, from 1914. The wireless, aeroplane and submarine would all have deadly roles in the coming wars. (Cressy 1914)

Pl 15 A 105mm gun from a First World War U-boat, presented to the town of Chepstow in Wales in commemoration of a local wartime hero. *U81* had a gun of this calibre.

Pl 16 'Caught in the act': a grainy image printed on grainy wartime paper, this photograph allegedly shows a U-boat preparing to sink a British merchantman that it has stopped. According to the original caption, the photo was taken by the ship's captain as he was rowed away from his doomed vessel. (Golding 1917, p 171)

Pl 17 Abandoning a wartime merchant ship, as portrayed by W. Luker Junior for the readers of *The Wonder Book of the Navy for Boys and Girls* (Golding 1917, p 75). The abandonment of the *Terence* was apparently less controlled. (Drawing by W. Luker Junior 1867–1948)

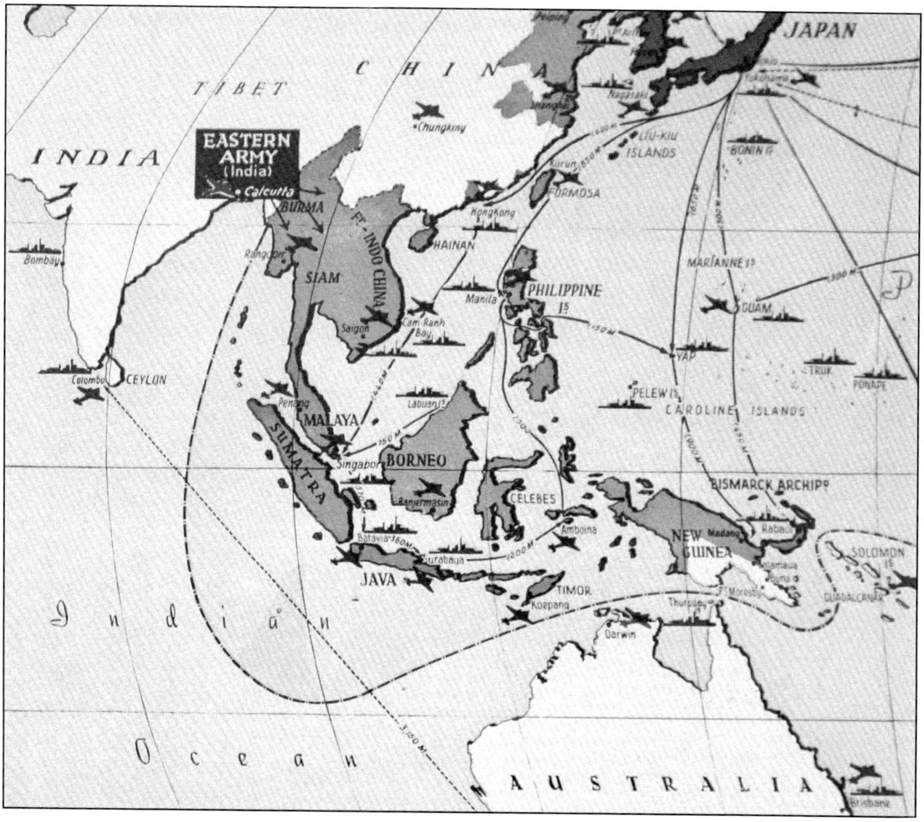

Pl 18 The extent of Japanese conquests in the western Pacific and south-east Asia in 1942, from a wartime map.

Pl 19 The stricken HMS *Cornwall*, photographed from a Japanese aircraft a few minutes before it sank. (© Imperial War Museum, HU2759)

Pl 20 Half cross-section of a tanker built using the Isherwood system, which made it possible to put the tanker engines at the stern. The 'expansion trunk' at the top allowed space for the oil volume to expand in hot weather. (Nicol 1912, p 91)

Pl 21 The *Torrey Canyon* begins to break up. (© *Catastrophe du Torrey Canyon*/ Bridgeman Images, XRE1955776)

Pl 22 A modern container ship: the *Eugen Maersk* docks at Felixstowe, September 2018.

Pl 23 The *MSC Napoli* aground in Branscombe Bay, 2007. (© Jack Sullivan/Alamy Stock Photo A4HBDX)

Pl 24 A container facility from the earlier era of containerization: the former Victoria Deepwater Terminal at Charlton, on the Thames, in 1980. It had conventional cranes, along with its container gantry.

Pl 25 Dockers tallying wool bales in the London docks, c. 1901.

Pl 26 Stacks of containers on a 'boxship': the *Eugen Maersk* at Felixstowe, September 2018.

Pl 27 'Naval reservists bidding good-bye to wives and children' during the First World War. (Golding 1917, p 256)

End of Empire

There was still no sign of the Japanese by 3 April, and Somerville began to think that the intelligence was mistaken. He sent the *Dorsetshire* and the *Cornwall*, and the old carrier *Hermes*, back to Ceylon. The *Dorsetshire* was overdue for a refit and the two other vessels had operational commitments elsewhere. The rest of the fleet went to the navy's secret base at Addu Atoll, so that some of the ships could take on water.

Captain Agar, in the *Dorsetshire*, found his orders 'puzzling', though he knew that Somerville was anxious to see the cruiser fitted with additional anti-aircraft guns and a new radar set. The two cruisers arrived at Colombo on the morning of Saturday, 4 April, and some of their sailors were given shore leave. Then news came through that a Catalina had sighted Nagumo's force, heading for Ceylon. The Eastern Fleet prepared to sail from Addu, and the two cruisers were ordered to rejoin it. They left Colombo Harbour at 10.00 pm and headed south. At the same time, most of the shipping in Colombo was sent to sea, to escape the expected bombing raid. The Eastern Fleet itself left Addu on 5 April. It was Easter Day.[16]

Japanese aircraft bombed Colombo on the morning of 5 April, but the Eastern Fleet could do nothing about that. Somerville received a new sighting report later that day, and altered course to shadow Nagumo's ships. He seems to have been contemplating a night torpedo attack on the Japanese, an operation in which the Fleet Air Arm excelled and the IJN did not. However, this was very risky: if the Japanese had found the Eastern Fleet in daylight, they could have annihilated it.

While Somerville manoeuvred his ships, the two cruisers continued south, aiming for a 4.00 pm rendezvous with the Eastern Fleet. The cruiser captains were experienced officers, Captain Augustus Agar VC in the *Dorsetshire*, the flotilla leader, and Captain P.C.W. Manwaring in the *Cornwall*. At 8.00 am a radio report of a 'strong enemy force to Eastward' led Agar to increase the force's speed to 27½ knots, the fastest that the *Cornwall* could go.

At 11.30 am on 5 April, watchers in HMS *Dorsetshire* spotted a dot dancing up and down on the horizon. It was a reconnaissance plane from the IJN ship *Tone*.

The search aircraft reported the position of the cruisers, and fifteen minutes later Admiral Nagumo's fleet began preparing an air strike. Because of delays in loading torpedoes, the admiral decided to send fifty-

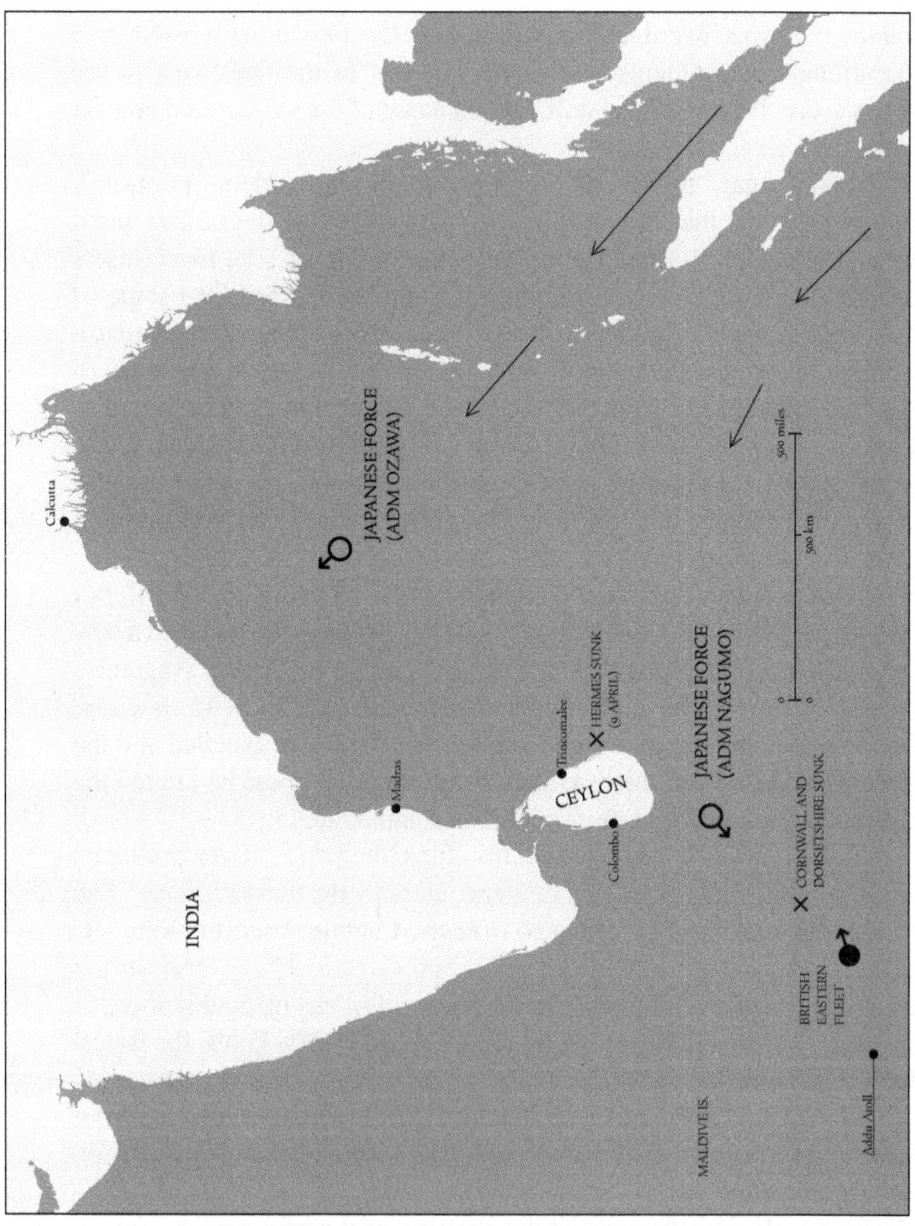

Fig 16 The situation at about midday on 5 April 1942, showing the approximate general positions and courses of the opposing fleets. The position of the loss of the carrier HMS *Hermes*, on 9 April, is also marked.

three Type 99 dive-bombers from the carriers *Akagi*, *Soryu* and *Hiryu* against the two British cruisers. Each plane carried a 250kg bomb.[17]

The cruisers were sailing about one mile apart by this time, closed up for action, and the crews ate a scratch Easter dinner at their duty stations. At about 1.00 pm, two more aircraft were seen some miles off, in different directions. One of them was believed to be British, and the sighting encouraged Agar to think that the main fleet and its fighter cover might not be far away. This persuaded him to press on to the prearranged rendezvous point – the alternative was to turn west and take the ships further from the enemy. At about the same time, confused signals began to appear on *Dorsetshire*'s radar screen. It was the echo of the Japanese strike force. Agar broke radio silence and sent out a sighting report.

Cornwall's radio operator started picking up strong Japanese transmissions at around 1.40 pm. Two minutes later, Japanese aircraft began diving down towards the cruisers. They came in waves of three, from the direction of the sun and over the ships' bows.

The cruisers opened fire, but their anti-aircraft guns achieved little, and only one or two Japanese planes were shot down (the diving angles of the bombers may have been outside the guns' range of elevation). The diving aircraft released their bombs at between about 600 and 1,000 feet (180–300m), machine-gunned the ships, and then pulled out.

The *Dorsetshire* tried to take avoiding action, but three bombs hit the ship in quick succession. The radio rooms and the aircraft catapult were obliterated, and power to most of the portside anti-aircraft guns was cut. Critically, the steering was also disabled.

More bombs followed, striking the boiler room, one of the 8-inch turrets and an anti-aircraft magazine. Within five minutes, the ship was slowing and out of control, tilting heavily to port and almost defenceless. Telephone lines were down, and the cruiser looked to be ablaze from the bridge to the stern. Shrapnel blew the valve off the ship's siren, and its unrestrained howling mixed with the roar of escaping boiler steam and the sounds of battle.

Down below in the ship, men struggled to escape. Francis Anstis and Tom Shirley, two boiler-room stokers, clambered up ladders from the depths of the cruiser to find their normal exit blocked by a ball of fire. They managed to pick their way round it, and reached the open deck via a small service ladder, only to be confronted with screaming wounded and shattered bodies.

More bombs hit the cruiser, along with some near misses, which probably breached the hull plating. Agar gave orders for the crew to prepare to abandon ship. Despite suffering from shrapnel wounds, Commander Jack Byas, the ship's executive officer, managed the uphill climb from port to starboard, where he organized groups to throw rafts overboard.

It's unlikely that many heard Agar's cry of 'Abandon ship' – the Tannoy system was out – but it was already clear that the ship was lost. Men jumped for the water, some of them from a height of 70 feet. Even as the ship foundered, a Royal Marine Bugler, G.W. Timms, kept firing his machine gun at the Japanese planes. Amazingly, he got out alive.

Seven or eight minutes after the first bombs were dropped, the *Dorsetshire* turned over on one side and started sinking by the stern. Agar and others made their way towards the bow, but they were flung into the water when the ship lurched upwards. Shortly after, it slid below the surface. A number of Japanese aircraft flew low over the sinking ship, machine-gunning survivors, wounding some and probably killing at least one man.

The terrible scenes on the *Dorsetshire* were matched by those in the *Cornwall*, which sank around five minutes later.

The *Cornwall* had tried to turn to starboard as the bombs began to fall, and the two forward 8-inch gun turrets were trained to port in a vain attempt to fire at the attackers (**Pl 19**). However, two bombs cut the electricity supply, taking out the telephone system, the main guns and the central control of the anti-aircraft weapons. Gun crews carried on firing, but to little effect.

The motors that controlled the rudder failed, and even hand steering had to be abandoned when the lights in the steering compartments went out. Within a few minutes, water was pouring into the engine and boiler rooms, and thick black smoke billowed out from two of the funnels.

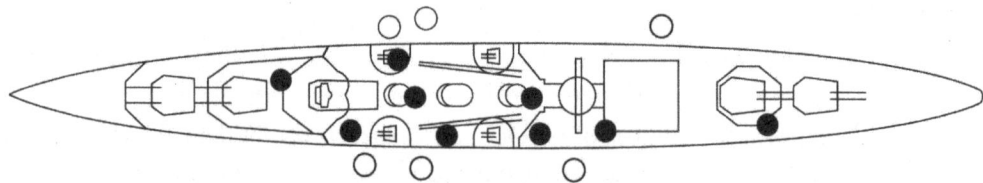

Fig 17 Schematic diagram to show the recorded direct hits (solid circles) and near misses (open circles) suffered by HMS *Cornwall*. Dive-bombing could be very accurate. (Based on information in TNA ADM 267/84)

There was carnage in the ship. First aid groups in the sickbay and recreation spaces were killed by bombs, and on the open deck, flames from explosions enveloped some of the gun crews. Fortunately, the battledress or anti-flash gear that they wore seems to have prevented too many serious burns – though some fires were so intense that no one could survive.

The direct hits were not as calamitous as the near misses. These lifted the ship 'bodily', shook it from end to end, and were probably what caused it to sink so fast. Commander Fair, *Cornwall*'s second in command, certainly believed that these underwater blasts tore open the old, rivetted hull plating and were the primary cause of the sinking.

Like their counterparts in the *Dorsetshire*, men throughout the *Cornwall* tried to cope with the overwhelming shock of the attack and still do their jobs, or at least to save shipmates and themselves. Nearly a quarter of the *Cornwall*'s dead were engine-room or boiler staff, probably killed outright by blasts or trapped as the ship went down – the equivalent proportion of such casualties in the *Dorsetshire* was at least one-third.

Up above, a bomb killed most of the bridge crew: the chief yeoman, Sam Langford, survived, but later lost both legs. Several decks below, the Transmitting Station staff, who controlled the main guns, were ordered to evacuate when the guns became inoperable. Fire consumed most of the TS staff, but Ken Dimbleby, a young South African sailor, and his Marine friend Bill Barrett, were able to get to the weather deck after a nightmare trek up three blazing levels. They reached daylight just in time to see the *Dorsetshire* sink. Bill Barrett later died of wounds in one of the boats.

Paddy Keeping, a 16-year-old sailor who served in one of the gun turrets, was wounded by a near-miss and almost left for dead. Luckily, another man realized he was alive and saved him. Shock made the boy lose his sight for several weeks, but fortunately it came back and he lived to see old age.

Cornwall's starboard outer propeller broke surface as the ship turned on to its port side and began to sink by the bow. Though the main wireless room was out of action, a position signal was broadcast four times from an emergency set. Captain Manwaring, already wounded himself, ordered the crew to escape.

The Japanese stopped their attack as soon as it was clear that the ship was doomed. They got into some sort of formation and flew over the survivors. There was no attempt to machine-gun the men in the water, as had happened with the *Dorsetshire*. About four minutes later, the cruiser turned on its beam-ends and went down by the bows, 'making remarkably little disturbance'. As with the *Dorsetshire*, oil floated up and congealed on the surface. It got into eyes, mouths and throats, making people cough and vomit.

Hundreds of men swam, floated or struggled in the water. A couple of the *Cornwall*'s boats, including an unfuelled motorboat, had been got away, along with six Carley floats, two large fenders and a variety of debris. The survivors swam to anything that floated, but it took more than seven hours to gather most of them in a group round the boats. Isolated parties were still being brought in the following day.

As many wounded as possible were transferred to the motor boat, where the doctors could work on them. A Fleet Air Arm Albacore aircraft appeared at about 4.00 pm. It circled round the two groups of survivors, and was followed later by another FAA plane. This encouraged the men, but rescue was still twenty-four hours away. More thick black oil began billowing up from the wreck a few hours later, though the swell of the waves kept the survivors clear of it.

The three medical officers in the *Cornwall* were RNVR men, Surgeon Lieutenant-Commander Glyn Rees, Surgeon-Lieutenant P.W. McEldowney (a dentist), and Surgeon-Lieutenant Paul Isaac. Rees and Isaac laboured for twenty-nine hours straight, tending the wounded in the motorboat, without food or rest. Their only breaks were to dive into the water to cool off. McEldowney was stranded on an outlying raft during this time (after the later rescue by HMS *Enterprise*, he, too, went to work for a day and night in the ship's sickbay).

The men 'had a short sing-song' before settling down for the night. Most seem to have remained calm. The water supply in the boats had been polluted by seawater and oil, but fortunately there were cases of tinned fruit in the emergency supplies. Doled out on the basis of one tin per ten men, each can was first punctured so that the juice could be drunk, and then it was cut open so the sailors could eat the fruit. Along with some corned beef, these were almost the only supplies available.

The two groups of survivors from the cruisers spent the hours after the sinking on floating islands, separated by a mile or two. Fortunately, the sea was calm, and everything was very quiet after the terrible noise of the attack. Some of the *Dorsetshire*'s boats – two whalers and a skiff –

had been launched, along with floats. There was also a lot of buoyant wreckage. Captain Agar set about getting the disparate groups of his men together, and swimmers began collecting floating debris. Agar had encouraged his men to learn to swim when the ship was in Ceylon, and this very likely helped some of them to survive.

The whalers were leaking and nearly awash, but the wounded men were put into them for lack of anything better. Many had horrible burns. Only one of the ship's medical officers had survived, Surgeon Lieutenant Christopher Wood, RNVR; like his colleagues from the *Cornwall*, he worked for the next day and more to try to relieve the suffering of the wounded. Agar credited him with saving many lives.

The *Dorsetshire* survivors were gathered into one compact group by 5.00 pm. They were surrounded by a lot of fuel oil, though Agar thought later that this was a blessing, as it helped to keep the sharks at bay. A tin of canteen dripping had bobbed to the surface and the fat was rubbed on bodies to serve as makeshift insulation in the cold of the night and as sunscreen by day. The boats had tinned milk and ship's biscuit as their provisions, along with some water, and this was rationed out. A few oranges were also found, and these were kept for the badly wounded. The captain urged his men to 'be prepared to stick it out for the night', with everyone conserving their strength. It was actually warmer, if more tiring, to stay paddling in the water, and men swapped between boats and sea from time to time in order to get some rest.

Perhaps a dozen of the wounded died between the sinking and the rescue, and all that could be done was to push their bodies into the sea to make way for the living. The courage and compassion shown by many of the survivors is illustrated by the story of Charlie Thorne, a South African Sick Berth Attendant (SBA) in the *Dorsetshire*, nicknamed 'Ginge'. According to the testimony of a crewmate, Thorne was pulled into one of the boats with burns on his hands, arms and legs and a bullet wound in one leg. There was another South African rating in the boat, who lay in agony – his foot had been almost severed and was dangling loose. Despite his own wounds, Thorne asked for a knife and neatly amputated the foot. Then he tore off his own shirt and trousers to make bandages for the stump. He cradled the man for hours, though sadly, the amputee died in the night. Thorne tended the other wounded for the whole of the next day, toiling naked under the hot sun, and later carried on working in the rescue ship's sickbay. The testimony to him was written by one of those he had saved.

With the exception of the Captain and doctor, the *Dorsetshire*'s officers stayed in the water, encouraging their men, and the majority of the survivors seem to have remained as positive as they could. Though it sounds like a line from a wartime propaganda film, Agar remarked that in the night, men could be heard calling out: 'Stick it out mates. Be British.'

The next day's heat was intense, and battledress trouser legs were cut up to provide head coverings. The *Cornwall* survivors spotted a lot of sharks in the vicinity, but the predators kept their distance, probably waiting to attack corpses.

Rescue was on its way. Somerville had decided to move east, both to evade the enemy and to find the cruiser crews. At about 6.00 pm on 6 April, the British ships *Enterprise*, *Paladin* and *Panther* found all of the survivors and saved them. If they had not been discovered for another day, it is likely a very large number of the men would have died from wounds, heat and thirst – or sharks.

A total of 1,546 officers and men served aboard the two cruisers, reflecting something of the makeup of the British Empire, or at least the white part of it. There were British officers and sailors from across the UK, along with Australians, Canadians, Maltese and large contingents of South Africans, 104 in the *Cornwall* and over 100 in the *Dorsetshire*. A total of 424 men from both ships died, including forty-eight South Africans and six Maltese.

The survivors were first taken to Addu Atoll, and then to South Africa. The Admiralty began to make lists of the living and the dead, both for its own manpower and administrative purposes and so that it could inform relatives. The sinkings were announced in the press on 9 April, but given the distance and numbers of men involved, it was not until July that final casualty lists could be published. Even then, there were some anomalies, where deaths could not be confirmed.

The Admiralty personnel files contain many moving letters and telegrams from relatives and friends. They were often written in clipped, formal phrases, belying the desperation that lay behind them. For some, the vagaries and slowness of wartime mail raised cruel hopes. In early September 1942, one young woman suddenly received a letter from her fiancé, who had been an officer on HMS *Cornwall*. It was dated

8 April, after the sinking. Six of her letters to him had already come back marked 'Missing, Presumed Killed on Active Service', and she wrote immediately to the Admiralty to find out if he really was dead. They had been engaged for three years. Five days later, an official letter confirmed her worst fears.

Some next of kin got the dreaded standard telegram:

PRIORITY
FROM ADMIRALTY. DEEPLY REGRET TO INFORM YOU THAT IT IS NOW CONFIRMED YOUR HUSBAND *... or son, or brother, was serving in one of the ships ...* AT TIME OF LOSS AND THAT HIS DEATH MUST NOW BE PRESUMED.

Telegrams like this went out across the UK, to South Africa and many other places. Once back in England, Captain Agar set about writing hundreds of condolence letters to the families of those lost, and did his best to stay in touch with survivors.

For many families, there was good news – 1,122 of the sailors survived. Some of these went home, to South Africa and other places. British survivors were only allowed to go home if they had been abroad for more than two years, had suffered two sinkings or were medically unfit. Captain Agar was outraged when he found this out, because it seems that many of the British survivors did not return home in 1942.[18]

Some survivors later suggested that the two cruisers were used as decoys to draw the Japanese fleet away from the Eastern Fleet. In truth, it seems that their loss was down to a mistake. Their presence so close to the enemy that Sunday was due to Somerville's original error in sending the two vessels back to Ceylon, and the more general failure to appreciate the range of Japanese naval aircraft. Given the shortage of British fleet units at the time, it is inconceivable that Somerville would have deliberately sacrificed two heavy cruisers. In the end, it was chance and inadequate Japanese reconnaissance that preserved the Eastern Fleet – Admiral Nagumo had no idea of where it was.[19]

The Royal Navy did not award any medals for bravery to the crews of the two cruisers. The courage and devotion of some of those who tended the wounded was recognized, with civilian awards for Surgeons Rees, Isaac and Wood. Sixteen other men were mentioned in dispatches.[20]

The loss of the two cruisers did not end the carnage at sea, though. On 9 April, the old carrier *Hermes* was bombed and sunk off Ceylon, along with two other warships and two support vessels. In the Bay of Bengal, Admiral Ozawa's raiding force sank twenty-three merchant ships in the space of five days.

It was, however, the end of the Japanese incursion into the Indian Ocean. Their ships withdrew. The growing overstretch of the Japanese navy over the next three and a half years, and the presence of a revived Eastern Fleet, meant that the IJN was never able again to pose a serious threat to vital Indian Ocean routes, nor to India or Ceylon.

Most of the Japanese aircrew who bombed the *Dorsetshire* and *Cornwall* were probably themselves dead within two months. *Akagi*, *Hiryu* and *Soryu* were three of the four IJN carriers sunk by US Navy aircraft at the Battle of Midway in early June 1942. The Japanese air groups were either lost in combat or by ditching, as they ran out of fuel.[21]

From mid-1942 to the spring of 1945, the naval war against Japan was principally an American operation. The vast industrial strength of the United States enabled it to equip forces to fight a transoceanic war on an unprecedented scale in the Pacific. India, South East Asia and the Indian Ocean remained in the British sphere of military influence, and the Eastern Fleet held the line against the Japanese there, but the Royal Navy faced huge problems during the Second World War. Home defence, the security of the Atlantic supply lanes and the war in the Mediterranean, all of these placed enormous strains on Britain's forces and resources. Something had to give, and that something was serious participation in the naval offensive against Japan until 1945.

As commitments eased in other theatres, a powerful British Pacific Fleet (BPF) was created and sent east in late 1944, and the Eastern Fleet was reconstituted as the East Indies Fleet. Both went on the offensive in 1945, and engaged in a great deal of hard fighting against an enemy that remained dangerous until the very end. However, the US Navy accepted the BPF's contribution grudgingly and only gave it a subsidiary role in operations. It became one task force supporting the work of what was now unquestionably the world's greatest naval power.

Britain retained a powerful navy for decades after the Second World War, and still deploys a nuclear deterrent at sea, but its days of global dominance were over by 1945. The Second World War left the country bankrupt, and even after it recovered, there was neither the money nor the political will to reassert past naval power. The rapid postwar disappearance of the empire, which had been an important part of the navy's raison d'être, also undermined the case for keeping a big fleet.[22]

The destruction of the *Dorsetshire* and the *Cornwall* were not turning points in themselves. The Royal Navy lost nearly one thousand vessels to enemy action during the Second World War, and more than 500 to shipwreck, accident and unknown causes.[23] The losses of these two heavy cruisers were, however, clear signs of the way the world was changing. Two complex and expensive products of the metal warship revolution were bombed and sunk within a dozen minutes: air power was coming to dominate war at sea.

On the strategic level, the retreat of the Royal Navy had enabled a powerful enemy force to penetrate waters that had been virtually a British lake since the eighteenth century. Little could be done to stop the Japanese raids, and British power came close to collapse in the region. Even though the Eastern Fleet managed to defend the vital Indian Ocean routes, the myth of European imperial superiority was broken, and the clock was ticking for the British Empire. The empire unravelled very quickly after 1945, with the independence of India and Pakistan in 1947 and a rollercoaster of British decolonization in the following decades, some of it by agreement, and some by force.[24]

The memory of the *Dorsetshire* and the *Cornwall* was kept alive after the war, as some of the survivors formed ships' associations. These enabled old shipmates to keep in touch and share experiences, but inevitably, time took its toll. The HMS Cornwall (1939–42) Association held its last formal reunion in 2002 and The HMS Dorsetshire Association in 2012.[25]

The Royal Navy had underpinned the development and existence of Britain's global empire since the seventeenth century. Likewise, the empire helped to sustain the navy, and the multinational crews of the *Dorsetshire* and the *Cornwall* made them archetypal imperial ships at a time when the empire was coming to its conclusion. However, in the end, the abiding impressions from the destruction of these cruisers are not the geopolitics, the technology or the horror. They are images of kindness, compassion, endurance and bravery shown by so many of the men who served in the two ships. It's encouraging to think that courage and humanity can still come through, whatever the circumstances. The aftermath of the loss of the *Dorsetshire* and the *Cornwall* showed the men of the Royal Navy at their best.

Chapter 6

The Spill
The Oil Tanker SS *Torrey Canyon* (1967)

On 18 March 1967, the giant tanker *Torrey Canyon* ploughed into the Seven Stones reef between the Scilly Isles and Cornwall. Over the next few days, the ship spilled a very large part of the 119,000 tons of crude oil that it carried, causing massive environmental damage.

However, the *Torrey Canyon* was not British-built, British-owned or British-crewed. Why, then, is it being featured in a book about British maritime history? To many of those living at the time of the ship's loss, the answer would have been obvious. The damage caused by the tanker had a huge and highly visible impact on coastlines in the English Channel, and the wreck and its aftermath were headline items in newspapers and on radio and TV for weeks. As a result, this was probably the first time that most people became aware of just how badly human activity could affect the oceans. For decades after, pictures of doomed seabirds, gasping out their lives on a beach covered in black oil, were iconic images of the threat to the marine environment. In recent years, plastic pollution of the seas has subsumed the threat of marine oil spills in the public consciousness, but plastic itself comes from the petrochemical industry. Evidence of humanity's intense involvement with oil will bob to the surface, across the globe, for centuries ahead. Literally.

Oils of various kinds had been used for lighting as far back as ancient times, but it was only in the mid-nineteenth century that oil from geological deposits came into widespread use as a fuel for lamps. This was first made possible in 1859, when drilling rigs struck oil near Titusville, Pennsylvania in the USA. The oil was stored in 42-gallon (US) barrels, and this barrel remains the unit for measuring oil output to this day. The crude oil was refined into paraffin or kerosene, which proved to be an excellent source of light.

The Spill

The American oilfields went from strength to strength, but others began to develop across the world. Baku, on the landlocked Caspian Sea in the Russian Empire, grew as an oil production centre from the 1870s. The oil was transported overland to Batum on the Black Sea, where it was loaded on to ships.

Initially, the oil travelled in wooden barrels or tin cases, but it was soon realized that it could be cheaper and more efficient to build large metal oil tanks within a ship's hull. Some early sailing tankers with wooden hulls and iron oil tanks were in service in the 1860s, but the first metal-hulled tanker used for carrying oil in bulk was the SS *Glückauf* of 2,704 deadweight tons (dwt: deadweight, a measure of the carrying capacity of a ship in terms of weight). The ship was designed and built by the British yard Armstrong, Mitchell & Co. in 1886 for a German line that acted as the agent for the giant US company, Standard Oil. The following year, the Hartlepool yard of W. Gray & Co. launched the first British-owned tank steamer, the *Bakuin*. These early tankers could be dangerous, but they represented the future. In 1885, just under 9 per cent of the oil sent from the USA to Europe was carried in bulk, the rest in barrels. By 1906 the total shipped had increased nearly two and a half times, though now over 99 per cent of it sailed as bulk cargo.

The world oil trade at the end of the nineteenth century was dominated by America and Russia, but major British oil companies also began to appear. The brothers Marcus and Samuel Samuels entered the oil transportation business in 1892, successfully shipping oil from the Black Sea to the Far East. In 1897 they formed the Shell Transport and Trading Company to run their fleet of tankers – the name 'Shell' was inspired by the family's former trade in exotic sea shells. Ten years later the company merged its interests with those of a Dutch concern, Royal Dutch Petroleum, which had begun producing oil in the Dutch East Indies (now Indonesia). Each firm retained a separate identity within the new company, which was called Royal Dutch Shell. It remains one of the biggest companies in the world.

The Anglo-Persian Oil Company Ltd was another early British oil firm, formed to look for oil in Persia (now Iran). The company made its first strike in 1908 and then it grew rapidly. It secured a highly lucrative contract to supply the Royal Navy with oil when the fleet started to convert from coal to oil in 1911. So important was the company's product that in 1914 the British government bought 51 per cent of the shares. The firm established its own tanker fleet in 1915, and would later be known as British Petroleum – now BP.

The invention of the internal combustion engine in the 1880s saw a new use for oil, just as the kerosene market was starting to decline in the face of competition from electric light. Motor cars, and later aeroplanes and airships, relied on petrol for their engines. Oil fuel also began to be used for firing the boilers of merchantmen and warships (as with the Royal Navy), and for powering the diesel engines of the new motor ships. By 1914, oil was a vital strategic material for both the civilian economy and warfighting, and it has remained so ever since.

In the last decades of the nineteenth century, Britain's interest in the Middle East was focused on the Suez Canal, opened in 1869, which substantially shortened the sea route between Britain and its Indian empire. This was one of the reasons why the British occupied Egypt in 1882. In the twentieth century, oil transformed the nature of Britain's strategic involvement in the region, and other powers followed suit. Much of the Middle East was under the rule of the crumbling Ottoman Empire until 1918, when it finally collapsed. Britain and France shaped the development – or underdevelopment – of the nominally independent Arab nations that emerged from it. Vast Arab and Persian oil reserves made the Middle East increasingly important as a source of petroleum.

Britain's 'informal empire' in the Middle East came to an end in the 1950s and 1960s, though not without conflict. The British and Americans engineered a coup in Iran in 1953 to topple a government that had nationalized the main oil refinery. Three years later Britain, France and Israel staged the futile Suez War after the Egyptians did the same with the Suez Canal. Since that time, Iran and the Arab nations have become richer, more independent and more powerful. Six of the top ten oil exporters in the world are still located in this region, which remains of great importance to the Western nations. The Arab-Israeli conflict, the rise of extremist versions of Islam and internal attempts to overthrow dictatorial regimes have also given other countries reasons to get involved there.[1]

Wherever it is produced, the primary instruments of oil distribution are pipelines and seaborne tankers. The distinctive profile of tankers like the *Torrey Canyon* has been around for more than a century, but early tankers often resembled ordinary merchant ships. The safest configuration for a tanker is to have the engines at the stern, and the oil tanks in front, to keep this source of heat as far as possible from the volatile cargo. Early tanker hulls could not take the strains imposed by this layout, and so the engine room had to be put amidships. This meant that the propeller shaft was routed through the aft oil tanks in order to reach the propeller. The oil tanks were – and still are – divided from each other by cofferdams, but no hull was completely oil-tight, and the shaft tunnel could fill with explosive vapour from the tanks. The problem was largely solved in 1908, when the Isherwood system of longitudinal framing was introduced. This made hulls stronger, and it became possible to put the engines at the stern (**Pl 20**).

Like other ships, the average sizes of tankers increased over the years. In 1892, Shell's first tanker, the *Murex*, was of 4,600 deadweight tons. Typical capacities rose from 8,000 dwt in 1918 to 14,000 by the mid-1930s and 16,000 dwt by the early 1950s. The world's first tanker of more than 100,000 dwt was launched in Japan in 1959, the same year that the *Torrey Canyon* was completed.

To begin with, most oil was refined near where it was produced and then transported in this ready-to-use form. After 1945, oil companies began building more refineries in the areas where most of the oil was consumed. It was cheaper to do this, and much of the oil carried by tankers changed from refined to crude.

Various studies over the years showed that tankers got cheaper over 100,000 dwt. The value of the increased cargo carried far outweighed the costs of building bigger hulls, or the increased engine power required, and crewing costs could be kept down by greater use of automation. The term 'supertanker' was coined as long ago as 1921, but it doesn't seem to have begun to come into common use until the early 1950s, and has always been used to refer rather loosely to whatever the current size of a big tanker happened to be. Industry terms are more precise. A vessel on the scale of the 120,000-dwt *Torrey Canyon* was defined as a 'Medium Crude Carrier'. 'Very Large Crude Carriers' started at 200,000 dwt and 'Ultra Large Crude Carriers' at 300,000 dwt. The profits from larger tankers even outweighed the additional costs resulting from fact that they were too big to pass through the Suez Canal. This is why the *Torrey Canyon* had to sail round Africa in 1967: it was a so-called 'Suezmax' vessel, and under regulations then current, drew too much water to transit the Canal.[2]

Britain was a leader in the construction of tankers until the 1950s. The subsequent decline of this part of British industry can be tracked in Shell's order book for tankers between 1950 and 1989. Over this period 167 tankers were launched for the company. Of those, eighty-two were British-built, but all bar eight of these were completed between 1950 and 1966, the last in 1982. The American-built *Torrey Canyon* was just one sign of a world in which Britain was beginning to decline as a builder of big ships.[3]

In 1967 the *Torrey Canyon* was still a relatively new ship, with the top classification awarded by Lloyds Register of Shipping – 100 A-I. It was launched in 1959 at Newport News, Virginia, in the USA, and then 'jumboized' (enlarged) in Japan in 1965, with a deadweight capacity of 120,890 tons of crude oil, split between eighteen tanks. The ship measured 974 feet from stem to stern (297m) and 125 feet (38m) at its widest. There was only one propeller, but the steam turbines in the engine room could drive the tanker along at a respectable top speed of 16½ knots.

The vessel was well equipped by the standards of the day. Besides the usual radio, there were two radar sets, one with a maximum range of 40 miles, a fathometer for checking the depth of water under the keel, a Sperry autopilot and LORAN. LORAN was a system that used radio signals to fix a ship's position at sea. First developed in the USA in the Second World War, it was not as accurate as astronomical navigation, but still good enough for ocean transits. The *Torrey Canyon* was no dangerous rustbucket. Even after the disaster, the embattled master of the tanker, Captain Pastrengo Rugiati, could still describe his ship as the best in the world.

The *Torrey Canyon* was a multinational ship, underscoring the complex nature of modern shipping. It flew the Liberian flag and was owned by the Barracuda Tanker Corporation, a Liberian company registered in Bermuda that was itself a subsidiary of California-based Union Oil. Fifty-five-year-old Captain Rugiati was a highly experienced Italian master mariner of forty years' service, commanding an Italian crew, with thirty-five men aboard at the time of the ship's loss. The only 'British' things about the tanker on its last voyage were the facts that British Petroleum had chartered the ship and owned the 119,328 tons of crude oil that it carried.

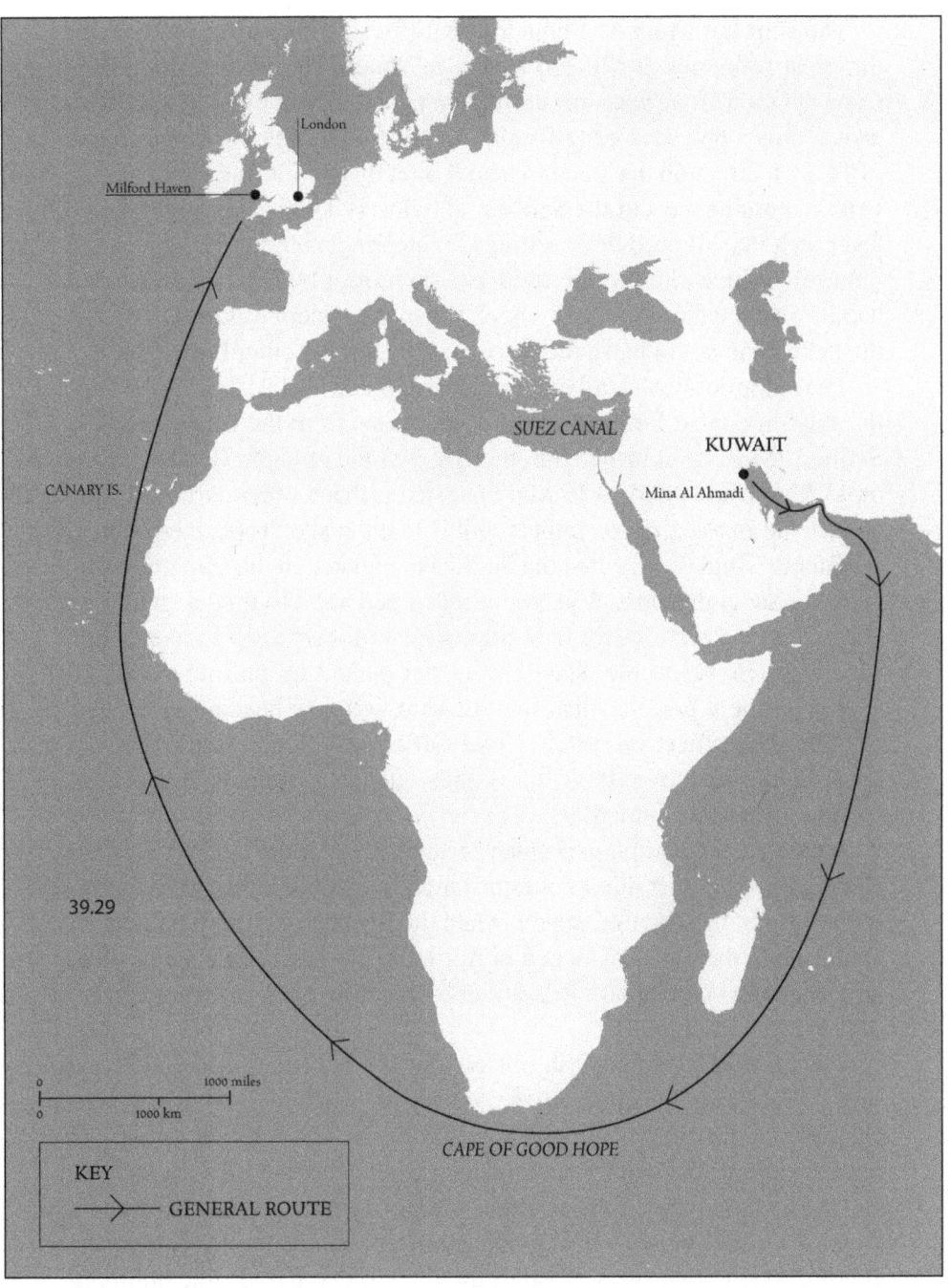

Fig 18 The general route taken by the *Torrey Canyon*.

The ship left Mina Al Ahmadi in Kuwait on 18 February, bound for the great refineries at Milford Haven in Wales. The passage round the Cape of Good Hope was uneventful. On the afternoon of 14 March, with arrival only a few days away, Rugiati set the Sperry autopilot on a course of 18¼°, a direction designed to take it directly towards the west coast of Britain, passing west of the Scillies. The Sperry Duplex Gyropilot had a lever on it that allowed three settings for steering: automatic, manual and 'control', which allowed the rudder to be moved by means of a control handle on the left of the ship's wheel. When the system was on automatic, the helmsman could leave the wheel and undertake other bridge duties.

The autopilot was clearly an impressive piece of 'kit', because it kept the ship on course for most of the 1,400 miles from the Canaries to the Scillies. 'Most' as it turned out, though, was not enough. Between noon on 17 March and 0600 on 18 March, it seems that a water current started to push the *Torrey Canyon* imperceptibly to the east of its planned course.

Captain Rugiati expected the Scillies to register on the ship's radar by 0600 on the eighteenth. When he went to bed at 0240 that morning, he left written instructions for the bridge watch officer to call him once this happened. However, the islands were not picked up until about 0630, at which time it became clear that the ship was now heading to the east of them. The officer on watch, Chief Officer Bonfiglia, turned the ship towards the western side of the islands, and rang Rugiati to ask what specific course he wanted.

A shipmaster or captain is always responsible for the fate of his or her ship, unless it is lost due to circumstances outside the master's control. In the case of the *Torrey Canyon*, when the Liberian government held an enquiry into the wreck at Genoa in April 1967, it laid the blame for what happened next on Captain Rugiati, and on confusion over the operation of the ship's autopilot.

Rugiati decided to go east, not west of the Scillies. This would have saved about half an hour on the voyage to Milford Haven. He later claimed that he did this in order to get there in time for high water – he needed time in the calm waters of the Haven to pump oil fore and aft, and if he missed the tide it would have been another five days before he could dock and unload. Chief Officer Bonfiglia challenged this at the enquiry, saying that the sea was calm enough that day for the pumping operation to be performed en route, and he (Bonfiglia) had been planning to do it that morning.

The Spill

The sea on the eastern side of the Scillies was deep enough for the *Torrey Canyon* to pass, but Rugiati was unfamiliar with these waters and there was one major hazard, the Seven Stones reef. The enquiry panel later suggested that the real reason the captain chose the easterly route was merely that it was more direct.

Rugiati came back on the bridge at 0700, and remained there. The watch changed at 0800 and Third Officer Alfredo Coccio took over from Bonfiglia. The ship was still running on autopilot, even though the Scillies and the Seven Stones were not far off. Rugiati's original bad decision was now compounded by another.

The captain could have taken the ship east of the Seven Stones, but instead decided to go through the 6½-mile gap between these rocks and the Scillies. Contemporary pilot books strongly advised masters against taking this route, but the *Torrey Canyon* did not have one relevant to this sea area. Rugiati briefly turned the autopilot from automatic to manual, and made the course correction, and then switched it back to automatic.

A couple of fishing boats now appeared off to port, and net floats were also seen on both sides of the ship (Rugiati would claim that there was a third fishing boat to starboard, though no one else seems to have spotted it). Given the time it takes to turn or halt the huge mass of a tanker, the boats represented collision risks.

It was proving difficult to get accurate position fixes, and it was only at about 0840 Rugiati discovered that the ship was a mere 2½ to 3 miles from the Seven Stones. He turned the autopilot back to manual at 0842, and made another hurried course correction. It would have been safer to turn eastwards, but instead he swung the vessel due north, a manoeuvre that took about three minutes. Then (he later said), Rugiati reset the machine to automatic.

Suddenly, at 0848, rocks were spotted ahead. Rugiati shouted to the helmsman to 'come to the wheel' and turn the ship hard left. The man did so, but the rudder did not answer, even though the rudder's position indicator did move. The helmsman didn't understand why this was happening, and called out to Rugiati. Unknown to the helmsman, the autopilot was set on 'control', not automatic, and in that mode the ship's wheel would not be able to steer the ship. Only the separate control wheel could do that.

The captain rushed to the wheel and flipped the lever to manual. It was too late. The ship drove on and at around 0850, still travelling at

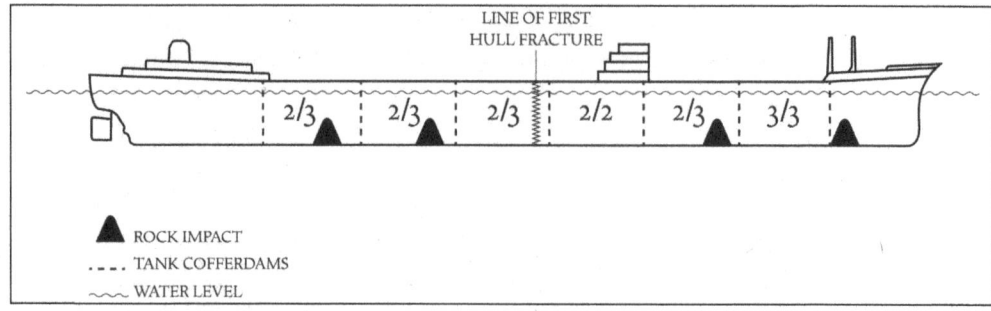

Fig 19 Schematic diagram of the *Torrey Canyon* on the rocks. The ship had six rows of tanks, each divided into three: the annotation '2/2', '3/3' indicates how many oil tanks in a given row were believed to be ruptured soon after the grounding. (Based on information in TNA 68/58 and other sources)

close to top speed, the *Torrey Canyon* ran on to Pollard's Rock, one of the Seven Stones. At least six oil tanks were ruptured immediately, and probably more. The contents of the tanker started spilling out into the English Channel.

The Liberian enquiry itemized what it saw as Captain Rugiati's failings: his routing decisions were poor (considering that he was unfamiliar with this sea area); he did not ask his officers' opinions; he did not reduce speed; there was no clear procedure regarding the autopilot. The last-minute confusion with the autopilot proved fatal. There was no set system for using it. Rugiati did not order the helmsman to switch to manual when he ordered the hard-left turn: he simply *assumed* that the man would do it, even when he had not been trained to do so.

Edward Cowan, a journalist who published an account of the disaster in 1969, suggested that the board of enquiry – for which Liberia itself had no set procedure – was balanced in favour of shipowning interests and the defence of the reputation of Liberia as a 'flag of convenience'. The British government, for example, was only allowed an observer at the enquiry, and could not take part directly. Also, the board did not follow up on issues such as comments about an earlier problem with the ship's steering gear, or the lack of a relevant pilot volume for the western end of the Channel.

A 1968 report by a Royal Navy expert on electrical engineering, Commander Michael Hunter-Jones, suggested that Rugiati either did not understand the correct operation of the autopilot in certain vital respects, or did not have the right manual aboard. In the end, the confusion was still down to Rugiati, though: he should have known precisely how this vital piece of equipment worked, and trained his bridge crew accordingly.[4] As it was, his distinguished career effectively perished with his ship that morning.

The Royal Navy handled the initial response to the grounding of the tanker. The naval command at Plymouth learned of the incident at 0920 on 18 March, and a navy helicopter was sent out to the ship an hour or so later to find out what was happening. A couple of Dutch salvage tugs, owned by Bureau Wijsmuller, also set out for the tanker. The Dutch firm offered a 'no cure, no pay' salvage attempt to the ship's owners, which was accepted.

The tanker's engine room was flooded, and it was without power, but at first there were real hopes that the ship could be refloated and taken safely off the rocks. At the same time, though, it was abundantly clear that oil was gushing into the sea – an estimated 30,000 tons leaked in the first few days.

The authorities knew that there was the danger of a pollution disaster, both at sea and on the nearby coasts of Cornwall and the Scillies. However, no one in the navy, or the country, had experience of dealing with oil pollution on this scale. The Royal Navy had dealt with small-scale spills in harbour, and in those cases the normal remedy was to spray the oil with detergent. This could cause it to break up and disperse if the oil slick was also subject to the turbulence of wind and waves. The problem was, it was also known at the time that detergent could be toxic to marine life.

The navy's 'Operation Mop Up' officially began two days after the accident, but spraying had started near the wreck on 18 March, and in the first forty-eight hours about 5,500 gallons of detergent were used (25,000l). The seaborne anti-pollution effort eventually developed into something on the scale of a small war, with forty-six military and civilian vessels mobilized under naval control, including seventeen trawlers, two destroyers, two frigates and three tugs. The majority of these were employed until 6 April, when 'Mop Up' ended. Falmouth was used as the base for storing detergent, and by late March there was a stock of 158,271 gallons available there. Ironically, BP supplied a lot of the detergent, making money out of dispersing its own oil.

None of the *Torrey Canyon*'s crew was injured, and they were all taken ashore between 19 and 21 March, with Captain Rugiati the last to leave. Tragically, the aftermath of the wreck was not free of fatalities. On 21 March, there was an explosion in the *Torrey Canyon*'s engine room. It blew a huge hole in the ship and a piece of shrapnel killed the Dutch salvage chief, Captain Hans Stal. Stal's shocking death was regarded by some as a major setback to the chances of the salvage operation. The other death occurred in early April, when Able Seaman Ward was killed in an accident on a 'Mop Up' tug at Falmouth.

Various ideas were considered for getting the oil out safely, alongside salvage, but none proved practical. Pumping the cargo out might have worked, but with the rocks nearby, it was not possible to get a large oil carrier close enough. It might have been technically feasible to anchor a vessel further out and lay a pipeline from the tanker, but there was simply no time to do this.

Another idea was to set fire to the oil. This was considered from the start, but there were legal problems, because the *Torrey Canyon* was a foreign ship lying outside UK territorial waters. It would have set a bad international precedent – and lead to legal action from the owners of the ship and cargo – to interfere with the ship before it had been formally abandoned.

Satisfying as the thought of setting fire to the problem might have been to some, it was not guaranteed to succeed. Captain Francis Broad, BP's marine superintendent, had experience of major tanker wrecks, and he advised that not all the oil might burn. He described the case of a wrecked tanker in the Persian Gulf that had blazed for two months until the flames went out, but only half of its oil was consumed. Even then, the fire left a sticky tarlike substance that could still pollute beaches. For a fire to really work, the hull of a tanker had to be opened up to let the air in.

On 26 March, the *Torrey Canyon* began to break up. The owners and salvors unofficially advised the navy that they intended to abandon the ship on 28 March. The way was now open for fire (**Pl 21**).

The idea of setting bombs in the oil tanks was considered, though quickly abandoned as being too dangerous. One government scientist, Mr Bridges, courageously tried to light the floating oil using incendiary bricks that he had developed. The process involved the scientist dangling underneath a helicopter while he dropped his devices directly on to the slick. Despite his bravery, the bricks did not work.

It was clear that aerial bombing was the only feasible way to start a major fire. Between 28 and 30 March, Fleet Air Arm and Royal Air Force

The Spill

aircraft mounted attacks on the *Torrey Canyon* using 1,000lb bombs, rockets and napalm. The rockets mostly missed, the napalm was quickly extinguished by the sea, and of the 160 bombs dropped, only sixty-nine hit the ship and actually went off. The remainder either missed or failed to explode. Official reports were generally upbeat about the bombing, though the numbers of misses and duds were not very encouraging, considering that the target was both undefended and stationary.

For all that, the result was spectacular, and seems to have been effective. The oil around and inside the ship caught fire and a huge column of black smoke rose 3,000 feet in the air. The problem was, it was estimated that only around 20,000 tons of oil were still left in the

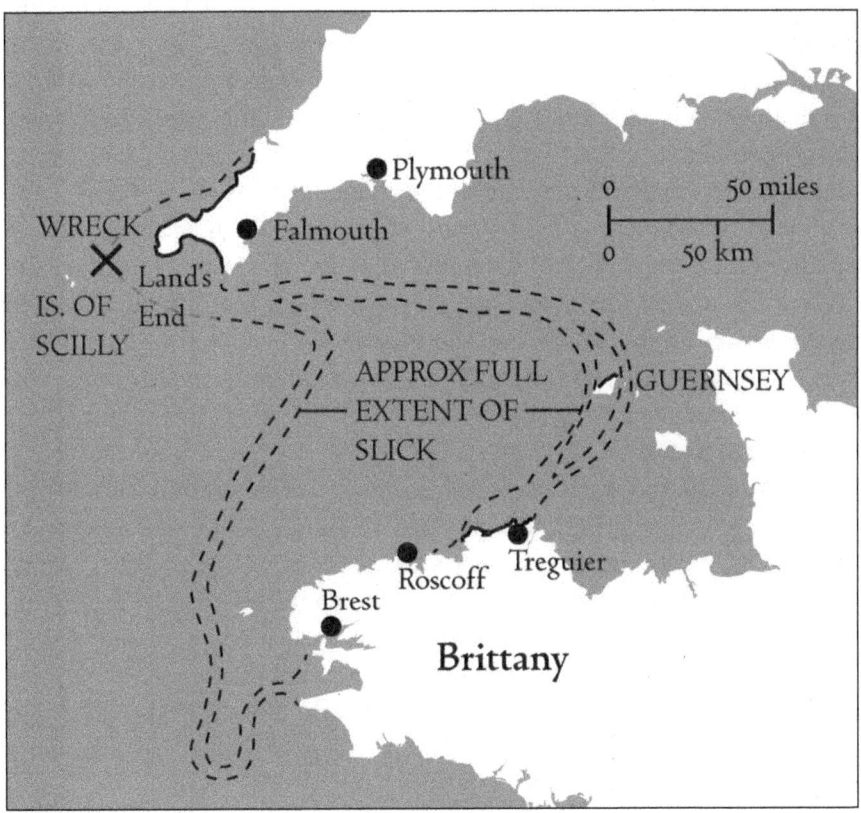

Fig 20 Map showing the approximate full reach of the *Torrey Canyon* oil slick. The broken lines mark the heaviest concentrations of oil at sea, but do not show the full spread of the less dense oil. The solid black lines on the coasts mark the heaviest of the pollution that reached land, but does not show every stretch of shore polluted by the lighter oil. (Based on Smith 1968, supplemented with information from TNA 68/59)

ship by that point. Around 99,000 tons had already poured out into the English Channel. Some of it had already found its way to beaches in Cornwall, and the 'black tide' would also reach Guernsey and Brittany.

A host of other organizations took part in the anti-pollution effort, as well as the navy and the RAF. The RNLI, the Coastguard, Trinity House (which runs lighthouses and lightships) and local authorities all got involved. Units of the army and Royal Marines were drafted into Cornwall to help, along with more than 300 firemen from thirty brigades and a US Air Force firefighting detachment.

A junior minister, Maurice Foley, was sent to Plymouth of 19 March to take charge. On the following day, thirty-two Cornish councils were called to a meeting to discuss the threat, and were issued questionnaires in order to find out what they needed. Prior to the *Torrey Canyon* incident, the general policy of central government was to push the responsibility for dealing with oil pollution entirely on to local authorities. In the end, the government decided to give the services of the armed forces for free, and agreed to cover 75 per cent of the councils' costs.

Some government officials were concerned about the capabilities, and even the competence of a number of councils. Despite this, the local authorities, armed forces and central government seem to have worked well together on the whole, and did their best to tackle the crisis. There was one major difficulty, though: a marine oil spill on this scale was unprecedented, and what was perceived as 'the best' could end as the complete opposite.

Oil was spotted on some beaches in the Scillies on 20 March, just two days after the spill, and a pincer-like formation of slicks began to envelop the north and south coasts of Cornwall. Only contrary winds held them back. The pincer started to close on the night of 24/25 March, with reports of oil on shore at Mounts Bay, St Just and Sennen Cove. In the end, 140 miles of coastline were polluted with the chocolate-brown crude, including around forty holiday beaches. Not all of the oil stayed on the beaches: some of it blew inland, coating windows and walls with a thin, oleaginous film.

Fortunately for Cornwall, the wind shifted on 26 March, and blew most of the oil away from its coast. This meant that no more than about 15 per cent of it actually came ashore in south-west England, though this was bad news for Guernsey and Brittany, which lay in the path of the wind.

The Spill

Cornish local authorities were supplied with at least 500,000 gallons of detergent by the government. The process of 'deterging' the beaches (to use a contemporary term) began with soldiers spraying the detergent. They were then followed by firemen, who tried to clear the resultant mix with high-pressure hoses. The detergent was toxic, but none of the other possible anti-oil remedies seemed to offer much hope of success.

It does seem that detergents were considerably over-used at many places on the coast, right up until the coastal operations ended in mid-May. A lot of marine wildlife actually survived the initial flood of oil, only to be killed off by the detergent, which turned the sea milk-white. By early April, the government was reminding local authorities of just how poisonous the detergent could be, but to little effect. Some local officials seem to have been more concerned to save the valuable local holiday trade by getting the beaches clean, irrespective of the effect on marine life. This was understandable, in one way: Cornwall was already a major holiday destination, with visitor numbers increasing by 50 per cent between 1954 and 1964. Inevitably, people working in the holiday industry were filled with foreboding as the oil washed ashore.

Many local people seem to have felt marginalized by the official response to the crisis. That, certainly, is one of the impressions that comes out of recent oral history interviews conducted with fifty individuals who lived on the Cornish coast in 1967, or took part in the clean-up operation. Those with specialist local knowledge of the tides, currents and weather on the coast were seldom consulted, and some resented the 'we know best' attitude of officialdom – especially as it was apparent that the authorities did not always know what to do.

Many local boatowners and fishermen benefitted from charters and high pay when their boats were hired for inshore spraying, though those on charter boats generally did not have the protective clothing available to the military or firemen. Some other people were apparently able to indulge in what they saw as the age-old tradition of 'wrecking'. They took a risk and boarded the *Torrey Canyon* before it was bombed, lifting things such as the compass, electrical wiring and even tins of barley sugar from its lifeboat rations. However, those in the local fishing industry also feared for the future of their trade, regarding the detergent as more toxic than the oil they were fighting.

Surprisingly, a series of detailed studies conducted soon after by the Plymouth Laboratory of the Marine Biological Association found that the longer-term effect of the oil and detergent on marine organisms was not that great. The coastlines affected consisted mainly of rocky cliffs or beaches, not estuaries: it was just luck that no estuaries were badly hit, because detergent concentrations would have reached catastrophic levels in such enclosed waters.

More recent research has suggested that the impact of the detergent was much more severe than the preliminary results suggested. Food chains were disrupted: micro-organism populations in 'undeterged' oiled beaches recovered in two to three years. By comparison, those in detergent-treated beaches took thirteen or fourteen years to get back to normal. This does not mean that there was anything benign about the oiled beaches, though, where the oil sank into the sand in many places and the air reeked of petroleum and decay. Sometimes, the only remedy was to bulldoze the affected material.

Besides the beaches, the most visible casualties of the *Torrey Canyon* oil were seabirds. The RSPCA, the Royal Society for the Protection of Birds (RSPB) and many volunteers were galvanized into action by the sight of birds struggling in oil. People scoured the beaches looking for oiled birds, trying to save as many as possible. As well as poisoning their food sources, the oil also gummed the birds' feathers, gave them blisters, burned their eyes and could fatally damage their internal organs. The RSPCA set up a cleaning centre for birds at Mousehole in the first week after the wreck, though even at the time it was estimated that 20,000 birds had already died. Other centres opened, and in the first month after the disaster, more than 8,000 oiled birds were taken to cleaning stations run by the RSPCA and the RSPB, though over a quarter of these died. Finding effective cleaning methods was matter of grim trial and error; some birds were too far gone to save, and had to be killed humanely.

Birds had long suffered from oil pollution, whether it came from accidents or deliberate discharges by tankers and other vessels cleaning their tanks with seawater. A 1964 estimate reckoned that millions of birds across the world were oiled every year. Figures for the total numbers of birds killed by the *Torrey Canyon* and other spills can never be known. As well as those found on the beaches, an unknown number must have died out at sea.

A 1984 study recorded 144 incidents around the UK between 1966 and 1983 in which oiled seabirds were found. Auks proved to be the most vulnerable species, probably because of the amount of time they spend floating on the sea. The period between December and March was shown to be the worst for oiling incidents in Europe as a whole. Possible explanations for this included the migratory habits of the birds themselves, the coagulating effect of cold weather on oil, and the tendency of ships to discharge more oil in the generally worse winter weather in order to regulate their stability.

Cornwall relied heavily on the tourist trade, and though at first the disaster kept holidaymakers away, it did not have a long-term adverse impact. As was pointed out at the time, 70 per cent of the county's beaches were left unpolluted. Cornwall, though, was not the only place affected.[5]

The oil hit Guernsey on 6 April, where it polluted a number of coastal areas. The island's government, the States of Guernsey, found that sewage trucks were quite effective at sucking oil off the sand, and eventually more than 800,000 gallons were removed in this way and dumped in a disused quarry. Despite clean-up attempts, the oil in that quarry was still killing birds in 2012.[6]

The oil also reached as far as Brittany, first arriving some three weeks after the spill. In response to pleas from scientists, however, the French government did not use detergents, at least to begin with. The initial official response was slow, but eventually more than 2,000 troops were despatched to Brittany to clean the beaches. A modified chalk powder was used to sink the oil in the sea, apparently with success, but in the end the French, too, began deterging their shores.[7]

Marine insurers paid out $8.25 million on the loss of the *Torrey Canyon*, of which four-fifths was paid by Lloyd's of London. The British and French governments pursued the Barracuda Tanker Corporation through the courts in search of compensation. At first, the company denied that it had any responsibility for damage done by the *Torrey Canyon*'s oil, claiming that the bombing had released most of it.[8]

The *Torrey Canyon* wreck left a legal tangle. The cleanup had cost huge amounts for both Britain and France (at least £6 million in the British case). The two countries had to arrest the *Torrey Canyon*'s sister ship, the *Lake Palourde*, in order to drag Barracuda into court. A hearing was held in London, but given the lack of suitable anti-pollution legislation at the time, the British and French governments had to sue the company under common law for negligence and causing a public nuisance. In the end, the company paid a total of £3 million in compensation, a large sum at the time, but nowhere near enough to cover the costs of dealing with the *Torrey Canyon* and its oil.

It was recognized that a new international legal regime was needed to govern marine pollution liability and compensation. The *Torrey Canyon* disaster led the British government to push the UN's International Maritime Organization (IMO) to establish a new convention for this. The 1969 International Convention on Civil Liability for Oil Pollution Damage was the result. This was later amended, and funds to compensate third-party victims of pollution were set up. British jurists also drafted an international Civil Liability Convention for marine pollution, which has been in force since 1970. Shipowners and crews became liable for oil pollution in both civil and criminal actions. As the Australian Judge Stephen Rares points out, there is no doubt that the *Torrey Canyon* disaster led to a change in international law.[9]

These changes definitely had an effect on the tanker trade. The International Tanker Owners Pollution Federation was established in 1968 to promote effective responses to oil spills and provide technical advice. By 2017, virtually all of the world's oil, gas and chemical tanker fleets belonged to the federation.

In 1967, the wreck of the *Torrey Canyon* was the worst oil tanker loss in history. Just over fifty years on, it now ranks as the seventh-worst, though some took place far out in the ocean and are little known. The most disastrous at the time of writing was the wreck of the *Atlantic Empress* off Tobago in the West Indies, with 287,000 tonnes of oil spilled. In Europe, the scale of the *Torrey Canyon* incident was exceeded by the *Amoco Cadiz* (Brittany 1978, 223,000 tonnes) and the *Haven* (Genoa 1991, 144,000 tonnes).

However, since 1970, statistics for spills of more than 7 tonnes have shown an encouraging trend. Each decade, the average number of spills has gone down from nearly seventy-nine per year in the 1970s to just under seven in the 2010s. It is estimated that around 5.74 million tonnes of oil were spilt in tanker accidents between 1970 and 2017, but just over half of this was in the 1970s and only 1 per cent of it dates from the 2010s. Over the same period, the volume of oil carried at sea has roughly doubled.

There is no doubt that over the last fifty years, the carriage of oil at sea has become much safer. This can be attributed to some degree to a rising environmental consciousness, but a lot of the change has come from the tanker industry itself. It is unlikely if this powerful, freewheeling trade would have changed as much had it not been for the increased regulation and penalties, and the greater certainty of prosecution, that came out of Britain's experience of the *Torrey Canyon*. The USA, for example, unilaterally imposed new conditions on tankers trading to America, and required them to have double bottoms (the better to resist grounding) and improved navigational equipment.

In 1982 the IMO succeeded in getting the fifteen countries that controlled more than half of the world's merchant fleets to sign up a new and binding convention. The International Convention for Prevention of Pollution from Ships, or MARPOL, stipulated that all tankers of 20,000 dwt and more built after 1980 should be able to fill empty spaces in tanks with inert gas, to prevent explosions. Tanks were also supposed to be washed with crude oil rather than seawater, to prevent the discharge of polluted liquid. Hull protection against collision was also increased by a requirement that ballast tanks had to be kept completely separated from oil tanks (two of the *Torrey Canyon*'s tanks were being used to hold water ballast at the time of the wreck). What the French called *la mareé noire*, the 'black tide', in 1967, has had a much more positive outcome than might have been expected at the time, and has helped to make the seas a relatively safer place.

Tanker spills are not the only sources of oil pollution at sea, though. Marine oil rigs have been around since the 1940s, and when they blow out the results can be devastating. In 2010 the BP rig *Deepwater Horizon* exploded and eleven of its crew were killed. The rig's well remained uncapped for nearly three months, releasing more than four times the total of the *Torrey Canyon* spill into the Gulf of Mexico. The scenes of blackened beaches, birds and other sealife were familiar to those who witnessed the 1967 disaster. A long fishing ban after the disaster had a savage economic and psychological impact on local communities.

Another, hidden threat comes from many of the ships sunk since the seaborne oil trade began, including vessels from the two world wars. Some of this oil will seep out as tanks and fuel bunkers rust, and some has already done so. In November 1951, tons of oil-impregnated seaweed were washed up on the eastern Scottish coast, south of Stonehaven, and coated many cormorants in oil. A local man suggested that this had come from the wreck of the tanker *Baku Standard*, which lay offshore.

The ship had been sunk by a U-boat in 1918, and it was thought that recent heavy storms had ruptured its tanks.[10]

The *Torrey Canyon* disaster still remains vivid in the memories of many people who were there – and many of those who watched it on TV. It also had an effect on the growing environmental movement in Britain and elsewhere. The wreck received global publicity, and the events were televised from start to finish. C.M. Jameson, a writer on nature and the environment, believes that though there were worse oil spills, the *Torrey Canyon* had a decisive impact on the drive for greater nature conservation in Britain.

The disaster took place at a time when more and more people were becoming aware of issues of pollution and environmental damage. The UK branch of the campaigning environmental organization Friends of the Earth was formed in 1971, and Greenpeace UK followed a few years later. The British government formed a standing Royal Commission on Environmental Pollution (which reported in 1970), and took steps to ensure that future responses to major pollution incidents were better informed and better co-ordinated. As part of this, the key responsibility for dealing with such threats was given to the departmental minister in a new Department of the Environment.[11]

However, the dying, oiled seabird has recently been supplanted as a key symbol of marine pollution by another deadly environmental threat: plastic. Some of this comes from vessels, in the form of lost nylon ropes and fishing nets, but much of it derives from domestic waste taken out to sea by rivers, including fragments of artificial fibres discharged when clothes are washed. The plastics can kill sea creatures and seabirds directly, by choking them or blocking their guts. More insidious are signs that plastic is entering the marine food chain – including seafood eaten by people. Terrible as oil spills are, they are not in the same league as this threat, though of course plastic is a product of the petrochemical industry. Out of a typical barrel of crude oil, only around 60 per cent ends up as motor fuel – the rest gets used in heating and in making items as diverse as plastics, rubber, deodorant and toothpaste.

In 2017 Sir David Attenborough's *Blue Planet II* programme for the BBC shocked millions of people with its graphic demonstration of the nature and extent of marine plastic pollution. It remains to be seen how much the raised public consciousness of the issue will lead to real action to tackle it, but it is not something that can be denied.[12]

The Spill

The world's economy still relies on oil to a very large extent and modern lifestyles depend on it to a huge degree, although most of us might not like to think about it. The burning of fossil fuels like oil also has also had a profound effect of the global environment, from smog in great cities to global warming.

The tanker, and its ability to move large amounts of petroleum across the globe, has played a significant part in the development of the oil-based economy: in 2005, two-thirds of oil exports still travelled by sea.[13] Ugly, smelly and potentially explosive, the tanker is still a key 'oil mule', serving our addiction to the stuff. Hopefully, in the next hundred years the world will move away from oil consumption, and the ghost of the *Torrey Canyon* will be laid at last. If that happens, the oil tanker will join the carrack, the galleon and the first rate as a curiosity of history.

Chapter 7

Oceans of Stuff

The Container Ship *MSC Napoli* (2007)

My laptop went wrong as I was writing this chapter. The problem was traced to a malfunctioning hard disk, which had to be replaced. This gleaming piece of junk now sits on my desk. Like so many other items in daily life today, it reflects the realities of world trade – the laptop is American, but the disk was manufactured in China, with design input from the Netherlands and Japan.

It is a machine made by globalization. In the last few decades this process has shifted the centre of the world economy away from Europe and North America and enabled China and other Far East nations to rise as industrial powerhouses. Container ships have played an important part in this transformation: my laptop almost certainly made its way to the UK in a shipping container (**Pl 22**).

The *MSC Napoli* was a British-registered container ship or 'boxship', owned by a British company, though there was not much else 'British' about it. The vessel suffered catastrophic damage in the English Channel during a storm in December 2007, and was towed to a spot just off the Devon coast. It shed some of containers, which washed ashore. The ship became a tourist attraction, and also the centre of a brief feeding frenzy as some people looted a number of the beached containers. The goods taken might have been modern, but this looting or 'wrecking' behaviour goes back centuries: the appeal of 'stuff' can be timeless.

The stacked boxes on container ships or boxships give them the appearance of a vast Lego model, painstakingly assembled by a giant child. The vessels are far from elegant and often compared unfavourably with the steamers of old, though even they had their critics. In 1912 the naval architect George Nicol wrote that 'With regard to changes of form, it must be admitted that the body of the modern cargo steamer is no thing of beauty. The sentiment which demanded fineness of form and grace of outline has passed away under the pressure of ever-increasing competition'. The same could be said about container vessels.[1]

The narrative of the *Napoli* and containerization reveals just how the oceans have become a highway for stuff as never before. The story also helps to underscore just how much Britain has changed as a seafaring and sea-trading nation since the SS *Terence* went down in 1917.

For decades after the end of the Great War in 1918, the British merchant marine remained powerful, though its fortunes were very mixed at times. In 1919 the National Maritime Board was established to act as a forum for shipping employers and unions to negotiate wages and conditions. Three years later, the title 'Merchant Navy' was conferred on the merchant fleet, in recognition of wartime service. However, economic turmoil in the 1920s and 1930s led to high unemployment levels and volatile trading conditions for the Merchant Navy, and on top of this there was growing competition from foreign fleets. Despite this, decline was only relative at that point. Britain still had the world's largest merchant fleet in 1939, and the Merchant Navy played a key role in helping the nation survive the Second World War.

There were not many serious foreign rivals in the years immediately after 1945. It was a good time for the British merchant fleet, and working conditions improved for seafarers. However, as other countries began to rebuild their economies, the nature of the maritime world changed.

'Flags of convenience' began to become more common. These are shipping registers maintained by countries that are much cheaper for shipowners, with less stringent requirements for safety standards, manning, crew training and other issues than those of once-major seafaring nations like the UK. Typically, they also levied lower taxes. Panama became the first flag of convenience nation, during the First World War, but the flag of convenience 'fleets' grew enormously from the late 1940s. In 2017 the three biggest merchant-ship registries belonged to the tiny nations of Panama, Liberia and the Marshall Islands. In 1957, the British-registered fleet was the still the largest in the world; sixty years on, in terms of deadweight tonnage (carrying capacity) it ranked eighteenth.

The process of shipowners 'flagging-out' to such registries had a huge impact on world shipping. In Britain, the size of the registered merchant fleet declined from 31.5 million grt in 1977 to 3.6 million in 2001. A 'tonnage tax' was introduced to encourage shipowners to commit to keeping their ships on the British register, and this seems to have had some success. Despite a drop caused by the 2008 financial crash, the December 2017 total stood at 16.2 million grt. However, the picture is complicated: some ships are owned in Britain, but registered elsewhere. In 2017 the total size of the fleet that was owned, parent-owned or managed in the UK amounted to about 4 per cent of world merchant shipping's cargo capacity.

Britain – the City of London in particular – remains a centre for ship management, shipbroking and marine insurance, with earnings coming back to the UK. It is significant that the one UN agency headquartered in the UK is the International Maritime Organization. Britain is still a player in the merchant shipping business, though with nothing like the dominance it once had, and it remains to be seen how Brexit may affect matters.

The twentieth century also saw the decline of the UK's merchant shipbuilding capacity. The industry went through tremendous ups and downs in this period, with boom conditions in both world wars, separated by a deep depression for much of the 1920s and 1930s. Conditions remained good into the postwar world, but the industry was dogged by outdated attitudes among management and workforce, low morale, insecurity of employment and a persistent reluctance or inability to invest in innovation. Foreign shipbuilding industries became serious rivals in the 1960s, particularly that of Japan: its industry had been rebuilt after the war on modern lines and was more geared to innovation.

The ways in which the industry was organized in Britain did not help long-term planning, investment or stability, either. Some firms were amalgamated in the 1960s: this was followed by nationalization as British Shipbuilders in 1977, and then denationalization in the 1980s. Many newly privatized yards could not survive. British Shipbuilders employed 87,000 people in 1977: by 2003, only 26,000 worked in the entire UK industry, and that figure includes yacht-builders.

Naval shipbuilding, though a shadow of what it once was, has survived in better shape than mercantile construction. It has received more government support, in order to maintain the supply of vessels for the Royal Navy. However, the story of British merchant shipbuilding is one of precipitate decline. In 1913, the Clyde alone launched around one-sixth of the *world*'s merchant tonnage: by 1997, the UK as a whole only built 0.7 per cent of the world total, with more than 80 per cent constructed by Japan and Korea.

Even more serious is the shortage of UK seafarers. Numbers of seafarers in the Merchant Navy stood at 192,000 in 1938. Two-thirds of these hailed from the UK, while a quarter came from India or China. In 1956 the total was 160,000, though actual productivity (the number of men required to run a given size of ship) had increased thanks to technology, and the proportions of British and foreign-born crew remained roughly the same (just over 27 per cent of them came from Asia and East Africa).

By 2016, the number of UK seafarers active at sea was 23,060, of whom 10,650 were certificated officers and 8,800 were ratings. The 2016 figures also showed that around one seafarer in six was female, though the majority of these were technical officers, catering or hotel staff, often serving on cruise liners. Most certificated sea officers were male (97 per cent), and around half of them were aged 45 or older. Whilst it is true that digital technology means that fewer people are needed to crew a ship, the decline in the UK's seafaring workforce is still absolute, and its age profile is not an encouraging sign for future.

The composition of the crew of the British-registered *Napoli* was symptomatic of the changes that have taken place. The only British seafarers aboard were two Scottish officer cadets. The rest came from Bulgaria, Turkey, India, the Philippines and the Ukraine. There is nothing new about the employment of foreign seafarers in British ships – it goes back centuries – but nowadays their use is widespread in the UK fleet. The Rail, Maritime and Transport Union (RMT) is concerned that British owners will use relaxed regulations to employ more and more non-UK crews on British-registered ships, because they are cheaper.[2] This is not to say, however, that there was anything wrong with quality of the crew of the *MSC Napoli* as it made its way down the English Channel in the teeth of a storm on 18 December 2007.

The *MSC Napoli* was built at Koje in South Korea by the Samsung Heavy Industries Co. It was originally called the *CGM Normandie* and registered in France. The vessel had capacity of 4,419 TEU (twenty-foot equivalent container units, the standard measure for container loads) and a gross tonnage of 53,409 tons. At around 275 metres in length (902ft) and 38 metres beam (124ft), the ship was slightly longer than the *Titanic* and a third wider. There were seven holds, six full-depth ones in front of the bridge and accommodation structure, and a shallower hold behind, above the engine. The containers in the *Napoli*'s full-depth holds were in stacks of thirteen, with five in each stack rising above the level of the open deck.

The *Napoli* was powered by a Sulzer diesel engine that gave it a service speed of 24.1 knots when built, though in its last year of service the ship operated with a maximum charter speed of 21.5 knots. The merchantman was a one-off design, scaled up from a smaller ship, and was a 'post-Panamax' vessel – that is, too wide to go through the Panama Canal. The ship went through various changes of ownership and name and was bought by Metvale Ltd in 2002. It was re-registered in the UK, under the management of Zodiac Maritime Agencies Ltd. Finally, in 2004 it became the *MSC Napoli*, when it was chartered by the Mediterranean Shipping Company (MSC).

To begin with, MSC used the *Napoli* on voyages between the Mediterranean and north-west Europe, but in November 2006 it was switched to a much longer route, stretching from Cape Town to northern Europe, with a dozen stops on the way. The *Napoli* left Cape Town on its last voyage on 29 December 2006, already four days behind schedule. Engine trouble had added a couple of days to this by the time it reached Felixstowe in Suffolk on 13 January. Scheduled stops at Hamburg and Le Havre were cancelled, due to the delay. The goods destined for those places were unloaded at its next port of call, Antwerp in Belgium, from where they were forwarded by road. The *Napoli* sailed from Antwerp on the morning of 17 December, making for Sines in Portugal. There were 2,318 containers aboard.

By late morning on 18 December the ship was around 45 miles off the Cornish coast, butting its way through force 10 or 11 winds. Waves of up to 11 metres (36ft) are entirely possible in such conditions. The *Napoli* was only making 11 knots, though the engine was pumping out enough power to give the ship 17 knots in calm conditions. Despite the awful weather, designated 'Storm Kyrill' in Europe, the master felt that his ship and its cargo were in no danger.

Just after 11.00 am, some very large waves hit the *Napoli*, followed around five minutes later by a loud cracking sound. A flood alarm went off in the engine space, as water began to enter the hold. The chief engineer went to investigate, and found a large crack in the starboard side of the hull.

Oceans of Stuff

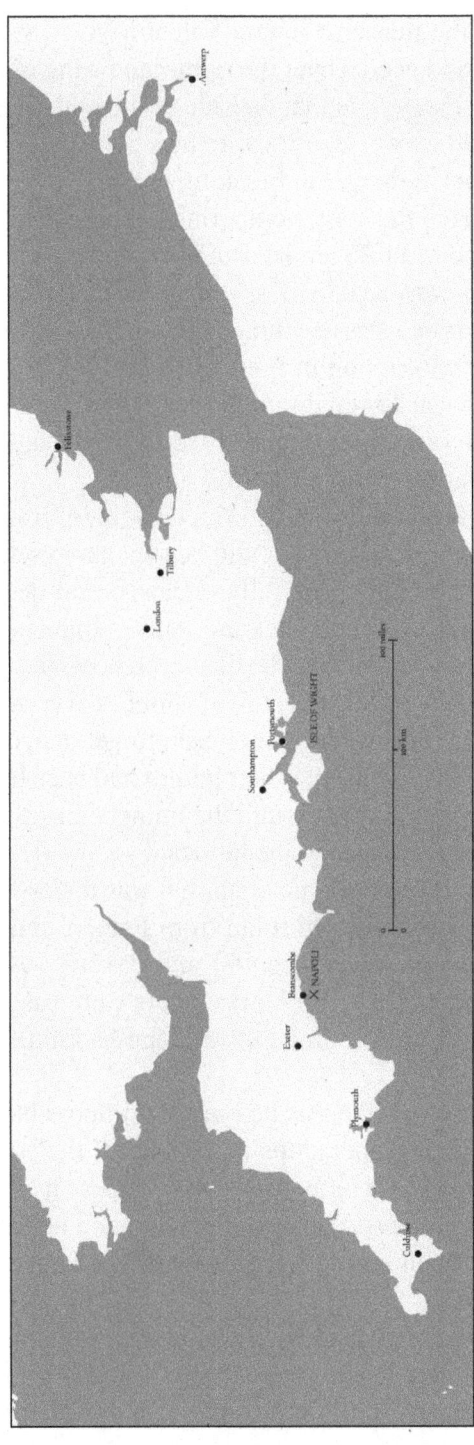

Fig 21 The last ports of call of the *Napoli*, and its final location off Branscombe Bay.

The chief rang the master, Captain Valentin Velev, who was on the bridge. Velev went and peered over the right-hand wing of the bridge. He could see the crack every time that the side of the hull rode up out of the waves. To make matters worse, a fracture now also appeared on the port side. The *Napoli* was in danger of breaking in two.

The captain ordered the crew, numbering twenty-six in all, to prepare to abandon ship, and at 11.25 am he sent out a distress call. Fortunately, Velev had drilled his crew well in lifesaving procedures, and the operation went smoothly. Everyone was accounted for, and a last message was sent out to the Ushant radio station in France. The sailors boarded the port-side lifeboat, which was lowered into the sea. There was a last-minute – literal – hitch when one of the ropes failed to disengage, but the chief engineer cut the boat free with his knife.

The lifeboat, now under its own power, drew away from the ship to a point about 1½ miles off, where its radio beacon and rescue transponder were switched on. The craft was fully enclosed and designed to hold thirty-two, but with everyone wearing bulky immersion suits and lifejackets, it was cramped inside. The boat soon became stiflingly warm, the atmosphere made worse by the reek of vomit as everyone succumbed to seasickness. Some of the survivors began to get dehydrated and feel faint. Luckily, a number of plastic water bottles had been brought aboard, and the men could get a drink, though the immersion suit gloves had to be cut off before they could open the bottles.

By this time, a full-scale rescue operation was under way, with a tug and a Super Frelon helicopter en route from France, and two Fleet Air Arm Sea King helicopters, Rescue 193 and Rescue 194, heading out into the English Channel. The FAA helicopters were based at the Royal Naval Air Station at Culdrose in Cornwall, and had nine crew between them.

Back in 1872, weather like this had made it impossible to rescue the crews of the *Russell* and other ships in trouble off the Northumberland coast (see Chapter 2). The job was made easier in 2007 thanks to technological developments such as radio, radar and helicopters, but the rescue was still difficult and dangerous, with the helicopters close to their operating limits.

Rescue 193 arrived first and tried to lower a 'highline' to the boat. A highline is a weighted leading rope, used to steady the descent of the winchline or winchman from a helicopter to a vessel, and it has to be caught and held by one of those below. The disorientation caused by extreme seasickness makes it very difficult to focus, and unfortunately the survivors tied the highline to the boat, rather than just hanging on to it. The line promptly broke under the strain. A second attempt with a highline also ended in failure.

Rescue 194 arrived shortly after, with a diver aboard, Petty Officer Jay O'Donnell. It was decided that O'Donnell would go down to the lifeboat and receive the highline. It was a perilous business, with the craft pitching up and down wildly, though O'Donnell finally got into the boat. The waves were so high that at one point, when the boat was on a crest, he found himself looking *down* at the helicopter.

With some difficulty, O'Donnell was able to grab the highline, and the winchline descended. While this was going on, a passing Finnish merchant ship, the *Birka Carrier*, paused in its voyage and used its bulk to shield the lifeboat from the worst of the weather. The survivors were not able to give much help to the Petty Officer, for by now most of them were sick, dehydrated and very groggy.

O'Donnell ensured that each man was lifted to safety, first to Rescue 194, and then to Rescue 193. By the time he was able to ascend, 193 was low on fuel, and its tanks were nearly empty by the time the machine reached Culdrose. O'Donnell's bravery was outstanding, and his fellow aircrew in both helicopters also risked their lives in the rescue.

The derelict container ship was subsequently taken in tow, but a plan to take it to Portland in Dorset was soon abandoned. There were fears that the ship might break in two and sink, with a risk of oil pollution, so it was taken to Branscombe Bay in Devon (**Pl 23**). On the morning of Saturday, 20 January, the *Napoli* was run aground about one nautical mile offshore from the village of Branscombe.[3]

Sightseers soon began to arrive at Branscombe, drawn by news reports about the *Napoli*. Fifty containers fell off the ship that night in strong winds, and drifted ashore. The bizarre mixture of cargo reaching shore illustrated the diverse range of goods carried by a container ship. It included food, BMW motorbikes, motor engine parts, pharmaceuticals, nitric acid, automobile airbags, hypodermic needles and heads for industrial mops. Some people started taking goods from containers that had spilled open, or in other cases they actually broke into ones that were still locked.

The authorities taped off the beach, but according to a subsequent Devon County Council (DCC) enquiry, there was a period of a few days in which the police seemed to be uncertain about their powers to stop this kind of improvised 'salvage'. The legal position regarding the removal of these items was not as straightforward as if they had been taken, say, from a burned building. The salvaged goods would only become stolen goods if they were not declared to the Maritime and Coastguard Agency's Receiver of Wreck within twenty-eight days.

News of the wreck spread across the country, and within a short time people were coming to Branscombe in large numbers, some from as far away as Manchester. These modern 'wreckers' gridlocked the village with what the DCC report describes as a '"white van" invasion', and some residents feared for their safety as aggressive looters carted off their wheelbarrows and wheelie bins to move goods from the beach. However, the official salvors arrived on the Tuesday, and the police closed the beach and local footpaths to the public. The free-for-all was stopped.

The spilling of so many containers was unprecedented in the UK, and exposed gaps in emergency planning systems. As the DCC report pointed out, something like twenty-four permanent or temporary official bodies became involved, a situation ripe with potential for miscommunication, misunderstandings and competition.

Oil recovery and oil boom teams were on site quickly, and prevented most of the fuel in the ship from escaping (it could hold up to 3,800 tonnes, and the tanks were nearly full). However, 302 tonnes did get out, and the effects of this were bad enough. The spill killed an estimated 18,000 seabirds, though the toll on wildlife could have been far worse if the ship had sunk outright. DCC's public enquiry found that the decisions made regarding the ship and its grounding were as good as they could have been in such difficult circumstances, though it was critical of some of the ways in which the aftermath was handled.

The pillaging of the containers was like a bizarre replay of history, as documented cases of wreck looting go back to the Middle Ages. Manorial lords, religious houses and others used to own the 'right of wreck' for defined stretches of coastline, which originally meant that if any shipwreck material was washed up on their coast, it became their property. In 1236 a 'law of wreck' changed that. It decreed that if a man or animal escaped alive from a shipwreck, then the ship and its contents were not *legally* 'wreck', and the original owners were given a set time within which they could reclaim their belongings.

Of course, this led to a lot of disputes. Many people, from landowners to the dirt poor, still grabbed the contents of wreck on the basis of 'finders keepers'.

Some 'wreckers' claimed to see shipwrecks as the working-out of God's will: it was a sin not to take advantage of them. In 1619, local people objected to the construction of a lighthouse on the Lizard in Cornwall. If it reduced the number of shipwrecks, they said, it would 'take away God's Grace from them… They have been so long used to reap purchase by the calamity of the ruin of shipping as they claim it hereditary'. Opportunism and greed played their part in wrecking, too, along with what seems to be a curious idea that the sea somehow washes away the legal bonds that normally link goods with their owners. Those who looted the *Napoli*'s containers were probably driven by similar impulses, though none seem to have claimed that God had allowed them do it.

It took a long time to empty the *Napoli* of its containers and fuel oil. An attempt to refloat the ship in July had to be abandoned, and in the end, it was broken up. The forward section was towed to Belfast for scrapping and the rest was dismantled in situ and removed. In all, the clear-up took fifteen months.

But what wrecked the *Napoli*? The conclusions of the UK's Marine Accident Investigation Branch (MAIB) were clear. In the prevailing conditions, the ship did not have sufficient strength to prevent the hull from buckling at the point between the front section and the engine room. At the time it was built, the ship classification society rules only required buckling strength calculations to be made for the midships area, and this did not include the engine room. The report concluded that there was an insufficient, or non-existent safety margin between the ship's design loading and its strength, and that the load on the hull was likely to have been amplified by a 'whipping' effect as the ship rose and fell in the heavy seas. The ship's speed should have been reduced in those conditions, though the MAIB acknowledged that the master believed that his vessel was operating within acceptable limits.

The MAIB put out a worldwide alert to classification societies to check the buckling strengths of certain ship designs. By April 2008, when the report was issued, over 1,500 ships had been checked, of which a dozen were found to need remedial work, ten were borderline, and a further eight container ships remained to be screened.

The fate of the *Napoli* shows how the sea can break even the biggest of ships. Hulls may look very solid, but they can become 'hogged' (drop down at bow and stern), they can sag (droop in the middle), and the waves can also twist them – a 'racking' force. All of this places huge strains on what in the end is no more than an arrangement of welded plates and bolted metal. Something might give.[4]

Over fifty years of development lay behind the *Napoli*. If, for some reason, you wanted to get your flags out for a 'World Container Day', 26 April would be a good choice. On 26 April 1956, an American trucking magnate named Malcom P. McLean loaded fifty-eight aluminium truck bodies on to an old tanker called the *Ideal-X* in the port of Newark, New Jersey. The ship then sailed to Houston in Texas where its cargo was loaded back on to trucks. McLean (1913–2001; he spelled his first name as 'Malcom') had grown frustrated with conventional ways of shipping things and wanted to try something new. He did not invent the container, but his key insight was to see that if container shipping was to work effectively, changes had to be made not just in ships, but in cargo-handling, ports and road and rail distribution.

McLean formed a new shipping line, Pan-Atlantic, later renamed Sea-Land Service in 1960. Containerization was not an overnight success. It took seven years for McLean's company to make a profit, and it was not until the 1960s that there was international agreement over sizes and designs for containers – something critical to their widespread adoption. This is when the TEU became a standard measure for containers, which can be up to 40 feet in length (or two TEUs).

Sea-Land's business was boosted by the Vietnam War. US forces in Vietnam discovered that containers and computerized tracking were the answer to problems in their supply system, which had been a logistical nightmare. Civilian traders also began to make more use of containers. The first transatlantic container ship sailed in 1966, though it was not until the late 1970s that the technology began to have a real impact on the shipping business **(Pl 24)**.

Container ships still have holds, like their historic predecessors, but these are not the battened-down spaces of old. Containers have standard fittings and are designed to slot together so that they can be stacked securely, when, as usually happens, the stacks rise higher than the open deck. They are loaded or unloaded by a specialized crane that can move

Oceans of Stuff

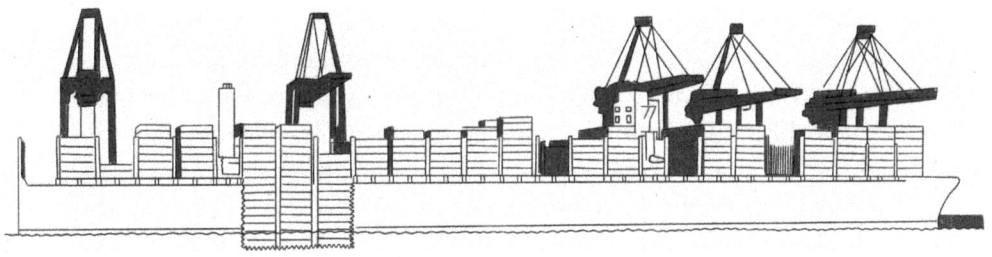

Fig 22 Sketch of a container ship, cut away to show the stacks below deck.

along or across a ship. When a ship is unloaded, the boxes are lifted off on to a transporter waiting between the crane's wide, insectile legs. This takes the box to a container yard, where it is stacked again. In the final phase of the process, the containers are loaded on to trucks and taken away to inland distribution centres or factories.

Containerization destroyed many long-established aspects of sea trade, including the ways in which shipping companies worked. In the nineteenth century, shipping lines developed trade cartels, agreeing between themselves to charge set rates for different kinds of cargo on a variety of routes. Known by the neutral-sounding term 'liner conferences', these were in fact large-scale fixes by shipowners aimed at maximizing their profits. Such cosy agreements could last for a long time. For example, the 1914 'Chamber of Shipping River Plate Charter-Party', in force in the days when the SS *Terence* sailed to South America, was still current in the 1950s. Liner conferences favoured shipping lines, not those who shipped or bought the goods they carried, and the conferences were often backed by governments that wanted to maintain the stability of the shipping business.

Containers radically simplified shipment rates. Many older cargo methods, and the rather byzantine pricing systems that went with them, were replaced by a few types of standard metal boxes with standard costs (the only exceptions were in specialist areas, like bulk cargoes). Business began to move from the conference liners to container ships, adversely affecting the bigger, more established shipping lines.

As shown by Marc Levinson in his fascinating book on containerization, *The Box*, the convenience of containers and the lowering of freight rates had a direct impact on other industries. Manufacturers no longer had to cluster near the ports that supplied their raw materials and parts. With transportation becoming much easier and cheaper, it was possible to move large parts of the production process, or even the entire process, to overseas locations where wages and other costs were lower. It also made new ideas like 'just in time' manufacturing feasible, whereby factories could rely on components arriving exactly when they are required, and do not have to keep inventories stored in expensive warehouses. This has all played a big part in modern globalization. The differences made by containers become very clear when one looks at how ships and ports operated in the pre-container era.[5]

Stowing cargoes aboard ship has always involved a complex balancing act, to ensure that the ship isn't overloaded, and that the cargo is evenly distributed and can be unloaded at the other end in the order it is needed – a 'last-in, first-out' principle. These fundamentals still govern container shipping, but matters were much more complicated in earlier times. For one thing, a shipmaster had to ensure that items were in good condition before they were stowed, as he became liable for the condition of a cargo once he had signed for it. 'Breakbulk' cargoes (those shipped in separate units) were packed in a dizzying number of ways. To take some examples: apples from Canada came in barrels or boxes; bananas travelled from the West Indies in crates; cotton came from Egypt in 700lb (318kg) bales; Malayan rubber was packed in big bales, cases or bags; Brazilian coffee set sail in bags of about 125lb (57kg); Burmese sago arrived in bags or casks; raw Australian wool was shipped in bales. This can all sound very romantic until you consider that these goods were produced by mostly ill-paid workers, transported by mostly ill-paid sailors and handled by mostly ill-paid dockworkers at either end of their voyage (**Pl 25**).

Proper stowage was governed by many considerations. A ship's holds had to be kept clean, well ventilated and dry, with a supply of 'dunnage' (lengths of timber, or mats of some kind) to keep sacks and other packages clear of the hard metal floors. Goods also had to be held in place – shifting cargo can overturn a ship. Barrels needed to be stacked in tiers, preferably in the bottom of the hold, so that any leakages dripped into the ship's bilges and not over other goods. Certain cargoes required special storage conditions: cotton bales were seen as a fire risk (from spontaneous combustion) and syrupy 'green' sugar (a less refined kind) could corrode a vessel's structure if it leaked. Cargoes that might taint each other, or react together, also had to be kept well apart. Creosote, in particular, could stink out a hold (Fig 11 shows a conventional arrangement of holds).

The handling of bulk cargoes was easier to mechanize than that of general goods. Coal-handling equipment was available from the mid-1880s and grain machinery from the early 1890s. However, breakbulk cargoes could only be loaded or unloaded by human beings, with the assistance of cranes, winches and other, fairly basic machinery. There were a few innovations, such as the introduction of pallets and forklift trucks in the 1950s London docks, but not many.[6]

Pre-Industrial Revolution ports were designed to handle breakbulk cargoes. Earlier medieval harbours seem to have been little more than beaching points for ships, but by the twelfth century wooden quays began to appear in northern Europe. Quays made it easier to load or unload ships – especially the bigger ones – but they were subject to the tide, which could make cargoes difficult to access at low water. Another, more serious problem, was that quay space was always strictly limited, causing delay in busy harbours as ships waited offshore to unload.

The concept of the 'legal quay' was introduced in England in 1558, as a place where trade could be conducted lawfully. The measure was intended to reduce port chaos and inhibit smuggling. It did not work. The smuggling of high-value goods was rife in Britain until the early nineteenth century, and legal quays did not to reduce congestion. This was especially true in London, the country's biggest port from the Middle Ages to the twentieth century. By the eighteenth century the capital had about a mile's worth of legal quays lining both sides of the Pool of London, east of London Bridge. Nevertheless, the Pool was often jammed with ships big and small (over 13,500 visited the port in 1797 alone), either awaiting their turn at a quay, or discharging into lighters, each of which still had to unload at a quay somewhere.

The answer was to create commercial docks, which provided additional quay space and had lock systems that ensured the water level stayed constant. Docks did exist before the 1700s, but they were used for shipbuilding or maintenance, not trade. A small commercial dock was built at Bristol in around 1710, but it was unsuccessful. Liverpool constructed its first trading dock in 1715, and had more success, but even here, really large docks did not develop until the 1780s.

Part of the advantage of dock systems lay in the fact that they could be made secure by surrounding them with high walls. Pilferage and theft were major problems, especially at London, where 'river pirates' preyed on ships. Merchants had long tried to improve and extend the quay space there, and in the early 1800s they finally achieved their goal, when the West India Dock, the East India Dock and the London Docks were built. The new docks transformed the capabilities of the port, and many others were constructed on the Thames over the next century and more.

Dock systems and their great brick warehouses and walls came to dominate the reaches of the Thames east of the Pool of London, extending the port eastwards and downriver. London's built-up area followed, as manufacturers and other businesses sprang up near the docks, and workers' housing was constructed close by. This created the 'East End', and the area that is still called Docklands, even decades after the demise of its eponymous docks.

Cargo-handling relied heavily on manual labour before containerization. There were 20,000 men at work in the London docks in the 1850s; a century later, the capital had about 50,000 dockworkers. However, much of the work was casual and unpredictable, relying on the ebb and flow of shipping movements. This meant that most labour requirements were decided from day to day, resulting at its worst in the morning 'scramble' at the dock gates as men jostled and sometimes scuffled to attract the eye of a hiring foreman.

Dock communities were characterized by poverty, but also by tradition. It was normal, for example, for certain dock jobs to pass from father to son, or to another male relative. Life in Docklands was hard, but there was also a powerful sense of cohesion among Dockland people, and this helped to lead to the development of strong dock unions in the nineteenth and twentieth centuries.

Life did improve somewhat for dockworkers and their families after the Second World War. The National Docks Labour Board was created in 1947 and this facilitated improvements in working conditions, including 'fall back' payments for casuals when they failed to get daily work. Casual work was finally ended in 1967, though it has been said that this helped speed the decline of the docks, because the 'flexibility' offered by casual labour had kept many cargo-handling companies afloat. Full-time workforces were more expensive.

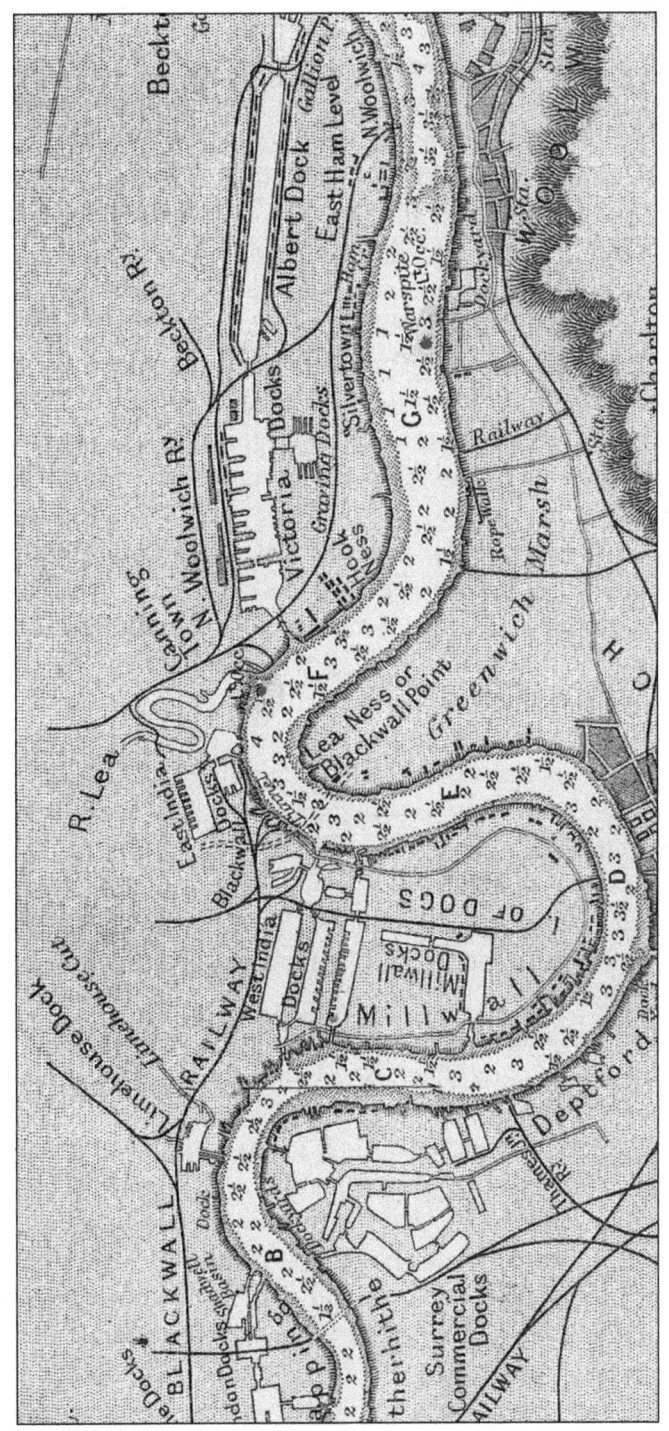

Fig 23 The Thames and the London docks in 1905, from a Thames pilot book.

Dockworkers were divided into three main groups: the stevedores, who could only work on ships, dockers who were able to work both on a ship and ashore, and lightermen, who operated the lighters used to unload vessels away from the quays, whether in dock or in the river. It took experienced men to know how to load all of the many awkward corners in a vessel, and the work was very labour-intensive. Unloading a ship, for example, needed a gang of ten to twelve working in the hold, and another dozen receiving the goods on the quayside. In addition, men were needed to take the cargoes to the 'sheds' and warehouses. Though cranes and pulley systems were used, much of the stacking and lifting of boxes and other packages relied on strong arms and strong backs. Injuries were common, from muscle strains to the danger of death as men worked in and around deep holds and heavy, moving loads.

Dockland life seems to have been fairly similar across the world, but pretty much all of it was swept away by containers. London docks, for one, were already in difficulty even before containerization really began to bite, because they could not accommodate the biggest new ships (and much later on, a ship the size of the *Napoli* would have been hard-pressed to get very far up the Thames, let alone enter any of the old docks). The closure of the small St Katharine's and London Docks was recommended as early as 1962, along with the development of a new deepwater port area at Tilbury in Essex, close to the mouth of the Thames. Four years later, with containerization on the horizon, it was estimated that the general cargo capacity of London's 160 dock berths and 300 river wharfs could be replaced by a mere twenty-one container berths.[7]

Before the container revolution, the effective limit for the size of merchant ships, both cargo liners and tramps, was around 14,000 dwt. This limit had nothing to do with technical considerations: it was down to the great length of time that it took to load or unload a ship using traditional methods. Docks did not generally work around the clock, and in an eight-hour day shift in good weather, a dozen stevedores might move 960 tons of cargo. On this basis, more than three days would have been needed to unload 3,000 tons, and that was without allowing for stoppages of one kind or another. In 1950, it was reckoned that cargo-handling in general was so slow that vessels spent only half of their time actually going anywhere - and a ship in harbour was a ship not earning.

Trade unions could see, very clearly, that containers threatened dock jobs. It was planned to develop Tilbury as the UK's main container port, but this was hamstrung for two years from January 1968 by the Transport and General Workers' Union, when it imposed a ban on handling containers. In the interim, Sea-Land Service negotiated a container-handling deal at a non-unionized, minor Suffolk port. This was Felixstowe, and it went on to become the UK's largest container port.

The port of Felixstowe was opened in 1886, with a dock served by a rail connection, but it never really flourished. By 1945 it was in disrepair, with serious problems caused by silting. The Felixstowe Dock & Railway Company was bought in 1951 by Gordon Parker, an East Anglian corn merchant, who set about redeveloping the port for the export of grain. The company expanded into other areas, and reclaimed land to build a 'roll-on, roll off' (roro) wharf. In 1967 it opened a 500-foot-long stretch of quay designed to handle containers, the first in England.

The total import and export tonnage handled in the port rose from 1.5 million tonnes in 1968 to 8.5 million in 1983. The throughput of containers over the same period rose from fewer than 50,000 to over 450,000, carried by fifty-five shipping lines that reached across the globe. This was in addition to companies operating in other trades. Compared to conventional ports, container ports gave ships faster turnaround times, employed fewer people and worked round the clock. They were also more secure, because containers are sealed and locked. Felixstowe's rise is a product of the container age.

This kind of operation rang the death knell for traditional ports. All of London's major upriver docks closed between 1967 and 1981. Dock employment likewise fell, from 32,000 registered dockworkers in London in 1955 to only 3,000 in 1985. The wider Docklands economy was closely linked to that of the docks, and for every dock job lost, three more went in local industry and transport. By 1981, the area had some of the highest unemployment rates in the country, with more than one man in five out of work.

The face of Docklands changed in other ways, as new financial businesses and office blocks moved in. Weather-sealed containers do not need buildings to house them, so the imposing nineteenth-century London warehouses became redundant and were converted into expensive flats. This kind of transformation has been seen in former docklands across the world.

The development of containerization was helped by the contemporaneous growth of computerized record-keeping, that made it much easier to keep track of goods. In many ways it is a highly rational and controlled system, but not everything in the container world is perfect. Containers can be used for trafficking people or for transporting drugs, weapons and other illegal items by criminals or terrorists, and computerized cargo systems can sometimes be hacked. The container yards themselves, with their enormous stacks of blank-sided metal boxes, look like cities of the dead, which is perhaps one reason why they seem to feature so often in film and TV thrillers.

The *normal* operation of the container industry also gives causes for concern. In Europe, there is no requirement to weigh containers before they are loaded on a ship. The shipper declares the weight of a container, and this is taken as the actual weight when the container is loaded. Part of the cargo of the *Napoli* offers a case in point. Six hundred and sixty containers from the ship were weighed by the MAIB, because they had remained dry. About one box in five was more than three tonnes different from its declared weight, with a twenty-tonne discrepancy in the worst case. In addition, fifty-three of the 700 containers were not in the positions they had been allotted at the time the loading stability calculations were made. It is, apparently, reckoned in the container industry that up to one in ten of the containers loaded on to a vessel might be out of place in this way.

Did this adversely affect the ship? MAIB thought that such variations in weight distribution would not have been sufficient, in the existing conditions, to have caused the hull fractures. However, the Board did feel that they would have impaired the safety levels in the ship's structure.

Though the MAIB did not assign legal blame for the loss of the *MSC Napoli*, it was harshly critical of the container industry. In MAIB's view, commercial pressures lay behind various decisions that had eroded the safety margins of the ship, including the decision to go as fast as possible in heavy seas. The overriding concern of the industry was to move as much as possible in the shortest possible time, and this was trumping safety at sea.[8]

Aside from the problems it revealed, the wreck of the *MSC Napoli* also showed, once again, the skills, courage and compassion of those in the rescue services who still go out in all weathers to save life at sea. Petty Officer Jay O'Donnell received the Queen's Gallantry Medal for risking his life to rescue of the crew of the *MSC Napoli*. The two helicopter commanders, Lieutenant Guy Norris and Lieutenant Commander Martin Rhodes, were awarded the Queen's Commendation for Bravery in the Air, for their courage and 'exceptional flying skills in atrocious weather conditions', and the crews of both helicopters also received joint awards.[9]

The *Napoli* incident is a reminder that there are certain constants in maritime affairs that are independent of technological, economic and other factors: seafarers will deliver goods where they are wanted; in the wrong conditions, the sea can still break the biggest of ships; people will risk their lives to save shipwreck victims; given the opportunity, some other people will behave badly and try to loot a wrecked ship. The ocean road has not changed as much as some might like to think.

That said, one cannot deny that real historical changes have occurred in the world's maritime economy in the last few decades. It would be simplistic to say that containerization is responsible for all of this, but it has certainly facilitated it, and the volume of container movements is an index of that change. In 1969, by volume of traffic, of the top ten container ports three were in the USA, four were in Europe (including Felixstowe), two were in Australia and only one was in Asia (Japan). By 2003, the top ten included six in Asia. In 2003, no UK port even made the top twenty. The centre of the world economy had moved to Asia, and to a significant degree it was the container ship that helped it move there.[10]

It is ironic just how much effort Europeans put into a quest for the riches of the East from the fifteenth century onwards. Nowadays, the East is coming to Europe, America and the rest of the world – though it may not bring riches in the longer term.

Ships and boats have moved 'stuff' around the world since prehistory, but the sheer volume of stuff on the move has increased exponentially in recent years. The size of the world merchant fleet doubled between 2004 and 2016. In the latter year there were about 58,000 vessels in service, with a carrying capacity of 1,778 million tonnes. The impact of that shipping on the world environment is staggering: it was said in 2017 that the annual output of pollution from ship exhausts is equal to that produced by Germany.[11]

Once upon a time, before the eighteenth century, a significant proportion of sea trade served elite markets –rich people who drank wine, wore silk or ate food cooked with spices. There were exceptions, like the trades in wool, cloth and salt, but much maritime commerce was distinctly 'high-end'. Sea trade nowadays is much more 'democratic'. Like it or not, most people in the world, even those in landlocked nations, are enmeshed in a vast maritime economy that profoundly affects their lives and the global environment. In this age of mass consumption, the container ships sail for us all (**Pl 26**).

Endpiece

It would be easy to end this book with a gloomy epitaph on the state of Britain as a maritime nation. Maritime empires, like all empires, come and go. The British Empire was no different: at the time when the English first began edging out into the ocean in the sixteenth century, it was Spain and Portugal that 'ruled the waves'. The USA superseded the UK as the world's greatest naval power in the mid-twentieth century, but it may well be challenged at sea in coming decades by China.

Remote as the oceans can seem, what happens there has always affected the rest of the world in some way. At the conclusion of his book on twenty-first-century sea power, *Super Highway*, Chris Parry quotes Sir Walter Raleigh on the subject. Even though he was writing four centuries ago, Raleigh's shrewd analysis still holds true: 'Whosoever commands the sea, commands the trade; whosoever commands the trade of the world commands the riches of the world, and consequently the world itself.'[1]

The sea, or at least the ways in which humans use it, can also offer some unpleasant surprises, as some things that people thought were extinct come back to life. One example of this is piracy, which has reappeared in the Indian Ocean, the Far East, and, most recently, the Caribbean, a product of failed or failing states. To take another theme, in Britain the Brexit debate delivered a sharp reminder, perhaps for the first time since the Second World War, that the country is an island and relies on ships to deliver a significant amount of its food. If shortages do arise, they will not be caused this time by marauding submarines, but by new tariff barriers and other consequences of 'crashing out' of the EU.

Over and above the recurrent economic and strategic issues related to the sea, there loom the crises of climate change and manmade environmental damage to the oceans. This is why the last two chapters of this book deal with environmental matters, rather than more 'traditional' issues of maritime history. Short of all-out nuclear war, these are the biggest threats facing both human society and nature in general, and they can only be solved – or, at least, mitigated – by exceptional levels of international co-operation. If they are not, the ocean may turn on humankind, with the seas invading more and more coastlines, and polluted marine food chains spreading disease.

This puts any concern about the status of one's country as a sea power, into sharp perspective. Having said that, Britain's involvement with maritime issues is still far from negligible. The country still has its place on the ocean road, and it could use its influence and expertise to help the world meet the coming environmental challenges of the twenty-first century, and the human consequences that flow from them.

Looking back over centuries of British maritime history, what comes first to my mind are the human stories that go with it. Departure for war, or even or for peacetime naval service, was of course a momentous event for sailors' families. It became a staple subject for cheap prints and souvenir pottery in the eighteenth and nineteenth centuries.

A photograph, printed in the upbeat and rather bullish *The Wonder Book of the Navy for Boys and Girls* from 1917 (**Pl 27**)[2] inadvertently captured the mixed emotions of such a moment. The men are naval reservists, called up for the Great War. The two sailors in the centre look relaxed and cheerful as they hold their children up for the camera, maybe excited at the prospect of action. However, the young woman on the right, perhaps the wife of the sailor she stands next to, looks grim. Her apprehension, if that was it was, is a counterpoint to the meretricious ideas about 'naval glory' that sometimes still pervade writings about maritime history.

The world is again living in another time of crisis, this one caused by the coronavirus Covid-19. At the time of writing, the outcome of the present epidemic is unknown. It is affecting the whole world, as far as is known, and one hopes that humanity will come out the other side of it with a much deeper realization of our shared vulnerability and our interdependence. Perhaps those of us lucky enough to live in the richer nations will learn to do with less, to share more, and to reduce our impact on the environment, which will still continue to face an unparalleled crisis, even after Covid-19 is beaten. This may sound utopian, but one of the things that history does show is that not all historical change is bad.

Endpiece

In 2003, I wrote a book about the maritime history of Britain and Ireland from the early Middle Ages. It concluded with an appeal to the peoples of those nations to take more account of the sea.[3] I paraphrase it here, not out of regard for my own writing, but because it seems appropriate to the times. However, it is no longer only addressed to the inhabitants of our small group of islands:

If this book has a message, it is that the people of the world should take much more account of the ocean that surrounds all of our lands, no matter how impossibly far away it may seem in landlocked nations. People need to take more notice of the life that lives in the ocean, of the people who work on it, and of what happens there. The sea has been – and remains – a highway, a source of food, a battleground, a dumping ground and a playground. It is also on our front doorstep.

Abbreviations

BNA	British Newspaper Archive, via www.britishnewspaperarchive.co.uk
MM	*Mariner's Mirror*
ODNB	*Oxford Dictionary of National Biography*
OED	*Oxford English Dictionary*, via oed.com
TNA	The National Archives, Kew
WSRO	West Sussex Record Office

Bibliography

Abell 1981 W A Abell, *The Shipwright's Trade*, London (Conway Maritime Press, London)
Adams 1986a G Adams, 'Cargo handling' in Al Naib 1986, pp 97-110
Adams 1986b G Adams, 'Reminiscences of a stevedore', in Al Naib 1986, pp 153-58
Agar 1959 A W Agar, *Footprints in the Sea* (Evans Brothers, London)
Al Naib 1986 S K Al Naib (ed), *Dockland: An Illustrated Historical Survey of Life and Work in East London* (North East London Polytechnic in conjunction with the Greater London Council, London)
Balfour-Paul 1999 G Balfour-Paul, 'Britain's informal empire in the Middle East' in Brown and Louis 1999, pp 490-514
Barker 1986 T Barker, "Docklands: origins and early history' in Al Naib 1986, pp 131-9
BCS 1996 British Chamber of Shipping, *Fleet and Manpower Enquiry* (British Chamber of Shipping, London)
Beckett 2019 F W Beckett, *Rorke's Drift and Isandlwana: Great Battles* (OUP, Oxford 2019)
Beer 1968 J V Beer, 'The attempted rehabilitation of oiled sea birds', *Wildfowl*, Vol 18, pp 120-24
Bergin 2011 T Bergin, *Spills and Spin. The Inside Story of BP* (Random House, London)
Berry 2015 W Berry, *The Pre-Dreadnought Revolution: Developing the Bulwarks of Sea Power* (The History Press, Stroud 2013)
Blake 1967 J B Blake, 'The medieval coal trade of north-east England: some 14th century evidence', *Northern History*, pp 1-26
Bone 1929 D W Bone, *Merchantmen-at-Arms: The British Merchants' Service in the War* (2nd edition, Chatto & Windus, London)

Bonsor 1983 N R P Bonsor, *South Atlantic Seaway: An Illustrated History of the Passenger Lines and Liners from Europe to Brazil, Uruguay and Argentina* (Brookside Publications, Jersey)

Bonwick and Steer 1959 G J Bonwick and E C Steer, *Ship's Business*, 3rd edition (The Maritime Press Ltd, Wokingham)

Boyd 2017 A Boyd, *The Royal Navy in Eastern Waters: Linchpin of Victory 1935–1942* (Seaforth Publishing, Barnsley)

Brown 1992 D K Brown, 'The Cruiser' in Gardiner 1992b, pp 55-70

Brown 1995 D K Brown (ed), *The Design and Construction of British Warships 1939–1945* (Conway Maritime Press, London)

Brown 1999 J M Brown, 'India' in Brown and Louis 1999, pp 421-26

Brown and Louis 1999 J M Brown and W R Louis (eds), *The Oxford History of the British Empire Vol IV – The Twentieth Century* (Oxford University Press, Oxford)

Brown 2011 L Brown, *County Class Cruisers*, Shipcraft 19 (Seaforth Publishing, Barnsley)

Burton 1994 A Burton, *The Rise and Fall of British Shipbuilding* (Constable, London)

Butel 1999 P Butel (trans I H Grant), *The Atlantic* (Routledge, London)

Clancy 2017 J Clancy, *The Most Dangerous Moment of the War: Japan's Attack on the Indian Ocean, 1942* (Casement Publishers, Oxford)

Coleman 1972 T Coleman, *Passage to America: A History of Emigrants from Great Britain and Ireland to America in the Mid-Nineteenth Century* (Hutchinson, London)

Corlett 1978 E Corlett, *The Iron Ship: The Story of Brunel's Great Britain* (Moonraker Press, Bradford-on-Avon)

Corlett 1981 E Corlett, *The Revolution in Merchant Shipping 1950–1980* (National Maritime Museum, London)

Corlett 1993 E Corlett, 'The screw propeller and merchant shipping', in Gardiner 1993, pp 83-105

Cottrell and Aldcroft 1981 P L Cottrell and D H Aldcroft (eds), *Shipping, Trade and Commerce: Essays in Memory of Ralph Davis* (Leicester University Press, Leicester)

Cottrell 1981 P L Cottrell, 'The steamship on the Mersey, 1815–80, investment and ownership', in Cottrell and Aldcroft 1981, pp 137-63

Cowan 1969 E Cowan, *Oil and Water: The* Torrey Canyon *Disaster* (William Kimber, London)

Bibliography

Cox 2013 C Cox, *History of Pennsylvania Civil War Regiments: Artillery, Cavalry, Volunteers, Reserve Corps, Colored Troops* (independently published)

Craig 1980 R Craig, *Steam Tramps and Cargo Liners 1850–1950* (National Maritime Museum, London)

Cressy 1914 E Cressy, *Discoveries and Inventions of the Twentieth Century* (Routledge, London)

Crouzet 1982 F Crouzet (trans A Foster), *The Victorian Economy* (Methuen, London)

DCC 2008 Devon County Council, MSC Napoli. *The Aftermath of the Beaching off Branscombe, East Devon, 20 January 2007* (Devon County Council, Exeter)

de Goey 2007 F de Goey, 'Trading vessels: modern vessels', in Hattendorf 2007 4, pp 179-87

DETR 1998 Department of the Environment, Transport and the Regions, *British Shipping: Charting a New Course* (Department of the Environment, Transport and the Regions, London)

DfT 2017a Department for Transport, *Shipping Fleet Statistics 2016* (Department for Transport, London)

DfT 2017b Department for Transport, *Seafarer Statistics 2016* (Department for Transport, London)

DftT 2018 Department for Transport, *Shipping Fleet Statistics 2018* (Department for Transport, London)

Dimbleby 1984 K Dimbleby, *Turns of Fate: The Drama of HMS Cornwall 1939–42* (Kimber, London)

Dodds and Maguire 1998 C Dodds and B Maguire, 'The Scottish shipbuilding industry', *Scottish Economic Bulletin*, No 57, The Scottish Office, via www.scotland.gov.uk

Doe 2017 H Doe, *The First Atlantic Liner: Brunel's Great Western Steamship* (The History Press, Stroud)

Donald 1997 D Donald (ed), *The Encyclopaedia of World Aircraft* (Blitz Editions)

Edgerton 2006 D Edgerton, *Warfare State. Britain, 1920–1970* (Cambridge University Press, Cambridge)

Elleray 1991 D R Elleray, *Littlehampton: A Pictorial History* (Phillimore, Chichester)

Farrant 1976a J H Farrant, *The Harbours of Sussex 1700–1914* (independently published, Brighton)

Farrant 1976b J H Farrant, 'The seaborne trade of Sussex, 1720-1845, *Sussex Archaeological Collections*, Vol 114, pp 97-120

Fayle 1920 C E Fayle, *History of the Great War: Seaborne Trade*, Vol I (John Murray, London)

Fayle 1923 C E Fayle, *History of the Great War: Seaborne Trade*, Vol II (John Murray, London)

Fayle 1924 C E Fayle, *History of the Great War: Seaborne Trade*, Vol III (John Murray, London)

Felixstowe 1985 Port of Felixstowe, *Port of Felixstowe Handbook 1985* (Port of Felixstowe, Felixstowe)

Flayhart 2002 W H Flayhart, 'The Inman Steamship Company Limited: innovation and competition on the North Atlantic, 1850–1886', *The Northern Mariner/Le marinier du nord*, Vol XII, No 4, pp 29-46

Foreman 1986 S Foreman, *Shoes and Ships and Sealing Wax: An Illustrated History of the Board of Trade 1786–1986* (HMSO, London)

Fowler 2011 S Fowler, *Tracing Your Naval Ancestors* (Pen & Sword, Barnsley 2011)

Friel 1983 I Friel, 'Documentary sources and the medieval ship: some aspects of the evidence', *IJNA* Vol 12, pp 41-62

Friel 2003 I Friel, *The British Museum Maritime History of Britain and Ireland 400–2001* (British Museum Press, London)

Friel 2015 I Friel, *Henry V's Navy: The Sea-Road to Agincourt and Conquest 1413–1422* (The History Press, Stroud)

Friel 2020 I Friel, *Britain and the Ocean Road: Shipwrecks and People, 1297–1825* (Pen & Sword, Barnsley)

Gardiner 1992a R Gardiner (ed), *The Shipping Revolution: The Modern Merchant Ship* (Conway Maritime Press, London)

Gardiner 1992b R Gardiner (ed), *The Eclipse of the Big Gun: The Warship 1906–45* (Conway Maritime Press, London)

Gardiner 1993 R Gardiner (ed), *The Advent of Steam: The Merchant Steamship before 1900* (Conway Maritime Press, London)

Gardiner 1994 R Gardiner (ed), *The Golden Age of Shipping: The Classic Merchant Ship 1900–1960* (Conway Maritime Press, London)

Gibbs 1957 C R V Gibbs, *Passenger Liners of the Western Ocean* (2nd edition, Staples Press, London)

Bibliography

Gilman 1992 S Gilman, 'Container shipping' in Gardiner 1992a, pp 42-62

Golding 1917 H Golding (ed), *The Wonder Book of the Navy for Boys and Girls* (Ward, Lock & Co, London)

Gordon 1996 A Gordon, *The Rules of the Game: Jutland and British Naval Command* (John Murray, London)

Green 2008 R Green, *Building the* Titanic*: An Epic Tale of Human Endeavour and Modern Engineering* (Carlton Books, London)

Green and Cooper 2015 A Green and T Cooper, 'Community and exclusion: the *Torrey Canyon* disaster of 1967', in *Journal of Social History*, Volume 48, pp 892–909

Greenhill 1993 B Greenhill, 'Steam before the screw', in Gardiner 1993, pp 11-27

Griffiths 1993a D Griffiths, 'Triple expansion and the first shipping revolution', in Gardiner 1993, pp 106-26

Griffiths 1993b D Griffiths, 'Marine engineering development in the nineteenth century', in Gardiner 1993, pp 160-78

Griffiths 1997 D Griffiths, *Steam at Sea: Two Centuries of Steam-Powered Ships* (Conway Maritime Press, London)

Halpern 1994 P G Halpern, *A Naval History of World War I* (University College London Press, London)

Harper 1999 M Harper, 'British migration and the peopling of the Empire', in Porter 1999, pp 75-87

Hattendorf 2007 J B Hattendorf (ed), *The Oxford Encyclopedia of Maritime History* (4 vols, Oxford University Press, New York)

Heaton 2004 P M Heaton, *Lamport & Holt Line* (P M Heaton Publishing) Abergavenny

Henry 1907 J D Henry, *Thirty-Five Years of Oil Transport: The Evolution of the Tank Steamer* (Bradbury, Agnew & Co, London)

HMSO 1976 HMSO, *British Vessels Lost at Sea 1939–45* (Patrick Stephens, Cambridge)

HoC 2017 House of Commons Library Debate Pack, *Future of UK Maritime Industry* (House of Commons, London)

Hope 1980 R H Hope, *The Merchant Navy* (Stanford Maritime, London)

Horn 1998 J Horn, 'British Diaspora: emigration from Britain 1680–1815', in Marshall 1998, pp 28-52

Hough 1959 R Hough, *Admirals in Collision* (Hamish Hamilton, London)

Hovgaard 1920 W Hovgaard, *Modern History of Warships* (E & F N Spon, Ltd, London)

Howarth 1992 S Howarth, *Sea Shell: The Story of Shell's Tanker Fleets 1892–1992* (Shell International Petrol Company, London)

Howarth and Howarth 1994 D and S Howarth, *The Story of P & O: The Peninsular and Oriental Steam Navigation Company* (Weidenfeld & Nicholson, London)

Howarth 1997 S Howarth, *A Century in Oil. The "Shell" Transport and Trading Company 1897–1997* (Weidenfeld & Nicholson) London

Howie 1986 Lord Howie, 'Dock labour history', in Al Naib 1986, pp 71-80

Howkins 2003 A Howkins, *The Death of Rural England: A Social History of the Countryside Since 1900* (Routledge, London)

Hull 1898 T A Hull, *The Pilot's Handbook for the English Channel* (J D Potter, London)

Hutchinson 1997 Hutchinson, G., *Medieval Ships and Shipping* (Leicester University Press, London and Washington)

Hythe 1913 Viscount Hythe (ed), *The Naval Annual 1913* (Griffin, Portsmouth)

ITOPF 2017 The International Tanker Owners Pollution Federation Limited, *Oil Tanker Spill Statistics 2017* (International Tanker Owners Pollution Federation Limited, London)

Jackson 1983 G Jackson, *The History and Archaeology of Ports* (World's Work Ltd, Tadworth)

Jameson 2012 C M Jameson, *Silent Spring Revisited* (A & C Black, London)

Jamieson 1998 A G Jamieson, 'An inevitable decline? Britain's shipping and shipbuilding industries since 1930' in Starkey and Jamieson 1998, pp 79-92

Jamieson 2004 A G Jamieson, 'Inman, William (1825–1881)', doi.org/10.1093/ref:odnb/14427, ODNB, accessed 21 January 2018

Jeffrey 1999 K Jeffrey, 'The Second World War' in Brown and Louis 1999, pp 306-28

Jones 2006 N Jones, *The Plimsoll Sensation: The Great Campaign to Save Lives at Sea* (Little, Brown, London)

Kennerley 2008 A Kennerley, 'Weston, Dame Agnes Elizabeth (1840–1918)' in ODNB 2008, https://doi.org/10.1093/ref:odnb/36842, accessed 10 December 2019

Bibliography

Lambert 2009 A Lambert, *Admirals* (Faber & Faber, London)

Lane 1964 F C Lane, 'Tonnages, medieval and modern', *Economic History Review*, 2nd Series, Vol XVII, pp 213-33

Laughton and Lambert 2004 K. Laughton, revised A. Lambert, 'Tryon, Sir George (1832–1893)', in ODNB 2004, https://doi.org/10.1093/ref:odnb/27782, accessed 15 December 2019

Lavery 2001 B Lavery, *Maritime Scotland* (Batsford/Historic Scotland, London)

Lavery 2004 B Lavery, *Hostilities Only: Training the Wartime Royal Navy* (National Maritime Museum, London)

Lavery 2006 B Lavery, *Churchill's Navy: The Ships, Men and Organisation 1939–1945* (Conway, London)

Lavery 2011 B. Lavery, *Able Seamen: The Lower Deck of the Royal Navy 1850–1939* (Conway, London)

Levinson 2006 M Levinson, *The Box: How the Shipping Container Made the World Smaller and the World Economy a Lot Bigger* (Yale University Press, Princeton)

Liberia 1967 Republic of Liberia, *Report of the Board of Investigation in the Matter of the Stranding of the SS TORREY CANYON on March 18, 1967* (Republic of Liberia, Monrovia)

Lloyd 1968 C Lloyd, *The British Seaman 1200–1860: A Social Survey* (Collins, London)

Lyon 1980 D Lyon, *Steam, Steel and Torpedoes: The Warship in the 19th Century* (National Maritime Museum, London)

Lyon 1993 D Lyon, *The Sailing Navy List 1688–1860* (Conway Maritime Press, London)

Lyon 2016 P Lyon, *Merchant Seafaring through World War 1, 1914–1918* (Kibworth)

MacGregor 1985 D R MacGregor, *Merchant Sailing Ships. Sovereignty of Sail 1775–1815* (Conway Maritime Press, London)

McCluskie 1998 T McCluskie, *Anatomy of the* Titanic (PRC Publishing Ltd, London)

Mallman Showell 2006 J P Mallman Showell, *The U-boat Century: German Submarine Warfare 1906–2006* (Chatham Publishing, London)

MAIB 2008 Marine Accident Investigation Branch, *Report on the Investigation of the Structural Failure of* MSC Napoli *English Channel on 18 January 2007,* Report No 9/2008, April 2008 (Marine Accident Investigation Branch, Southampton)

Marder 1961 A J Marder, *From the Dreadnought to Scapa Flow. Volume One: The Road to War 1904–1914* (Oxford University Press, London)

Marder 1965 A J Marder, *From the Dreadnought to Scapa Flow. Volume Two: The War Years: To the Eve of Jutland 1914–1916*, (Oxford University Press, London)

Marder 1969 A J Marder, *From the Dreadnought to Scapa Flow. Volume Four: 1917: The Year of Crisis* (Oxford University Press, London)

Marder 1970 A J Marder, *From the Dreadnought to Scapa Flow. Volume Five: Victory and Aftermath January 1918 to June 1919* (Oxford University Press, London)

Marder 1980 A J Marder, *Old Friends, New Enemies.: The Royal Navy and the Imperial Japanese Navy. Volume One: Strategic Illusions 1936–1941* (Oxford University Press, Oxford)

Marder, Jacobsen and Horsfield 1990 A J Marder, M Jacobsen and J Horsfield, *Old Friends, New Enemies. The Royal Navy and the Imperial Japanese Navy. Volume Two: The Pacific War, 1942–1945* (Oxford University Press, Oxford)

Markus 2015 U Markus, *Oil & Gas. The Business and Politics of Energy* (MacMillan International Higher Education, London)

Marshall 1998 P J Marshall (ed), *The Eighteenth Century: The Oxford History of the British Empire*, Vol 2 (Oxford University Press, Oxford)

Matthias and Pearsall 1971 P Matthias and A W H Pearsall, *Shipping: A Survey of Historical Records* (David & Charles, Newton Abbot)

Miller 1988 F M Miller, 'Immigration through the Port of Philadelphia', in Stolarik 1988, pp 37-54

Miller 2014 R F Miller (ed), *States at War, Volume 3: A Reference Guide for Pennsylvania in the Civil War* (University Press of New England, Lebanon NH)

Moss 2007 M S Moss, 'Napier, David (1790–1869)', ODNB, doi.org/10.1093/ref:odnb/19749

Moss and Hume 1986 M Moss and J R Hume, *Shipbuilders to the World: 125 years of Harland and Wolff, Belfast 1861–1986* (Blackstaff Press Ltd, Belfast)

Nicol 1912 G Nicol, *Ship Construction and Calculations*, 2nd edition (James Brown & Son, Glasgow)

Bibliography

O'Donnell 2011 J O'Donnell, *Rescue 194* (Penguin, London)
Ogden 1992 P Ogden (ed), *London Docklands: The Challenge of Development* (Cambridge University Press, Cambridge)
Ogden 1992a P Ogden, 'Introduction: some questions of geography and history', in Ogden 1992, pp 1-6
Osler and Barrow 1993 A Osler and A Barrow, *Tall Ships Two Rivers: Six Centuries of Sail on the Rivers Tyne and Wear* (Keepdate, Newcastle)
Parkes 1970 O Parkes, *British Battleships. Warrior 1860 to Vanguard 1950: A History of Design, Construction and Armament* (2nd edition, Seeley Service & Co., London 1970)
Parry 2014 C Parry, *Super Highway: Seapower in the 21st Century* (Elliott & Thompson Ltd, London)
Peattie 2001 M R Peattie, *Sunburst: The Rise of Japanese Naval Air Power, 1909–1941* (Naval Institute Press, Annapolis, Md)
Petrow 1968 R Petrow, *The Black Tide: In the Wake of the* Torrey Canyon (Hodder & Stoughton, London)
Plimsoll 1973 S Plimsoll, *Our Seamen: An Appeal* (Kenneth Mason, Havant)
Poole 1937 Unknown author, *One Hundred Years of Showmanship: Poole's 1837–1937* (via https://ore.exeter.ac.uk/repository/handle/10472/183)
Poole 1970 S L Poole, *Cruiser: A History of British Cruisers from 1889 to 1960* (Hale, London)
Porter 1999 A Porter (ed), *The Nineteenth Century: The Oxford History of the British Empire*, Vol 3 (Oxford University Press, Oxford)
Preston 2015 D Preston, *A Higher Form of Killing: Six Weeks in World War I That Forever Changed the Nature of Warfare* (Bloomsbury, London)
Punch n d *Punch* magazine, *Mr Punch at the Seaside* (*Punch* magazine, London)
Redford and Grove 2014 D Redford and P D Grove, *The Royal Navy: A History Since 1900* (I B Tauris, London)
Richardson 2015 M Richardson, *The Hunger War: Food, Rations & Rationing 1914–1918* (Pen & Sword, Barnsley)
Roberts 2017 J Roberts, *British Warships of the Second World War* (Seaforth Publishing, Barnsley)
Roddie 1976 A Roddie, 'Jacob, the Diver', *MM*, Vol 62, pp 255-69.

Roskill 1956 S W Roskill, *The War at Sea: History of the Second World War*, Vol II (HMSO, London)

Roskill 1998 S Roskill, *The Navy at War 1939–1945* (Wordsworth, Ware)

Rössler 2001 E Rössler, *The U-boat: The Evolution and Technical History of German Submarines* (Cassell Military Trade Books, London)

Sheail 2007 J Sheail, 'Torrey Canyon: the political dimension', *Journal of Contemporary History*, Vol 42, pp 485-504

Smith 1968 J E Smith (ed), *'Torrey Canyon' Pollution and Marine Life: A Report by the Plymouth Laboratory of the Marine Biological Association of the United Kingdom* (Marine Biological Association, Cambridge)

Smith, Watts and Watts 1998 K Smith, C T Watts and M J Watts, *Records of Merchant Shipping and Seamen* (Public Record Office, London)

Spector 1985 R H Spector, *Eagle Against the Sun: The American War with Japan* (Vintage, New York)

Spence 2015 D O Spence, *A History of the Royal Navy: Empire and Imperialism* (I B Tauris, London)

Starkey 1993 D J Starkey, 'Industrial background to the development of the steamship', in Gardiner 1993, pp 127-35

Starkey 1999 D J Starkey (ed), *Shipping Movements in the Ports of the United Kingdom 1871–1913. A Statistical Profile* (University of Exeter Press, Exeter)

Starkey 2007 D J Starkey, 'Economic history', in Hattendorf 2007 1, pp 617-24

Starkey and Jamieson 1998 D J Starkey and A G Jamieson, *Exploiting the Sea: Aspects of Britain's Maritime Economy since 1870* (University of Exeter Press, Exeter)

Stevens 1946 E F Stevens, *Shipping Practice* (5th edition, Sir Isaac Pitman, London)

Stolarik 1988 M M Stolarik (ed), *Forgotten Doors: The Other Ports of Entry into the United States* (Balch Institute for Ethnic Studies, Cranbury)

Stowe and Underwood 1984 T J Stowe and L A Underwood, 'Oil spillages affecting seabirds in the United Kingdom, 1966–1983', *Marine Pollution Bulletin* Vol 15, pp 147-52

Bibliography

Strange 1992 J Strange, 'Oil tankers, chemical carriers and gas carriers' in Gardiner 1992a, pp 63-83

Sumrall 1992 R F Sumrall, 'The battleship and the battlecruiser' in Gardiner 1992b, pp 14-36

Tarrant 1989 V E Tarrant, *The U-boat Offensive 1914–1945* (Weidenfeld & Nicholson, London)

Taylor and Trim 1944 L G Taylor and F H Trim, *Cargo Work. The Care, Handling and Carriage of Cargoes* (Brown, Son, and Ferguson, Ltd, Glasgow)

Thompson 1974 H J F Thompson, *Little Hampton Long Ago* (independently published, Littlehampton)

Thompson 1993 H J F Thompson, (ed) M Taylor, *Richard Isemonger and the British Slaves* (Jack Thompson Memorial Fund, Littlehampton)

Thornton 1959 R H Thornton, *British Shipping* (2nd edition, Cambridge University Press, Cambridge)

Tucker 2000 S C Tucker, *Handbook of 19th Century Naval Warfare* (Sutton, Stroud)

Van der Vat 2000 D Van der Vat, *Standard of Power: The Royal Navy in the Twentieth Century* (Pimlico, London)

Walker 2001 F M Walker, *Song of the Clyde: A History of Clyde Shipbuilding* (2nd edition, John Donald Publishers, Edinburgh)

Watson 1994 P B Watson, 'Bulk cargo carriers' in Gardiner 1994, pp 61-80

Wells 1994 J Wells, *The Royal Navy: An Illustrated Social History 1870–1982* (Wrens Park Publishing, Stroud 1994)

Weston 1909 A Weston, *My Life Among the Bluejackets* (James Nisbet & Co Ltd, London)

Williams 1904 A Williams, *The Romance of Modern Invention* (C Arthur Pearson, London)

Winton 1977 J Winton, *Hurrah for the Life of a Sailor! Life on the Lower-Deck of the Victorian Navy* (Michael Joseph, London)

Woodman 2010 R Woodman, *More Days, More Dollars: The Universal Bucket Chain, 1885–1920* (The History Press, Stroud)

Wyllie and McKinley 2016 J Wyllie and M McKinley, *Codebreakers: The Secret Intelligence Unit that Changed the Course of the First World War* (Ebury Press, London)

Notes

A note on tonnage measurement

1. Lane 1964.

1. 'Steam has conquered storms and tides': The Passenger Liner *City of Glasgow* (1854)

1. The figures for passengers and crew are based on a count of the passenger lists published in UK newspapers and the *New York Times*. *Sacramento Daily Union*, 14 August 1854, via cdnc.ucr.edu.
2. Unfortunately, I have not been able to find Mrs Collis's first name or the names of the lost children.
3. *The Spectator*, Vol 18, 22 February 1845, p 180.
4. This section is based on Horn 1998 and Harper 1999.
5. Coleman 1972, pp 120, 128-54, 189-217, 295-98 and 287-94; *An Act for Regulating the Carriage of Passengers in Merchant Vessels*, 1842; CO 384/91, 8089, Colonial Land and Emigration Office *Report* 1850, pp 1-2.
6. Coleman 1972, 120, 128-34; TNA CO 384/88, 10,008.
7. *Western Times*, 3 April 1830, p 1; *Exeter and Plymouth Gazette*, 1 May 1830, p 1; *Morning Post*, 24 April 1833, p 4; *Exeter and Plymouth Gazette*, 2 July 1836, p 2; *Western Times*, 14 April 1838, p 3.
8. This section is based on Horn 1998 and Harper 1999.
9. This section is based on: Greenhill 1993, Corlett 1978, pp 21-39, Abell 1981, pp 108-41 and Corlett 1993; CO 384/92, 3573.
10. Cottrell 1981.
11. *Public Ledger and Daily Advertiser*, 14 June 1811, p 4; OED; Butel 1999, pp 232-38.

Notes

12. Moss 2007; Lavery 2001, 81-95.
13. Griffiths 1997, p 35; *Glasgow Herald*, 15 April 1850, p 1; Doe 2017, pp 84-85 and 100-01.
14. *Glasgow Herald*, 15 April 1854, p 2; Doe 2017, pp 46-48; TNA CO 384/89, 2568; quoted in the *Leicestershire Mercury*, 2 February 1850, p 1 and *Aberdeen Press and Journal*, 6 March 1854, p 3; *Glasgow Herald*, 15 April 1850, p 1; Burton 1994, p 71; Corlett 1993, p 105; Griffiths 1997, p 36; information on the Tod and McGregor records thanks to Mr W Bill, Archive Services, University of Glasgow.
15. *York Herald*, 6 April 1854, p 1; *Southern Reporter and Cork Commercial Courier*, 23 April 1850, p 3; *Glasgow Herald*, 24 May 1850, p 4; *Northern Star and Leeds General Advertiser*, 28 September 1850, p 6.
16. Liverpool and the slave-trade: see Friel 2020, Chapter 7; Butel 1999, pp 223-57; Jackson 1983, pp 46-48, 77-80 and 120-22; Cottrell 1981, p 149.
17. *Waterford Standard*, 2 April 1890, p 3; *Larne Times*, 2 June 1834, p 9; *Liverpool Mail*, 28 November 1839, p 4 and 25 September 1840, p 4; *Gore's Liverpool General Advertiser*, 4 June 1846, p 4; *Liverpool Mercury*, 22 October 1847, p 6; *Liverpool Mail*, 25 March 1848, p 8; Jamieson 2004; *Liverpool Mercury*, 15 October 1850, p 8; *Liverpool Mail*, 17 January 1852, p 1; Flayhart 2002; TNA CO 384/90, 4034; Merseyside Maritime Museum, Archives and Library C/EX/L/4/67. No. 328.
18. *Greenock Advertiser*, 5 November 1850, p 1; *Stirling Observer*, 21 November 1850, p 2; *York Herald*, 8 March 1851, p 1; *Hull Advertiser and Exchange Gazette*, 21 March 1851, p 1; *Bolton Chronicle*, 30 October 1852, p 4; CO 384/91, 3105, Liverpool and Philadelphia company letter to the Colonial Land and Emigration Commissioners, 7 March 1853; Gibbs 1957, pp 112-16.
19. TNA CO 384/89, 2568; CO 384/90, 4034; CO 384/91, 3105.
20. CO 384/89, 2568; CO 384/91, 3105.
21. CO 384/91, 3105; Smith, Watts and Watts 1998, p 34.
22. *Lloyds List*, 14 February 1854, p 2; CO 384/91, 3105; *Morning Post*, 14 February 1854, p 5; *Shipping and Mercantile Gazette*, 17 February 1854, p 4; *Liverpool Mail*, 18 February 1854, p 6; *London Evening Standard*, 21 February 1854, p 6.
23. Coleman 1972, pp 236-42; costs: TNA CO 384/93, 1125

24. *Leicestershire Mercury*, 14 January 1854, p 2.
25. British list – e g – *Morning Advertiser*, 10 May 1854, p 5; *New York Times* passenger list, 1854, via www.oldmerseytimes.co.uk/cityofglasgow.html: the cabin/saloon passenger numbers listed in British versions come to 62, but the *New York Times* list adds two unnamed infants.
26. *North Wales Chronicle*, 4 March 1854, p 4.
27. *North Wales Chronicle*, June 1853, pp 1 and 5.
28. 1853 list: CO 384/91, 3105; 1854: *Morning Advertiser*, 10 May 1854, p 5.
29. See Friel 2020, *passim*.
30. TNA CO 384/91, 3105; *London Daily News*, 2 March 1854, p 3; *Morning Post*, 10 May 1854, p 6; *Morning Advertiser*, 22 April 1854, p 3.
31. *Freeman's Journal*, 1 April 1854, p 4; *London Evening Standard*, 14 April 1854, p 2; *Morning Post*, 15 April 1854, p 5; *Globe*, 15 April 1854, p 1; *Aberdeen Press and Journal*, 19 April 1854, p 10; *London Daily News*, 19 April 1854, p 6; *Globe*, 21 April 1854, p 3; *Belfast Commercial Chronicle*, 22 April 1854, p 2; *Globe*, 24 April 1854, p 3; *Galway Mercury*, 29 April 1854, p 4; *London Daily News*, 2 May 1854, p 6; *Morning Post*, 2 May 1854, p 5; *Dundee, Perth and Cupar Advertiser*, 2 May 1854, p 2; *Stirling Observer*, 4 May 1854, p 2; *Dublin Evening Packet and Correspondent*, 4 May 1854, p 3; *Shipping and Mercantile Gazette*, 8 May 1854, p 4; *North Wales Chronicle*, 6 May 1854, p 4; *Globe*, 10 May 1854, p 2; *Morning Advertiser*, 10 May 1854, p 5; *Shipping and Mercantile Gazette*, 11 May 1854, p 3; *Freeman's Journal*, 11 May 1854, p 3; *Liverpool Mercury*, 12 May 1854, p 15; *Hull Advertiser and Exchange Gazette*, 12 May 1854, p 10; *Dublin Mercantile Advertiser*, 12 May 1854, p 3; *Liverpool Mail*, 13 May 1854, p 6; *Newry Examiner*, 13 May 1854, p 3; *Cork Examiner*, 15 May 1854, p 3; *Scottish Guardian*, 16 May 1854, p 2; *Dublin Weekly Nation*, 3 June 1854, p 5; TNA CO 384/92, 4115.
32. *Dublin Evening Post*, 28 September 1854, p 3.
33. Corlett 1978, pp 36-37; McCluskie 1998, pp 39-40; Green 2008, p 136.
34. *Morning Chronicle*, 31 August 1854, p 6; *Freeman's Journal*, 31 August 1854, p 2; *London Daily News*, 31 August 1854, p 5; *Liverpool Mercury*, 1 September 1854, p 6; *Morning Post*, 4 September 1854, p 5.
35. *Inverness Courier*, 9 November 1854, p 3.

36. *Worcester Journal*, 27 May 1854, p 5; *Newry Examiner*, 3 June 1854, p 2; *Wilts and Gloucestershire Standard*, 1 July 1854, p 10; *Carlisle Journal*, 7 July 1854, p 8; *Carlisle Journal*, 14 July 1854, p 8; *Worcestershire Chronicle*, 23 August 1854, pp 1 and 4; *Sheffield Independent*, 2 September 1854, p 5; *Morning Advertiser*, 7 December 1854, p 7.
37. *Sacramento Daily Union*, 14 August 1854, via cdnc.ucr.edu; *Globe*, 19 May 1854, p 1; *London Daily News*, 19 May 1854, p 6; *London Daily News*, 22 May 1854, p 3; *Liverpool Mercury*, 23 May 1854, p 5.
38. Flayhart 2002; Jamieson 2004.
39. Butel 1999, p 242.
40. *Liverpool Mercury*, 4 July 1854, p 6; *Aberdeen Press and Journal*, 2 August 1854, p 3.
41. Miller 2014, p 365, note 168; Cox 2013, p 275.

2. Message in a Bottle: The Collier Brig *Russell* of Littlehampton (1872)

1. *Alnwick Mercury*, 21 December 1872, p 4; *West Sussex Gazette*, 19 December 1872, p 3, 2 January 1873, p 3 and 19 June 1873, p 3; TNA MT 9/94, p 121; TNA MT 9/78. Board of Trade *Wreck Abstract for Year 1872*, pp 171 and 188.
2. *Alnwick Mercury*, 21 December 1872, p 4.
3. West Sussex Record Office (WSRO) SR 14; other data regarding the crew and their families has been taken from the 1871 and 1881 Censuses, via findmypast.org; marriages and baptisms: *Transcript of the Parish Registers of St Mary Littlehampton. Marriages*, The Parish Register Transcription Society, Vol SXW 190, Part 2; St Martins Lane: WSRO SP/1315, sale particulars of 1892; 1870 lease: WSRO UD/LH/10/1,2; Isemonger will: WSRO STM 14, pp 388-90.
4. Lyon 1993, p 130; *Pigot & Co's Royal, National and Commercial Directory – Sussex*, 1839, *Post Office Directory, - Sussex*, 1845, 1852, 1862, 1866, 1874 and 1878, *Kelly's Directory of Sussex, 1855*; Thompson 1974, pp 14, 16, 19, 25 and 30; Thompson 1993, pp 5-6 and 17; WSRO UD/LH/10/1,2; LH/1/1/6, pp 1, 9 and 102.
5. Rates: WSRO PAR 127/30/9-18.

6. Farrant 1976a, pp 12-14 and 31-35; Littlehampton Museum D2519, 'New Song: The Littlehampton Horse Ferry'; *Punch* n d, pp 38-42; Elleray 1991, Introduction and photo 22.
7. MacGregor 1985, pp 83-85 and 136-49; Osler and Barrow 1993, pp 21-24 and 29.
8. WSRO CE1/1/1, pp 38, 81 and 110; CE 1/1/2, p 47; CE 1/1/3, p 45; Osler and Barrow 1993 and MacGregor 1985, *loc. cit.*; *Lloyds Register of British and Foreign Merchant Shipping*: volumes for 1799, 1829, 1830, 1835, 1840-41 and 1847-48; *Newcastle Courant*, 13 March 1824, p 4.
9. WSRO CE/1/1/3.
10. Crouzet 1982, pp 252-54; Starkey 1999, pp 354-55.
11. Blake 1967, pp 1-26; Osler and Barrow 1993, pp 10-11, 27-29.
12. Farrant 1976b.
13. *West Sussex Gazette*, 13 February 1873, p 3.
14. Osler and Barrow 1993, pp 66-68; Plimsoll 1973, Preliminary, p 30; Foreman, 1986, pp 72-74; Smith, Watts and Watts 1998, pp 52-56; Jones 2006 is a modern biography of Plimsoll, and details his campaign.
15. WSRO SR/14.
16. WSRO SR/14.
17. WSRO SR/14; *West Sussex Gazette*, 19 June 1873, p 3.
18. *West Sussex Gazette*, 19 December 1872, p 3 and 2 January 1873, p 3.
19. *West Sussex Gazette*, 19 June 1873, p 3.
20. *West Sussex Gazette*, 19 December 1872, p, 3, 2 January, p 3 and 9 January 1873, p 3; WSRO SR/14; Jones 2006, pp 12-15, on 'coffin ships' and insurance.

3. The Mastermind and the Insubordinate Stoker: The Battleship HMS *Victoria* (1893)

1. *Portsmouth Evening News*, 24 June 1893, p 3.
2. Gordon 1996, pp 193-214; Laughton and Lambert 2004; TNA ADM 1/7173, pp 139-40.
3. TNA ADM 188/275/168858; www.britishmedals.us/collections/BW/hmsv/curran.html: site developed by Jim Murray and maintained by Ross Wilson: Curran entry by Bryan Williamson.

Notes

4. Line of battle: see Friel 2020, Chapter 3; Parkes 1970, pp 330-36; Berry 2013, pp 17-46, 49, 52, 61, 66-69; Tucker 2000, passim; Hovgaard 1920, pp 15, 61-72; Lambert 2009, pp 254-55, 257-58, 262-64 and 279-83.
5. See Friel 2020, Chapter 6; Lavery 2011, pp 20-29, 41-44, 66-69, 104-05; Winton 1977, pp 77-78.
6. Information on the disaster in this chapter is based on in the court-martial papers, TNA ADM 1/7171, ADM 1/7172, ADM 1/7173 and ADM 229/37, with supporting diagrams, charts and drawings in TNA MFQ 1/235, MFQ 1/238, MFQ 1/239, MP I/93 and MP II/93. Other information has come from Hough 1959, pp 61-155 and Gordon 1996, pp 243-74. Hovgaard 1920, pp 69-72, provides a near-contemporary technical commentary by an expert on warship design. Force of the collision: Berry 2013, pp 45 and 68-69.
7. TNA ADM 1/7173, pp 85-6.
8. TNA ADM 1/7173, pp 39-40 and 50; J. Marchant, 'Bubbling seas can sink ships', *New Scientist*, 26 September 2001, www.newscientist.com/article/dn1350-bubbling-seas-can-sink-ships/, accessed 13 December 2019.
9. Hough 1959, pp 79-111; TNA FO 226/216; www.memorialsinportsmouth.co.uk/city-centre/victoria.htm, accessed 13 December 2019; *Portsmouth Evening News*, 1 January 1894, p 3; ghost story: *Liverpool Echo*, 29 July 1893, p 4; *Weston Mercury*, 29 July 1893, p 7; *Sheffield Independent*, 29 July 1893, p 5; *Birmingham Daily Post*, 4 August 1893, p 5.
10. TNA ADM 1/7173; Hough 1959, pp 118-55; Gordon 1996, pp 250-94; Laughton and Lambert 2004; Lambert 2009, pp 284-85; Parkes 1970, pp 337-39.
11. TNA ADM 157/1948/54; ADM 157/1952/1 and /36; ADM 157/1935/2, /5 and /65; ADM 157/1934/24; www.memorialsinportsmouth.co.uk/city-centre/victoria.htm; TNA ADM 1/7173.
12. *Portsmouth Evening News*, 24 June 1893, p 3 and 1 January 1894, p 3; *Leeds Times*, 16 December 1893, p 5; Kennerley 2008; *Western Morning News*, 14 September, p 8, and 2 October 1893, p 8; *Army and Navy Gazette*, 7 October 1893, p 3; *Woman's Signal*, 10 May 1894, p 9; Weston 1919, pp 173-80; Fowler 2011, pp 60-61 and 80-81; www.nationalarchives.gov.uk/help-with-your-research/research-guides/royal-navy-ratings-pensions; Wells 1994, pp 87-89, 122, 162 and 239-40; www.aggies.org.uk.

13. TNA ADM 188/275/168858; www.britishmedals.us/collections/ BW/hmsv/curran.html: site developed by Jim Murray and maintained by Ross Wilson: Curran entry by Bryan Williamson.
14. *The Star*, 31 August 1895, p 3; Beckett 2019, p 114; *The Era*, 14 October 1893, p 17 and 26, and 4 November 1893, p 26; *Eastern Daily Press*, 18 November 1893, p 4; *Western Daily Press*, 13 February 1894, p 4; Poole 1937; *Swindon Advertiser*, 17 March 1893, p 1; *Bath Chronicle*, 12 April 1894, p 7; *Gloucester Citizen*, 24 April 1894, p 4 and 17 May 1894, p 4; *Worcestershire Chronicle*, 9 June 1894, p 2; *Ross Gazette*, 28 June 1894, p 4; *Weston-super-Mare Gazette*, 25 August 1894, p 4; *The Cornish Telegraph*, 6 September 1894, p 5; *Exeter and Plymouth Gazette*, 26 October 1894, p 4; *North Devon Gazette*, 27 November 1894, p 5; *Western Gazette*, 7 December 1894, p 1; *South Wales Daily Post*, 26 December 1894, p 1; *The Era*, 26 January 1895, p 24, 16 February 1895, p 19, 2 March 1895, p 19, 22 February 1896, 10 October 1896, p 25, 13 March 1897, p 23 and 20 March 1897, p 22; *Pontypool Free Press*, 5 April 1895, p 5; *Coventry Evening Telegraph*, 13 July 1895, p 1; *Jersey Weekly Press*, 31 August 1895, p 5; *Isle of Wight Observer*, 19 October 1895, p 8; *Eastbourne Gazette*, 13 November 1895, p 8; *Hastings and St Leonard's Observer*, 30 November 1895, p 5; *Sheffield Daily Telegraph*, 26 December 1895, p 7; *Sheffield Independent*, 7 January 1896, p 7; *South London Press*, 30 May 1895, p 5; *Gravesend Reporter*, 20 June 1896, p 5; *Newcastle Daily Chronicle*, 25 December 1895, p 5; *Shields Daily Gazette*, 25 January 1897, p 1 and 10 February 1897, p 2; *Hexham Courant*, 17 February 1897, p 5; *Hull Daily Mail*, 20 April 1897, p 4; *Aberdeen Press and Journal*, 5 June 1997, p 10; www.britishmedals.us/collections/BW/hmsv/curran.html, accessed 12 November 2019; later service records: TNA BT 377/7/120057 and BT 377/7/102399.
15. Parkes 1970, p 330; Tucker 2000, pp 186-194, 217-23, 233-37 and 254-56.
16. Nicholas Blanford, 'Divers discover British shipwreck after 111 years, *Daily Star* (Lebanon), 4 September 2004; there is also a good Wikipedia entry on the *Victoria*, complete with an animation showing the sinking, at https://en.wikipedia.org/wiki/HMS_Victoria_(1887).

Notes

4. 'Last signal giving position...': The Merchant Ship SS *Terence of Liverpool* (1917)

1. Fayle 1920, pp 2-5; Fayle 1923, pp 390-400; Fayle 1924, pp 477-78; Richardson 2015, pp 98-129; Crouzet 1982, pp 147-84.
2. *Hull Daily Mail*, 11 July 1914, p 5; *Lloyd's List*, 15 October 1910, p 10; *Belfast Telegraph*, 3 June 1910, p 5; *Dundee Evening Telegraph*, 17 May 1911, p 2; www.legislation.gov.uk: Merchant Shipping Act 1906, Part III and Schedule I.
3. Craig 1980, pp 11-17 and 31-43; Crouzet 1982, pp 252-55, 264-67, 306-16, 345-58; Mathias and Pearsall 1971, p 59; Bonsor 1983, pp 77-101; Heaton 2004, *passim*; Merseyside Maritime Museum, Maritime Archives and Library, Information Sheet 23, Lamport and Holt; Howarth and Howarth 1994, pp 108-09.
4. Merseyside Maritime Museum Archives and Library B/LAH/5/5/1, *General Instructions to Masters in the Service of Lamport and Holt*, February 1914, pp 2-10; Foreman 1986, pp 63-78; Woodman 2010, pp 188-9, 209, 290-91 and 336-37; Friel 2003, pp 205-08 and 277; Bone 1929, pp 86-93; Lyon 2016, pp 7-13; BT 100/258: example of a crew agreement – the White Star liner SS *Olympic*, 1913; *Northern Whig*, 28 June 1911, p 8; career of William Frodsom: UK and Ireland, Masters and Mates Certificates 1850-1927, No 07599, National Maritime Museum, Liverpool Record Office 387CRE/1, crew agreement of the *Abbey Cowper* of Liverpool, 1880, 1871 Maryport and 1901 and 1911 Liverpool Censuses, all via ancestry.co.uk; TNA BT 351/1/48153; TNA BT 165/785: *Terence* logs, November 1913 to November 1914; BT 165/1426 - *Terence* logs, July 1915 to October 1916.
5. TNA ADM 137/3987, NID 12414; NMM BT 400/3673/6A and B.
6. TNA BT 165/785; BT 165/1426; Bone 1929, p 86.
7. *Shields Daily Gazette*, 28 April 1902, p 3; Glasgow University Archive Services person information GL 909; *Lloyd's Register of Shipping 1903–04*; Walker 2001, pp 37, 39, 162-63 and 229-40; TNA BT110/423 and Merseyside Maritime Museum Archives and Library C/EX/L/4/101, p 113: 1902 Register documents.
8. Bonsor 1983, pp 86-101; Starkey 1993; Griffiths 1993 a and b; Craig 1980, pp 11-17 and 31-43; Crouzet 1982, pp 252-55, 264-67, 306-16, 345-58; Mathias and Pearsall 1971, p 59; Howarth and Howarth 1994, pp 108-09.

9. Williams 1904, pp 7-27; Cressy 1914, pp 299-321.
10. This section is based on: Tucker 2000, pp 163-85; Hythe 1913, p 392; Preston 2015, pp 19, 42, 34-35, 70-73, 142 and 277; www.uboat.net; Rössler 2001, pp 10-38, 330 and 344; Tarrant 1989, pp 7-76; Mallman Showell 2006, pp 8-12 and 20-66; TNA ADM 173/2010: log of HM Submarine *E 54*, 29 April – 31 May 1917; ADM 137/3914: Admiralty History Sheets for *U81*; ADM 137/3872: *Interrogations of Survivors of Submarines. U Boats*, pp 1-10, 182 and 208; Wyllie and McKinley 2016, pp 15-20, 157-61 and 237-38; Tucker 2000, p 251; TNA ADM 116/1463: Admiralty war instructions for British merchant ships August 1914 to August 1914; ADM 137/2832: *War Instructions for British Merchant Ships, 1 August 1916*, p 19; Bone 1929, pp 92-93; ADM 137/2832: Admiralty war instructions for British merchant ships August 1916 to April 1917; Marder 1961, pp 328-36, 358-67; Marder 1965, pp 55-59, 64-70, 74-76, 102-03, 127, 342-67; Marder 1969, pp 63-106, 108-66, 181-292; Marder 1970, pp 77-120; Redford and Grove 2014, pp 58-66 and 79-87; Friel 2015, pp 44, 46, 102 and 113; Halpern 1994, pp 69-70, 84-87, 351-70; early convoys: see Friel 2020, Chapters 1 and 7.
11. TNA ADM 137/3987, ADM 137/2832: *War Instructions for British Merchant Ships, 1 August 1916*; cargo: BT 365/10, pp 7, 17, 33, 47, 52, 72, 98, 113, 118, 182 and 195; www.measuringworth.com/calculators/ppoweruk.
12. TNA ADM 137/3987: the three main sources for the attack are the transcripts of radio messages (NID Form 1a), the *Particulars of Attacks on Merchant Vessels by Enemy Submarines* form (April 1916 edition) and Frodsom's 'Master's statement'; Lyon 2016, pp 82-84, 124-26 and 181-83; U-boat shells: TNA ADM 137/3872, p 208; casualty figure: Commonwealth War Graves Commission, cwgc.org.
13. TNA ADM 173/2010: log of HM Submarine *E 54*, 29 April – 31 May 1917; ADM 137/3914: Admiralty History Sheets for *U81*; ADM 137/3872: *Interrogations of Survivors of Submarines. U Boats*, pp 1-10, 182 and 208.
14. Marder 1961, pp 328-36, 358-67; Marder 1965, pp 55-59, 64-70, 74-76, 102-03, 127, 342-67; Marder 1969, pp 63-106, 108-66, 181-292; Marder 1970, pp 77-120; Redford and Grove 2014,

pp 58-66 and 79-87; Friel 2015, pp 44, 46, 102 and 113; Halpern 1994, pp 69-70, 84-87, 351-70.
15. Redford and Grove 2014, pp 30-31, 33, 40-41 and 77-79; Richardson 2015, pp 130-69.
16. *Singapore Free Press and Mercantile Advertiser*, 14 February 1928, p 2; *Liverpool Daily Post*, 20 April 1945, p 4; *Newcastle Journal*, 23 June 1917, p 7.
17. HMSO 1976, pp 89-90; merchant fleet casualty figure: Commonwealth War Graves Commission, cwgc.org; Tarrant 1989, pp 77 and 132.

5. End of Empire: The Heavy Cruisers HMS Dorsetshire and HMS Cornwall (1942)

1. TNA ADM 358/3178.
2. Now the independent nation of Sri Lanka, but then a British colony called Ceylon.
3. Spector 1985, pp 154-55.
4. Roskill 1956, pp 1-27.
5. Brown 1999, pp 423-26 and 435-46; Jeffrey 1999, p 319; *Liverpool Daily Post*, 20 July 1942, p 2; http://adb.anu.edu.au/biography/stevens-sir-bertram-sydney-8650; Marder, Jacobsen and Horsfield 1990, pp 143-44.
6. As pointed out forcefully in Boyd 2017, xiv-xv and pp 305-409.
7. Lyon 1980, pp 13-19, 20-54, 104-117; Lyon 1993, pp 104-15, 169-75; Tucker 2000, pp 53-72, 77-80, 85-97, 134-62, 170-73, 201-03, 210-11, 214-226, 234-35; Sumrall 1992, pp 14-15 and 24; Brown 1992, p 55.
8. Redford and Grove 2014, pp 112-15; Poole 1970, pp 66-67; Brown 2011, pp 1-8, 10-11, 59-60; Brown 1995, pp 7-17, 98-101, 118-19; Roberts 2017, pp 76-103; Edgerton 2006, pp 21-41; HMSO 1976, pp 37-42. www.navalhistory.net/WW2CampaignRoyalNavy.htm; Van der Vat 2000.
9. Roskill 1998, p 448.
10. Lloyd 1968, pp 267-84; Wells 1994, *passim*; Winton 1977, pp 103-04; Brown 1995, pp 10-11; Lavery 2004, *passim*; Lavery 2006, pp 128-59; ROFT: personal information.

11. Tucker 2000, pp 201, 239-241, 245-53; Hythe 1913, pp 257-61; Marder 1980, p 341.
12. Marder 1980, pp 341-54; Peattie 2001, pp 18-20.
13. Boyd 2017, p 402; HMSO 1976, pp 4, 6-10, 42; Roskill 1998, pp 110-11; Spector 1985, p 6; Halpern 1994, pp 441-44; Peattie 2001, pp 39-42, 94-95, 140-41, 169-70, 172, 211, 258, 281-82, 284-85 and 333, n 27; Donald 1997, pp 31-32.
14. HMSO 1976, pp 10-24; Roskill 1956, pp 1-27; Spector 1985, pp 127-34; Boyd 2017, pp 295-98 and 334-51.
15. Boyd 2017, pp 364-655 (Roskill 1956, p 23, has slightly different figures) and 367; Peattie 2001, p 211.
16. Marder, Jacobsen and Horsfield 1990, pp 116-51; Boyd 2017, pp 366-85, and 400-09; Roskill 1956, pp 26-31; Agar 1959, pp 294-305.
17. Boyd 2017, pp 368-80 and 400-09; Marder 1980, pp 506-12 Agar 1959, p 306; TNA ADM 1/12269.
18. The account of the sinkings and their aftermath is based on: TNA ADM 53/115816, ADM 1/12269, ADM 267/784, ADM 199/623, ADM 358/3229, ADM 358/524, ADM 358/523, ADM 358/3178, and ADM 1/14283; Marder, Jacobsen and Horsfield 1990, pp 116-51, 171-72, 306 and 555; Peattie 2001, *loc cit*; Agar 1959, pp 305-21; Dimbleby 1984, pp 145-218; Clancy 2017, 66-130; Captain Agar thought that the brave Marine Timms went down with the *Dorsetshire*, but his survival is confirmed by ADM 358/3229.
19. Expressed in Dimbleby 1984, pp 199-204.
20. TNA ADM 1/12269; Lavery 2004, pp 162-63 and 269-82; Lavery 2006, pp 107-27.
21. Roskill 1956, p 28; Spector 1985, pp 166-78.
22. Redford and Grove 2014, pp 215 *et seq*; Marder, Jacobsen and Horsfield 1990, pp 566-70; Spector 1985, pp 537-38.
23. HMSO 1976, p 42.
24. Brown and Louis 1999, pp 44-45 and 728-39; Spence 2015, pp 173-96.
25. *Navy News*, February 2002, p 27; http://dorsetshire.byethost31.com, The HMS Dorsetshire Association, Newsletters 2011/12 and 2012/13.

Notes

6. The Spill: The Oil Tanker SS *Torrey Canyon* (1967)

1. Howarth 1997, pp 12-95; Henry 1907, pp 3 and 5; Watson 1994; Markus 2015, pp 62 and 79; Balfour-Paul 1999; Brown and Louis 1999, p 36.
2. Watson 1994; Strange 1992; Markus 2015, pp 40-41; 'supertanker': OED and a keyword search of British Newspaper Archive; Cowan 1969, pp 26-31.
3. Jamieson 1998; Shell tanker figures derived from Howarth 1992, pp 204-08.
4. Liberia 1967, pp 1-2; Petrow 1968, p 12; verbatim transcript of the proceedings of the board of investigation in TNA TS 68/56; TS 68/57 – origin of crew; TS 68/59, report by Commander Michael Hunter-Jones RN, 14 August 1968; Cowan 1969, pp 180-99.
5. TNA TS 68/59, *Report on the Grounding of the TORREY CANYON and the Measures Subsequently Taken to Combat Oil Pollution*, Commander-in-Chief, Plymouth, February 1968, *passim;* Report by Commander Michael Garnett OBE, Staff Officer (Operations) at Plymouth; Green and Cooper 2015; Smith 1968, pp 11-22, 37-90 and 174-84; Petrow 1968, pp 72-82; TS 68/58, Report of Captain Francis Broad, Maritime Superintendent of the BP Tanker Company Ltd, 23 January 1968; TS 68/58, Coastguard reports; TNA CAB 168/183, items 18 and 38; Beer 1968; Stowe and Underwood 1984; *Birmingham Daily Post*, 25 March 1967, p 20; *Birmingham Daily Post*, 27 March 1967, p 12; Petrow 1968, pp 72-82, 87-88, 91-109, 113-37 and 207-27; Cowan 1969, pp 124-69; Sheail 2007; A Vaughan, 'Torrey Canyon disaster – the UK's worst-ever oil spill 50 years on', *The Guardian*, 18 March 2017, www.theguardian.com/environment/2017/mar/18/torrey-canyon-disaster-uk-worst-ever-oil-spill-50th-anniversary; B Bell and M Cacciottolo, 'Torrey Canyon spill: the day the sea turned black', 17 March 2017, www.bbc.co.uk/news/uk-england-39223308.
6. TNA TS 68/60, item 54b; Jameson 2012, p 45.
7. Petrow 1968, pp 139-56, 207-25 and 234; Cowan 1969, pp171-79.
8. Cowan 1968, pp 185-206 and 227-33.
9. S Rares, 'Ships that Changed the Law - The Torrey Canyon Disaster', www.fedcourt.gov.au/digital-law-library/judges-speeches/justice-rares/rares-j-20171005.

10. ITOPF 2017, *passim*; Strange 1992, pp 74-75; Bergin 2011, pp 146-268; *Dundee Courier*, 10 November 1951.
11. Green and Cooper 2015, pp 903-05; Jameson 2012, pp 46-47; Howkins 2003, p 205; Sheail 2007, pp 486-87 and 496-504.
12. Markus 2015, p 39 (toothpaste etc); www.bbc.co.uk/programmes/p04tjbtx.
13. Markus 2015, p 44.

7. Oceans of Stuff: The Container Ship MSC *Napoli* (2007)

1. Nicol 1912, p 76.
2. de Goey 2007, p 185; Starkey 2007, p 623; Moss and Hume 1986; Dodds and Maguire 1998; www.tradepartners.gov.uk: Marine Sector Overview 2002; Burton 1994, pp 177-245; Walker 2001, pp 181-86, 205-09 and 214-21; HoC 2017, p 4; DfT 2017a; Thornton 1959, pp 88-122 and 203-04; BCS 1996; DETR 1998; Hope 1980, pp 24-27 and 31; Friel 2003, pp 277-81; DfT2017b; DfT 2018; MAIB 2008, Annex B; O'Donnell 2011, p 162; P Toynbee, 'How Britain sank the shipping industry by waiving the rules', *The Guardian*, 30 August 2016, www.theguardian.com/commentisfree/2016/aug/30/malaviya-twenty-britain-sank-shipping-industry; RMT (Rail, Maritime and Transport Union), 'Maritime union RMT demands action as further decline in seafarer numbers revealed in DfT statistics today', press release 25 January 2017.
3. The chief sources for this account are the Marine Accident Investigation Branch Report, MAIB 2008, *passim* and O'Donnell 2011, pp 153-247; also: www.devonnewscentre.info/msc-napoli-remembered-10-years-on; *Sunday Times* 28 January 2007, via www.marineprofessionals.co.uk.
4. DCC 2008, *passim*; Friel 1983, pp 56-60; 1619 reference quoted in Roddie 1976, p 272; http://braemar.com/msc-napoli/- Braemar press release of 31 July 2014; MAIB 2008, pp 45-46.
5. Levinson 2006, pp 1-7, 36-53, 67-75, 137-45, 164-65, 171-88, 228-29 and 254-78; Bonwick and Steer 1959, between pp 104 and 105.
6. Taylor and Trim 1944, pp 3-13 and 73-75; Stevens 1946, pp 120-29; Adams 1986a and b.

Notes

7. Hutchinson 1997, pp 105-110; Jackson 1983, pp 14, 33, 43-62; Barker 1986; Adams 1986a and b; Howie 1986; Levinson 2006, pp 17-35.
8. Gilman 1992, p 46; Corlett 1981, pp 8-13; Adams 1986a, pp 97-99; Levinson 2006, pp 201-07; Ogden 1992a, pp 4-6; Felixstowe 1985, pp 28-49, 59-71, 92-94 and 130-33; Parry 2014, pp 40-42 and 234-47; MAIB 2008, pp 28-29, 32-33 and 42-43.
9. O'Donnell 2011, pp 225-35; *BBC News*, 18 January 2017: 'MSC Napoli 10 years on: Rescue mission 'burnt into memory', www.bbc.co.uk/news/uk-england-devon-38657674; *The London Gazette*, Thursday 19 July 2007, Supplement No 1, 10416.
10. Levinson 2006, pp 209 and 273.
11. DfT 2017a.

Endpiece

1. Parry 2014, p 340.
2. Golding 1917.
3. Friel 2003, p 285.

Index

British and Irish placenames refer to historic counties, where relevant; placenames from outside the British Isles and Ireland are located in their modern states. References to plates are given as 'Pl', followed by the number.

admirals *see also* under individual surnames, 38–39, 44–47, 50, 57, 85–86, 87–88, **Pl 9**
admiralties, 67
Admiralty, The *see also* Royal Navy, 41–42, 49, 67, 69–70, 85, 94–95
Addu Atoll, 87, 94, Fig 16
Africa, Africans, 101
Africa, East, East Africans, 121
Africa, South, South Africans, 3, 78, 82, 91, 93–94, 95
Africa, West, 72, 73, Fig 14
Agar, Captain Augustus, 87–90, 93–95
Aichi D3A, Type 99, 85, 87–92, Figs 15 and 17
aircraft and air power, 77, 78, 81, 84–85, 86–92, 95, 96, 97, 100, 107, 108–09, 124–25, 137, Fig 15, **Pls 14 and 19**
aircraft weapons, 77, 78, 84–85, 89, 108–09, Fig 15
aircrew, 84–85, 87–92, 96, 124–25, 136–37
air raids, 84–85, 87
Albacore, Fairey, 92
Alnwick Mercury, 22
Amble, Northumberland, 21–22, 30, 37
America, North, and North Americans, 1, 2, 3, 4, 5, 9, 10–11, 15, 16, 18, 19, 49, 59, 63, 68, 78, 79, 85, 99, 102, 118, 128, 137, Fig 14
America, South, and South Americans, 58, 61, 129, Fig 14, **Pl 11**
America, United States of, 1, 3, 4, 10, 19, 13, 49–50, 61, 64, 68, 69, 80, 84, 96, 99, 98, 100, 102, 115, 137, 139
American Civil War, 10, 20, 43
American War of Independence, 2
Andrew, Chief Engineer John, 15–16
Anglo-Persian Oil Company *see also* British Petroleum, 99–100
Anstis, Francis, 89
Anti-Submarine Division, Admiralty, 70
Antwerp, Belgium, 122, 123, Fig 21
Arabia, Arabs, 100
Archimedes' Principle, reversal of, 48–49
Argentina, 72, 73, Fig 14
Arkless, William, 22, 34–36
armament *see* naval weaponry
armour, 39, 40, 41, 42, 43, 56, 80, 81
arms control, international, 80–81
Armstrong, Mitchell and Co, 40–41, 99
Armstrong-Whitworth, 81
army, armies, 83, 86, 110
Army, British, 40, 52, 110

Index

Arun, River, 24, 25, 27, Fig 4, **Pls 6 and 7**
Arundel, West Sussex, 24, 27, 33
Asia, 44, 78–79, 83, 96, 121, 137, 139, **Pl 18**
Atlantic Ocean, 3, 4, 5–6, 7, 10, 12, 14, 15, 17, 18, 19, 58, 67, 73, 77, 82, 96, 128, Figs 3 and 14
Attenborough, Sir David, 116
Australia, Australians, 2, 3, 15, 39, 64, 78, 79, 85, 86, 94, 114, 130, 137, **Pl 18**
Austro-Hungarian Empire, 43
autopilot, 102, 104–07

Baker, George, 18
Baltic Sea, 27, 67
Barracuda Tanker Corporation, 102, 108, 113–14
Barrett, Marine Bill, 91
Barrow-in-Furness, Lancashire, 81
Barwise family, 18
Batum, Russia, 99
Beach Town, Littlehampton, 25
Bechter, William, 15
Beirut, Lebanon, 45, Fig 8
Belchamber, Charlotte, 23, 24, 36–37, **Pl 5**
Belchamber, William, 23, 24, 25, 30, 32, 33–37, **Pl 5**
Belfast, County Down, Ireland, 81, 127
Belgium, Belgians, 64, 122
Belmullet, County Mayo, Ireland, 76
Bengal, Bay of, 86, 96
bereavement and the bereaved, 1, 17, 18–19, 38–39, 50–52, 94–95, 140
Bethesda, Caernarvonshire, Wales, 15, 17
Bideford, Devon, 4, **Pl 3**
Birkenhead, Lancashire, 81
Black Ball Line, 5
Black Sea, 42, 99, Fig 8
'black tide, the', 115
blockade, 57, 68–69, 77, 80

Blue Planet II, 116
Board of Trade, 16, 18, 28–30, 33–35, 60, Fig 5
boats *see* ship and boat types
Bombay, India (now Mumbai), 76
Bondicar Point, Northumberland, 22
Bone, Captain David, 61, 62, 63
Bonfiglia, Chief Officer, 104–05
Bourke, Captain Maurice, 39, 44–45, 46, 48–49, 50
Branscombe, Branscombe Bay, Devon, 123, 125–26, 127, Fig 21, **Pl 23**
Brazil, 58, 64, 72, 73, 130, Fig 14, **Pl 11**
Brentwood, Essex, 50
Brexit, 139
Bridges, Mr, 108
Bristol, 131
Bristol Channel, 67
Britain, British Isles, the British, ii, ix, 2–3, 4, 5, 6, 10, 15, 18, 19, 26, 27, 28, 30, 38, 39, 42, 44, 49, 50, 51, 54, 55, 56, 57, 58, 59, 61, 63, 64, 65, 67, 68–69, 70, 75, 77, 78–79, 80, 81–82, 83–84, 84–85, 86, 89, 94, 95, 96–97, 98, 99, 100, 102, 104, 106, 113–14, 115, 116, 118, 119, 120–21, 131, 139, 140, 141, Figs 3, 6, 14 and 18.
Britannia Royal Naval College, 82
British Pacific Fleet, 96
British Petroleum/BP, 99–100, 102, 107, 108, 115
British Shipbuilders, 120
Brittany, France, 25, 110, 113, 114
Broad, Captain Francis, 108
Brunel, Isambard Kingdom, 5, 18
Bulgaria, Bulgarians, 121
bulk cargoes, 5, 27, 99, 129, 131
Buenos Aires, Argentina, 72, 73, Fig 14
Bureau Wijsmuller, 107, 108
Burma (now Myanmar), 78, 130
Burtenshaw, Ann, 21, 23
Burtenshaw, Thomas, 23, 25, 30, 32, 37
Byas, Commander Jack, 90

Cammell-Laird Ltd, 81
Canada, Canadians, 4, 94, 130
canals, 27, 44, 45, 66, 100, 101, 122, Fig 8
Canary Islands, 104, Fig 18
Cape of Good Hope, 104, Fig 18
Cape Town, South Africa, 122
cargo-handling and stowage, container, 128–29, 135, 136, **Pls 22, 24 and 26**
cargo-handling and stowage, pre-container, 130–35, **Pls 11 and 25**
Caribbean *see* West Indies
Caspian Sea, Russia, 99
casualties, 1, 3–4, 21–23, 28, 36–37, 44, 47–49, 50–51, 54, 68, 76, 89–95, 108
Catalina flying boat, 86, 87
cattle trade, 64–65
Celebes Islands, 86
cemeteries, 37, 49
Ceylon (now Sri Lanka), 78, 85–86, 87, 93, 95, 96
Channel Islands, 25, 53, 54–55
charity and charitable institutions, 4, 19, 37, 51–52, 61, 116
Chatham, Kent, 81
Chepstow, Monmouthshire, Wales, **Pl 15**
children, 1, 2, 13, 18, 19, 23, 32, 36–37, 44, 51, 52–53, 62, 68, 83, 91, 140, **Pl 27**
China, the Chinese, 79, 82, 83, 118, 121, 139
China Station, 82
Christianity, 127
Churchill, Winston, 85
cinematograph film, 53–54
classification societies, 112, 127
climate change *see also* environment, 139
cloth trade, 138
Clyde, River, 6, 10, 65, 81, 120
coal, coal trade, 4, 5, 7, 16, 23, 24, 26, 27–30, 32, 33, 44, 61, 64, 66, 80, 99, 131

coastal change, 140
coastal trade, 27, 30, 36
Coccio, Third Officer Alfredo, 105
codes and ciphers, 39, 67, 70–71
Cole, Marine Francis, 50
Collis, Charles, 20
Collis family, 1, 13, 20
Collis, Mrs, 1
Collis, William, 1, 18, 20
Colombo, Sri Lanka, 85, 86, 87
Colonial Land and Emigration Commission, 3, 12
colonies, colonization and decolonization, 2, 3, 12, 79, 81, 83, 97, 163 n 2.
'Commissioned Officer', 54–55
communications *see also* codes and ciphers, signals, wireless
container system and container ports, ii, 61, 66, 118–20, 121–22, 125–26, 127–28, 129, 130, 132, 134–36, 137–38, Fig 22, **Pls 22, 24 and 26**
convicts, 2
Continuous Service Act, 44
convoys, 68, 69–70, 76–77
Cornwall, England, 73, 98, 107, 110–13, 122, 124, 125, 127
coronavirus, Covid-19, ix, 140
cotton industry/trade, 10, 58, 130
court-martials, vi, 39–40, 50
'CQD', 67
crimes and misdemeanours, 62–63, 136
County Class, 81
Crimean War, 19, 39, 51
'Cruiser Rules', 68
Culdrose, Cornwall, 124, 125
Cunard, 6
Cunard Building, Liverpool, **Pl 12**
Curran, Stoker James, 38, 40, 52–56, 57, **Pl 10**
customs officers and procedures, 12, 22, 32, 34–35
Cyprus, Cypriots, 64

Index

Dakar, Senegal, 72, 73, Fig 14
DAMS, 'Defensively Armed Merchant Ships', 69–70, 74
Dardanelles, 42, 45, Fig 8
Darwin, Australia, 78
David & William Henderson Ltd, 65, **Pl 13**
Deepwater Horizon, 115
deserters, desertion, 40, 52, 63
detergent, 107, 110–12, 113
Devon, England, ii, 4, 51, 118, 125
Devon County Council, 125–26
Devonport, Plymouth, England, 51, 81
diesel engines, 66, 71, 100, 122
digital technology, 118, 121, 128, 136
Dimbleby, Ken, 91
diplomacy and diplomats, 49
disabled people, disability, 13, 93–94
disarmament, 80–81
discipline *see also* punishment, 39, 44, 48, 62–63, 75, 82–83
disease *see also* health, ix, 3, 4, 140
dive–bombing, 84–85, 86, 88, 89, 90, Fig 17
dockers *see* dockworkers
docklands, general, 10, 134, 135–36
Docklands, London, 132–36, Fig 23, **Pl 25**
dockworkers, 130, 132–35, **Pl 25**
dockyards, royal and commercial, 10, 38–39, 52, 66, 81, 85, 131–35, Fig 23, **Pls 4, 12 and 25**
drunkenness, 63–64, 71
Duke Street, Littlehampton, 23
Dundalk, County Louth, Ireland, 18
Dundee, Scotland, 40, 52, 56
Durban, South Africa, 78
Dutch East Indies (now Indonesia), 78
Dutch navy, 85

East End, London, 132
Eastern Fleet, British, 85–87, 95–96, 97
East India Dock, 132, 133, Fig 23
East Indies Fleet, British, 96

Eckstein, Monsieur and Mademoiselle, 15
Ede, Thomas, 23, 32
education and training, civilian and naval, 30, 39, 42, 44, 55, 69, 82, 106, 107, 119
Egypt, 100, 130
Ellis, Marine William, 51
Ellyat, Mark, 57
Elswick, Northumberland, 40
Elswick Ordnance Company, 41
Emden, Germany, 71
empire, ideology of, 3, 79
emigration, emigrants *see* migration
emigration agents, 2, 15
emigration officers, 3
engineers, ships', 15–16, 44, 48, 106–07, 122, 124
entertainment *see* theatre
England, the English, 1, 2, 3, 18, 20, 27, 53–54, 81, 95, 110, 131, 139, Fig 5
English language, 2, 3, 63, 81
English Channel, 25, 98, 106, 110, 118, 121, 124
Environment, Department of the, 116
environment, marine and coastal, ix, 98, 107–117, 139–40
environmental activism, 116
environmental pollution, 107–17, 126, 137, 139–40
Essex, England, 50
Etajima Naval Academy, Japan, 84
European Union, 139

factories, 129, 130
Fair, Commander, 91
Falmouth, Cornwall, 107, 108
famine, 4
Farne Islands, Northumberland, 30, Fig 5
fascism, 80
fathometer, 102
Felixstowe Dock & Railway Company, 135

171

Felixstowe, Suffolk, 122, 123, 135, 137, Fig 21, **Pls 22 and 26**
Field, Mrs, 18, 19
Finland, Finns, 64
fire at sea, 9, 89–91, 108
firemen (shipboard), 16, 61, 62, 63–64, 73
firemen (land), 120, 121
First World War, Great War, 38, 56, 58, 59, 61, 66, 69, 70, 77, 80, 83, 84, 119, 140, **Pls 14, 15, 16, 17 and 27**
fishermen, 111
fishing industry, 111, 115, 116
fishing vessels, 105
flags, signal *see* signals
flags of convenience, 102, 106, 119-20
Flamborough Head, Yorkshire, 30, Fig 5
Flatholm Island, Bristol Channel, 67
Fleet Air Arm, 84–85, 86, 87, 92, 118–19, 124–25, 136–37
Foley MP, Maurice, 110
food and drink, shipboard, 12–13, 16, 59–60, 82
food trade, 10, 58–59, 77, 125, 130, 138, 139
Force Z, 85
France, the French, 19, 25, 27, 42, 56, 59, 80, 83, 100, 113, 115, 121, 124, **Pl 2**
Francis, Christian, 57
franc-tireur, 75
Friends of the Earth, 116
Frodsom, Mrs Mary, 62, 77
Frodsom, Captain William, 58, 63–64, 73–77
Fryatt, Captain, 75
Funchal, Madeira, **Pl 2**

Genoa, Italy, 114
George, Lloyd, 76
Germaniawerft, Kiel, 71
Germany navy *see also* High Seas Fleet, U-boat, 42, 56–57, 80, 82, 83

Germany, Germans, 12, 15, 22, 42, 56–57, 58, 67–69, 70, 71–77, 80, 82, 83, 85, 99, 137, **Pl 2**
ghost report, 50
Gilfillan, Chief Steward Archibald, 16
Glasgow, Lanarkshire, Scotland *see also* Clyde, 6–7, 9, 18, 65
globalization, 118, 130, 138
Godalming, Surrey, 27
government, national and local, 3, 4, 6, 9, 12–13, 16, 17–18, 19, 24, 28–30, 33–35, 39, 44, 59–60, 62–63, 70, 99–100, 104, 106, 108, 110–11, 113–14, 116, 120–21, 125–27, 132, 136, Fig 5
Grafton, Joseph, 32, 35
Gray & Co, W., 99
Greece, the Greeks, 45
Greenpeace UK, 116
Greenwich Royal Naval College, 82
Guernsey, Channel Islands, 54–55, 110, 113
Guernsey, States of, 113
Guildford, Surrey, 27
gunners, naval, 44, 48, 69, 73, 74, 89, 90, 91
guns *see* naval weaponry

Hamburg, Germany, 12, 122
Hamilton's Panorama, 53
Hampshire, England, 51
Harland & Wolff Ltd, 81
Hartlepool, County Durham, 32, 99
Harvey family, 26
Hauxley Haven Northumberland, 22, 29, 30, Fig 5
Hawkins-Smith, Staff-Commander, 47
health *see also* disease, 13, 57, 95
health, mental, 1, 20
Heath, Lieutenant, 49
Herefordshire, England, 51
highline, 124–25
High Seas Fleet, German, 57, 67
Hillery, Marine William, 50–51

Index

HMS Cornwall (1939–42) Association, 97
HMS Dorsetshire Association, 97
holiday trade, 25, 110, 111, 113
Honfleur, France, 25
Hong Kong, China, 78
Houston, USA, 128
Howe, Frank, 53
Howell, Hugh, 64
Hughes, Marine Ferdinand Edward Boileau, 50
Hull, George, 26
Hull, Yorkshire, 12, 15, 53–54
Huntcliffe Foot, Yorkshire, 21
Hunter-Jones, Commander Michael, 106–07

icebergs, 16–17
immigration, immigrants *see* migration
Imperial Japanese Navy, 83–85, 86–87, 96
India, Indians, 44, 79, 82, 86, 96, 97, 100, 121, **Pl 18**
Indian Ocean, 82, 86, 96, 97, 139, **Pl 18**
Indonesia *see* Dutch East Indies, Java
Industrial Revolution, industrialization, 42, 83, 118, 131
'informal empire', 100
Inman, William, 11–12, 16, 19
insurance, marine, 24, 35, 39, 113, 120
International Convention for the Prevention of Pollution from Ships, 115
International Convention on Civil Liability for Oil Pollution, 114
International Maritime Organization, 114, 115, 120
International Oil Tanker Owners Pollution Federation, 114
Iran *see also* Persia, 99–100
Ireland, the Irish, 2, 3, 4, 6, 9, 10, 11, 14, 15, 18, 20, 30, 51, 69, 71, 73, 75, 76, 77, 141, Fig 3

iron and steel production, 6, 42, 58, 65, 91
iron ships and shipbuilding, 1, 5, 9, 17, 39, 42, 43, 65, 79, 99
Isaac, Surgeon-Lieutenant Paul, 92, 95
Isemonger, Charlotte, 23
Isemonger, Thomas, 23–24, 26, 30, 33–37, **Pl 6**
Isemonger, Thomas Tupper, 24
Isherwood System, 101, **Pl 20**
Islam, 100
Israel, 100
Italian navy, 80, 83
Italy, Italians, 43, 51, 54, 59, 66–67, 80, 83, 84–85, 102, 114

Jameson, C. M., 116
Japan, Japanese, 64, 67, 78–80, 82, 83–84, 85–94, 95–97, 101, 102, 118, 120–21, 137, **Pls 18 and 19**
Japanese army, 83, 86
Java, Javans, Indonesia, 78, 79
Jellicoe, Admiral Sir John, 57, 69
John Brown Ltd, 81
Johnson, Gunner Frederick Masterman, 48, 49
Jones, Mr E., 15
Jones, Surgeon Henry, 16
Jones VC, William, 53
Jutland, battle of, 57

Keeping, Paddy, 91
Kent, Marine Joseph, 50
Kent, England, 23
Kiel, Germany, 71
Killard Point, County Down, Ireland, 75–76
Kintyre Peninsula, Argyll, Scotland, 18
Koje, South Korea, 121
Korea, South, 121

Lamport and Holt, 58, 60–61, 62, 64–65, **Pls 12 and 13**
Lancashire, England, 11, 76

Land's End, Cornwall, 67, Fig 20
Lane, Marine Charles, 51
Langford, Sam, 91
Lavernock Point, Glamorgan, Wales, 67
law and laws, 3, 9, 13, 30, 33–35, 44, 56, 60, 62, 63–64, 80, 113–14, 119, 126, 131
Lawlor, Patrick, 18
Lawlor, Thomas, 18
Lawson, Captain George, 26
Lee, John William, 76
legal quay, 131
Liberia, 102, 104, 106, 129
lifeboats and lifesaving, shore-based *see also* Royal National Lifeboat Association, 22, 29, 30
Light Brigade, Charge of, 54
lightermen *see* dockworkers
lighthouses, 110, 127
Limited Liability Acts, 60
linen trade, 10
line of battle, 43
liner conferences, 129
Lissa, battle of, 43
Littlehampton, West Sussex, 2, 22–26, 27, 31, 32, 34–35, 37, Figs 4 and 6, **Pls 5, 6 and 7**
Littlehampton Cemetery, 37
Littlehampton Harbour Board, 24
Liverpool, 1, 3, 4, 5, 10, 11, 12, 13, 15, 16, 58, 60, 62, 72, 73, 131, Fig 3, **Pls 4 and 12**
Liverpool and Philadelphia Steamship Company, 1, 9, 11, 13, 14, 17, Figs 1, 2, 3
Liverpool, Brazil and River Plate Steam Navigation Co Ltd *see also* Lamport and Holt, 58
Lizard, The, Cornwall, 127
Llanelli, Carmarthenshire, Wales, 32
Lloyd's List, 59–60
Lloyd's of London, 113
Lloyds Register of Shipping, 102
Lodge, Marine Henry, 50

London Bridge, 131
London, Brighton & South Coast Railway, 24–25
London Dock, 134
London Maritime Association, 24
London, Lord Mayor of, 50, 51
London Naval Treaty, 81
London, Pool of, 131, 132
London, port of, ii, 10, 27, 59–60, 131–36, Fig 23, **Pls 24 and 25**
London, United Kingdom, 50, 53, 113–14, 120
Londonderry, County Londonderry, Northern Ireland, 51
LORAN, 102
Low Countries, 27
Luker Junior, W, **Pl 17**

McEldowney, Surgeon-Lieutenant P W, 92, 95
McGregor, John *see also* Tod and McGregor, 6
McLean, Malcom P, 128
mail, carriage at sea, 1, 6, 12, 60, 94–95
Malaya (now Malaysia), 78, 79, 130
Malta, Maltese, 44, 49, 50, 51, 54, 94
MAN diesel engines, 71
manpower, mercantile, 121
Manchester, England, 126
Manwaring, Captain P C W, 87, 91
Marconi, Guglielmo, 66–67
'*mareé noire, la*', 115
Marine Accident Investigation Branch, 127, 136
Marine Biological Association, 111–12
marines, 50–51, 69, 90
marine science, 111–12
Maritime and Coastguard Agency, 126
Markham, Rear Admiral Albert, 44–50
Marmaris, Turkey, 45
MARPOL, 115
Marsh, William, 23, 32
Marshall Islands, 119
Maryport, Cumberland, 62

Index

Matthews, Captain Bernard, 7
medical officers and orderlies, 59–60, 92–94
medicine *see also* health, disease
Mediterranean Fleet, British, 38, 39, 42, 44
Mediterranean Sea, 38, 45, 96, 122, Fig 8
Mediterranean Shipping Company *see also MSC Napoli*, 122
merchant fleet officers *see also* shipmasters, 7, 15–16, 30, 36, 60, 63–64, 65, 75, 104, 105, 106, 131, **Pl 17**
Merchant Navy, merchant fleet, British, 5, 27, 32, 58, 59–63, 67, 68, 69, 70, 75, 76–77, 115, 119–21
'Merchant Navy' title, 119
merchants, 24, 132, 135
Merchant Shipping Act 1854, 60
Merchant Shipping Act 1906, 60
merchant shipping fleet, world, 119–20, 137
Mersey Docks and Harbour Board Building, **Pl 12**
Metvale Ltd, 122
Mexico, Gulf of, 115
Middle East, 86, 100
Midway, battle of, 96
migration, migrants, 1–4, 5, 7, 9–10, 11–17, 18–19, **Pl 3**
migration, ideologies of, 4–5
militarism, 80
Milford Haven, Pembrokeshire, Wales, 104, Fig 18
Milton Road, Liverpool, 62
Mina Al Ahmadi, Kuwait, 104, Fig 18
Montevideo, Uruguay, 72, 73, Fig 14
Montanas, The, 53
Morrison, Captain Kenneth, 15
motor cars, 100, 116
Moulson family, 18
Mounts Bay, Cornwall, 110
Mousehole, Cornwall, 112
Myanmar *see* Burma

Nafplio, Greece, 45
Nagumo, Admiral Chuichi, 86, 87, 89, 95, Fig 16
Napier, David, 6
Napoleonic War, 24, 41, 43, 80
National Amalgamated Sailors' and Firemen's' Union, 62
National Docks Labour Board, 132
National Maritime Board, 119
nationalism, 100
nationalization, 120
naval administration, 39, 40, 50–52, 56, 70, 76, 94–95
naval battles, 39, 41, 43, 57, 71–76, 82, 84–85, 87–91, 96
Naval Defence Act, 56, 80
naval diplomacy, 44
naval expeditions, 78, 86
naval expenditure, 41, 81, 96–97
naval intelligence, 39, 70–71
Naval Intelligence Department, 39
naval manpower, 44, 83, 94
naval memorials, 49
naval officers, 38–39, 43, 44–47, 49, 50, 52, 54–55, 57, 67, 68, 69, 82–83, 87, 90, 92–94, 137
naval sailors, 43–44, 51–53, 69, 82–83, 140, **Pl 27**
naval shipbuilding, 24, 40–41, 66, 71, 81–82, 120
naval strategy, 41–42, 44, 57, 67–69, 80, 86, 96, **Pl 18**
naval tactics, 39, 41, 43, 45–46, 69–70, 73, 74, 76, 84–85, 87, Fig 9
naval weaponry, guns and turrets, ii, 41, 42–43, 44, 47, 56, 69, 70, 71, 73, 74, 80, 81, 87, 89, 90, 91, Fig 17, **Pl 15**
naval weaponry, rams, 41–42, 46–47, Fig 9, Fig 10,
naval weaponry, torpedoes, 41, 58, 67, 68, 71, 73, 74, 76, 79, 82, 84–85, 86, 87
navigational techniques and equipment, 34, 102, 104–05, 106, 115, 133, Fig 23

Navy, French, 42
Navy, German, 42, 56, 57, 58, 67–71, 75, 77, 82, 83
Nelson, Horatio, 69, 84
Netherlands, the Dutch, 78, 85, 99, 107, 108, 118
neutral nations, neutrality, 63, 68
Newark, USA, 128
Newell, Charles, 23, 32
New Jersey, USA, 128
Newport News, USA, 102
newspapers, 15, 18, 32, 54–55
New York, USA, 7, 10, 58, 63–64, Fig 3, Fig 14
Newcastle upon Tyne, Northumberland, 26
Newfoundland, Canada, 17, 18, 67
Nicol, George, 118–19
Normandy, France, 25
Norris, Lieutenant Guy, 137
Northamptonshire, England, 39
North Sea, 67, 71
Northumberland, England, 26, 21–22, 30, 124
North Wales Chronicle, 15, 17
nuclear weapons, 96
Nutter, William, 32

O'Donnell, Petty Officer Jay, 125, 127
oilfields and wells, 98–99
oil fuel, 80, 100
oil rigs, 115
oil spills, 49, 76, 106–17, 126, Fig 20
oil trade, 58, 80, 86, 92, 93, 98–102, 114–15, Figs 19 and 20, **Pls 20 and 21**
Olivieri, Chief Bandmaster Giuseppe, 51
Operation C, 86–96
Operation Mop-Up, 107–110
Ottoman Empire *see also* Turkey, 42, 45
Ozawa, Admiral Jisaburo, 86, 96, Fig 16

Pacific Ocean, 78, 96, **Pl 18**
pacifism, 19, 80

paddle vessels, 4–5, 42, **Pls 7 and 8**
paddle warships, 42
Pakistan, 97
Panama, 119
Panama Canal, 66, 122
Pan-Atlantic *see* Sea-Land Service
Parker, Gordon, 135
Parliament *see* government
Passenger Acts, 3, 9, 12–13
passengers, ix, 1–20, 25, 60, 64, 67, 68, 121, **Pls 1, 2 and 3**
Pearl Harbor, Hawaii, 78, 85, 86
Peckham, London, 50
Pennsylvania Regiment, 114th, 20
people-trafficking, 136
Persia *see also* Iran, 99–100
Persian Gulf, 80, 86, 108
Philadelphia, USA, 1, 10, 11, 13, 15, 16, 17, 18, 19, 20, Fig 3
Philippines, Filipinos, 78, 121
Pier Road, Littlehampton, 25
pilots and pilotage, maritime, 34, 105, 106, 133, Fig 23
pilots, aircraft, 94
pipelines, 100, 108, 117
piracy and pirates, 122, 139
plastic, plastic pollution, 98, 116
Plimsoll, Samuel, 28
Plimsoll Line, 28
Plymouth, Devon *see also* Devonport, 107, 110, 111
Police, 126
Pollard's Rock, 106, Fig 19
pollution control measures, local and international, 107–13, 114–15, 125, 126
Poole, Joseph, 53, 55
Poole's Myriorama, 53–56, **Pl 10**
Portland, Dorset, 125
ports, port facilities, 10, 25, 33, 38–39, 52, 81, 85, 131–35, Fig 23, **Pls 3, 4, 5, 6, 7, 8, 11, 12, 22, 24, 25 and 26**
Port Sanitary authorities, 59

Index

Portsmouth Dockyard, Hampshire, 38–39, 81
Portsmouth Evening News, 38–39
Portsmouth, Hampshire, 49, 51–52, 53
Portugal, Portuguese, 122, 139
Potato Famine, Irish, 4
poverty, 36–37, 51–52, 59–60, 63, 64, 115
prisoners, imprisonment, 59, 62, 75, 76
privateering, 68
prizes and prize money, 43
progress, ideology of, 24–25
propaganda, 79
Protestantism, Protestants, 20
public houses, 25
Punch magazine, 25
punishment, 44, 55, 62

Quakers, 10, 19
Queenstown/Cobh, County Cork, Ireland, 73
Queen Street Wharf, Philadelphia, 1

racism, 79
radar, 81, 89, 102
radio *see* wireless
radio direction-finding, 70–71, 102
Rail, Maritime and Transport Union, 121
railways, 12, 13, 24–25, 27, 128, 135
Raleigh, Sir Walter, 139
rams *see* naval weaponry
Rares, Judge Stephen, 114
Rea family, 18
Receiver of Wreck, 126
recruitment and conscription, naval, 43, 44, 82, 83
Rees, Surgeon Lieutenant-Commander, Glyn, 92, 95
rescue efforts and organizations, 17, 22, 30, 49, 67, 94, 124–25, 136–37
Rescue 193, 124–125, 127
Rescue 194, 124–125, 127
religion, 51, 127

Rhodes, Lieutenant Commander Martin, 137
Richardson family/Richardson Brothers, 10–11, 12–13, 19
Richardson, Thomas, 10–11
Richardson, Watson & Co, 10
River Road, Littlehampton, 25, **Pl 6**
'river pirates', 132
Rio de Janeiro, Brazil, 72, 73, Fig 14
Robinson family, 26
rocket and mortar stations, 22
'ROFT', 83
Room 40, Admiralty, 70–71
Rorke's Drift, battle of, 53
Royal Air Force, 108–09, 110
Royal Albert Dock, Liverpool, 10, **Pls 4 and 12**
Royal Australian Navy, 82
Royal Commission on Environmental Pollution, 116
Royal Dutch Petroleum, 99
Royal Dutch Shell, 99, 101, 102
Royal Liver Building, Liverpool, **Pl 12**
Royal Mail Steam Packet Company, 6, 61
Royal National Lifeboat Institution, 22, 29, 30, 110
Royal Marines, 49, 50–51, 69, 90, 91, 110
Royal Naval Reserve, ii, 63, 83, 140, **Pl 27**
Royal Naval Volunteer Reserve, 83, 92, 93
Royal Navy, 24, 38–57, 67–71, 76–77, 78–97, 99–100, 106–07, 108, 110, 120, 140, **Pls 9, 10, 18, 19 and 27**
Royal Patriotic Fund, 51–52
Royal Society for the Prevention of Cruelty to Animals, 112
Royal Society for the Protection of Birds, 112
Rugiati, Captain Pastrengo, 102–07
Russia, Russians, 56, 64, 83, 86, 99

177

sailing capabilities/techniques, 4, 5, 6, 21–22, 25–26, 33–36
sailing vessels, 4, 5, 6, 11, 12, 15, 16, 17, 21–22, 25–27, 32, 42, 43
sailors' families, 21, 23, 36–37, 50–52, 94–95, 140, **Pls 5 and 27**
sailors, foreign, in British ships, 64, 121
sailors' homes, 23, **Pl 5**
sailors' and officers' pay, mercantile and naval, 15–16, 36, 37, 44, 51, 52, 61, 62, 64, 119
sailors' and officers' possessions, 64
Sailors' Rests, 51
St Just, Cornwall, 110
St Katharine's Dock, London, 134
St Malo, France, 25
St Martin's Lane, Littlehampton, 23, 37, **Pl 5**
salt trade, 138
Salvador de Bahia, Brazil, 72, 73, Fig 14
salvage, marine, 107–08, 109
Salvation Army, 4
Samuels, Marcus, 99
Samuels, Samuel, 99
Santos, Brazil, **Pl 11**
São Paulo, Brazil, **Pl 11**
science and scientists, 48–49, 108, 111–12, 113
Scilly, Isles of, 98, 104–05, 107, 109, 110, Fig 20
Scotland, the Scottish, 2, 6–7, 9, 11, 15, 18, 40, 53–56, 71, 115, 121, **Pl 10**
seabirds, 98, 112–13, 126
Sea-Coal Lane, London, 27
Sea King, Westland, 124–25, 127
Sea-Land Service, 128
Seamen's Missions, 61
Second World War, 77, 78–97, 102, 139, **Pls 2, 18 and 19**
Sempill Mission, 84
Sennen Cove, Cornwall, 110
servants, indentured, 2
Seven Stones Reef, 98, 105–06, Fig 19
Sheffield, Yorkshire, 18

Sheffield Independent, 55
Shell Transport and Trading Company, 99, 101
ship design, structures and materials, 1, 5, 6, 9, 17–18, 25–26, 27, 34, 35–36, 41–43, 64–65, 81, 90, 91, 99, 100–101, 115, 127–28, 136, **Pl 20**
sharks, 93, 94
ship and boat types
   aircraft carrier, 78, 85–86, 87–88, 89, 96
   barge, 27
   battlecruiser, 85, 86
   battleship, ii, 38–39, 40–43, 44–49, 54, 56–57, 79, 80, 82, 84–85, Fig 7, Fig 9, Fig 10
   boxship *see* container ship
   brig, 2, 21–22, 25–26, 33–36, **Pls 3 and 7**
   carrack, 117
   chemical tanker, 114
   collier *see also* brig, 25–26, 28–30
   container ship, 118–19, 121–30, 134–38, Fig 22, **Pls 22, 23 and 26**
   cruise liner, ix, 9, **Pls 1 and 2**
   cruiser, 79–82, 86–92, 95, Fig 17, **Pl 19**
   destroyer, 79, 86, 107
   dreadnought, 56–57, 67
   ferry, 18
   fishing craft, 105
   galleon, 117
   gas tanker, 114
   line of battle ship, 42, 43, 117
   liner, passenger, ii, ix, 1–20, 70, 121, Fig 1
   oil tanker, 98–99, 101–17, 128 **Pls 20 and 21**
   oil tankers, definitions of types, 101
   schooner, 22
   submarine *see also* U-boat, 58, 59, 67–77, 80, 83, 139, Fig 13, **Pls 14, 15 and 16**

Index

supertanker, 101
tug, 33, 107, **Pls 7 and 8**
U-boat, 58, 59, 63, 67–77, 80, 83, 116, Fig 13, **Pls 15 and 16**
yacht, 120
shipboard life and living conditions, 3–4, 7–9, 12–13, 26, 59–60, 71, Fig 2
shipbroking, 120
shipbuilding, 2, 5, 6–7, 24, 26, 35, 36, 40–41, 42, 43, 65, 71, 81–82, 99, 102, 115, 120–21, 127, 131
shipmasters, 7, 15, 30, 35, 36, 62, 75, 77, 102–08, 122, 124, **Pl 16**
ship models, 53
ships' boys and apprentices, 32, 44, 83
shipowners, 10–11, 19, 23–24, 26, 28, 35, 37, 60, 119
shipping costs, 129–30, 134–35
shipping lines and companies, 5, 10–11, 60–61, 102, 113–14, 122, **Pl 12**
ships – gear, rig and propulsion, ii, 4, 5, 7, 25–26, 33–34, 41, 42, 47, 89–91, 100–01, 104, 121–22
ships – interior layout and décor, 7–9, Fig 2
ships, kitchen/eating facilities, 9, 59–60
ships – launching, 7, 40, 65, 81, 99, 101, 102, 120
ships – lifeboats, ii, 3, 9, 75–76, 92–94, 124–25, **Pl 17**
ships
   Achilles, SS, 75
   Akagi, IJN, 87, 89, 96
   Amoco Cadiz, SS, 114
   Atlantic Empress, SS, 114
   Bakuin, SS, 99
   Baku Standard, 115–116
   Beccles of Seaham, SS, 22
   Birka Carrier, M/F, 125
   Bismarck, 82
   Blue Bonnet, tug, 33
   California Packet, 3

   Camperdown, HMS, 45–47, 49, 53, Figs 9 and 10
   CGM Normandie see also *MSC Napoli*, 121
   Chirripo, SS, 76
   City of Glasgow, 1, 2, 5, 6–19, 21, 65, Figs 1, 2, and 3
   City of Manchester, 1, 11, 19
   Cornwall, HMS, 78, 79, 80–81, 82, 85, 87–93, 94–95, 96, 97, Figs 16 and 17, **Pl 19**
   Devastation, HMS, 43
   Dorie, SS, 76
   Dorsetshire, HMS, 78, 79, 80–81, 82, 85, 86–90, 91, 92, 93–94, 96, 97, Fig 16
   Dreadnought, HMS (I), 54
   Dreadnought, HMS (II), 56–57, 79
   E54, HM Submarine, 76
   Edinburgh, HMS, 49
   Enterprise, HMS, 92, 94
   Eugen Maersk, MV, **Pls 22 and 26**
   Father Matthews of Seaham, SS, 22
   Glückauf, SS, 99
   Great Britain, 5, 17–18
   Great Western, PS, 5, 6, 7
   Haven, SS, 114
   Hermes, HMS, 87, 88, 96, Fig 16
   Hiryu, IJN, 87, 89, 96
   Hoche, SS, ii
   Ideal-X, SS, 128
   Jumna, tug, Pl 7
   La Gloire, 42
   Lancastria, RMS, ix, **Pls 1 and 2**
   Lake Palourde, SS, 113
   Lusitania, RMS, 67, 68
   Matchless of Seaham, SS, 22
   MSC Napoli, 118, 119, 121–26, 127–28, 134, 136–37, Fig 21, **Pl 23**
   Murex, SS, 101
   Nautilus, PS, 5
   Ocean, SS, 22
   Paladin, HMS, 94

Panther, HMS, 94
Repulse, HMS, 85
Prince of Wales, HMS, 85
Russell, SS, 21–23, 25–27, 28, 30–36, Figs 5 and 6, **Pl 7**
Sans Pareil, HMS, ii, 40–42
Sirius, PS, 6
Soryu, IJN, 87, 89, 96
Terence, SS, 58, 61, 62–65, 66, 67, 69, 71–77, 119, **Pl 13**
Titanic, RMS, 2, 18, 19, 53, 121
Tone, IJN, 87
Torrey Canyon, MV, 108, 100–116, 117, Figs 18, 19, 20, **Pl 21**
U81, 67, 71, 74, 75–77
Unicorn, SS, 3–4
Victoria, HMS, ii, 38–42, 44–57, 79, **Pls 9 and 10**
Warrior, HMS, 39, 42, 43
ships, toilets and plumbing, 9
shipwrecks, 1, 16–18, 28, 29, 46–49, 54, 67–69, 74–75, 76–77, 82, 89–94, 97, 104–08, 114, 115–16, 122–26, 137, Fig 3, Fig 5, Fig 17, Fig 19, **Pls 17, 19, 21 and 23**
Shipwrecked Mariners' Society, 37
shipwrights, 32
shipyards, 6, 7, 24, 40, 65, 71, 81–82, 99, 120
Shirley, Tom, 89
Short, Ann, 21, 23,
Short, Thomas, 23, 32
signals and signalling *see also* wireless, 39, 46, 67, 73, 89, 91, 102
signals intelligence, 70–71, 86, 87, 89
Sines, Portugal, 122
Singapore, 78, 85
slavery, slave trade, 10
smuggling, 131, 132
Somerville, Admiral James, 85–87, 94, 95
'SOS', 67
South Downs, Sussex, 24
Spain, the Spanish, 64, 139

Spectator, The, 2
Sperry Duplex Gyropilot, 104–07
Sri Lanka *see* Ceylon
Stal, Captain Hans, 107, 108
Standard Oil Co, 99
steam engines, 4–5, 6, 7, 13, 16, 41, 42, 44, 61, 64, 65, 66, 73
steam turbines, 56, 66, 102
steam vessels/propulsion, 1, 4–7, 41, 44, 56, 64–66, **Pls 7, 8, 11, 13 and 16**
steel ships and shipbuilding, 40–43, 46, 64–66, 79, 81, 91, 100–01, 118–19, 121, 127–28, 137, Fig 11, **Pls 13, 20, 21, 22 and 23**
steerage passengers, 3, 9–10, 11, 12–13
stevedores *see* dockworkers
Stevens, Sir Bertram, 79
stewards/stewardesses and hotel staff, 7, 16, 121
Stewart, Mrs, 16
stokers, 16, 38, 40, 44, 48, 49, 54, 56, 61, 63, 89, **Pl 10**
Stonehaven, Kincardine, Scotland, 115–16
Storm Kyrill, 122
storms, 1, 2, 4, 10, 13, 21–22, 33, 34, 35, 36, 37, 116, 121, 122
Suez Canal, 44, 66, 100, 101, Fig 8
Suez War, 100
Sulzer diesel engine, 122
Sunderland, Northumberland, 22, 32, 33, 34, 62, **Pl 8**
Super Frelon, Aérospatiale, 124
surgeons, 3, 13, 16, 92–93, 95
Surrey, England, 27
Surrey Street, Littlehampton, 23, 25
Sussex, West and East, 23, 24, 27, 33
swimming, 48–49, 93, **Pl 2**

Taranto, Italy, 84–85
tattoo, 40
taxes, tolls and customs, 119, 120
telegraph, 22, 49–50, 78
television, 98, 116, 136

Index

terrorism, 75, 136
TEU, definition of, 128
Texas, USA, 128
Thames, River, 40, 132–34, Fig 23, **Pl 24**
theatre and entertainment, 38, 52–56, 57, **Pl 10**
Thompson, Robert Henry, 34
Thorne, SBA Charlie, 93–94
'Three Graces', Liverpool, **Pl 12**
Tilbury, Essex, 134, 135
timber trade, 30, 32
Timms, Marine Bugler G W, 90
Titusville, USA, 98
Tobago, 114
Tod and McGregor, 6–7, 7–10, 11, 18, 19, 65
Tod, David, 6
Tod, First Officer Patrick, 15
Tokyo, Japan, 78
tonnage or capacity measurement, viii, 5, 26, 40–41, 128
'tonnage tax', 120
torpedoes *see* naval weaponry
trade disputes, 62, 121, 132, 135
trade, food, 58–59, 73, **Pl 11**
trade, general, 58–59, 65–66, 137, 138, 139
trade, ideology of, 59
trade protection *see also* convoys, submarines, 81
trade, raw materials *see also* coal, oil, wool, 58–59, **Pl 25**
trades unions, 62, 119, 121, 135
Trafalgar, battle of, 57
tramp shipping, 59–61, 70, 134
Transport and General Workers' Union, 135
treaties, 68, 80–81
trimmers, 16, 61
Trinity House, 110
Tripoli, Tripoli Bay, Lebanon, 45, 49
troll, 19
Trotter, Colonel, 49

Tryon, Vice-Admiral Sir George, 38–40, 44–47, 50, 54–55, 57, **Pl 9**
Turkey, Turks *see also* Ottoman Empire, 121
Turpin, John, 33, 34
turrets *see* naval weaponry
Tyne, River, 26, 27, 40, 81

Ukraine, 121
Union Oil Co, 102
United Nations, 114, 120
United States Air Force, 110
United States Navy, 80, 85, 96
urban topography, 23, 25
Ushant, France, 124

Valentia Island, Ireland, 71–72, Fig 14
Velev, Captain Valentin, 122, 124, 127
Vestey group, 61
Victoria Deep Water Terminal, Charlton, London, ii, **Pl 24**
Vietnam War, 128
Vickers-Armstrong Ltd, 81
Victoria Park, Portsmouth, 49
voyage times, 1, 10, 16

Wales, Welsh, 2, 12, 15, 17, 27, 32, 53, 66–67, 104, **Pl 15**
Wall Street Crash, 61
Walrus, Supermarine, 81
Ward, Able Seaman, 108
warehouses, 10, 25, 130, 132, 134, 135–36, **Pls 4 and 6**
Washington Naval Treaty, 80–81
Wear, River *see also* Sunderland, **Pl 8**
Weisbach, Kapitänleutnant Raimund, 67, 68, 71, 75–77
West India Dock, 132, 133, Fig 23
Weter family, 15
Wickham family, 18
West Indies *see also* individual territories, 2, 114, 130, 139
West Sussex Gazette, 23, 27, 33

Western Front, 75
Weston, Dame Agnes, 51–52
widows/widowers, 1, 18–19, 21, 51–52, 94–95
Wilson, J Havelock, 62
wireless, 66–67, 70–71, 71–73, 124, Fig 12, **Pl 14**
women, 7, 16, 21, 23, 36–37, 40, 140
women serving at sea, 7, 16, 121
Women's Royal Naval Service, 83
wooden ships and shipbuilding, 5, 25–26, 32, 35–36, 42
Wood, Surgeon-Lieutenant Christopher, 93

wool trade, 58, 73, 130, 138, **Pl 25**
Wreck Abstracts, Board of Trade, 28–30, Fig 5
wreck, law of, 126–27
wreckers, wrecking, 111, 125–26, 137,

Yorkshire, England, 12, 15, 21, 30, 53–54

Zodiac Maritime Agencies Ltd, 122
Zulu (film), 53